THE TROJAN TEN

THE

TROJAN TEN

THE 10
THRILLING
VICTORIES
THAT CHANGED
THE COURSE
OF USC
Barry
FOOTBALL
LeBrock
HISTORY

NAL | NEW AMERICAN LIBRARY

New American Library
Published by New American Library, a division of
Penguin Group (USA) Inc., 375 Hudson Street,
New York, New York 10014, USA
Penguin Group (Canada), 90 Eglinton Avenue East, Suite 700, Toronto,
Ontario M4P 2Y3, Canada (a division of Pearson Penguin Canada Inc.)
Penguin Books Ltd., 80 Strand, London WC2R 0RL, England
Penguin Ireland, 25 St. Stephen's Green, Dublin 2,
Ireland (a division of Penguin Books Ltd.)
Penguin Group (Australia), 250 Camberwell Road, Camberwell, Victoria 3124,
Australia (a division of Pearson Australia Group Pty. Ltd.)
Penguin Books India Pvt. Ltd., 11 Community Centre, Panchsheel Park,
New Delhi - 110 017, India
Penguin Group (NZ), cnr Airborne and Rosedale Roads, Albany,
Auckland 1310, New Zealand (a division of Pearson New Zealand Ltd.)
Penguin Books (South Africa) (Pty.) Ltd., 24 Sturdee Avenue,
Rosebank, Johannesburg 2196, South Africa

Penguin Books Ltd., Registered Offices:
80 Strand, London WC2R 0RL, England

First published by New American Library,
a division of Penguin Group (USA) Inc.

First Printing, August 2006
10   9   8   7   6   5   4   3   2   1

Insert photos courtesy of the University of Southern California

LIBRARY OF CONGRESS CATALOGING-IN-PUBLICATION DATA:
LeBrock, Barry.
The Trojan ten : the 10 thrilling victories that changed the course of
USC football history/Barry LeBrock.
p.   cm.
ISBN 0-451-21960-0
1. University of Southern California—Football—History.   2. Southern California
Trojans (Football team)—History.   I. Title.
GV958.U57L43 2006
796.332'630979494—dc22   2006010037

Set in 11 pt Garamond
Designed by Patrice Sheridan

Printed in the United States of America

TO MY FAMILY: 5, 15, 4

CONTENTS

Contents

ACKNOWLEDGMENTS

I'd like to thank so many people for their help as I wrote this book.

Tim Tessalone's USC Athletic Department was giving of their collective time, knowledge and energy. Chris Huston was particularly helpful with his firm grasp on USC football history and thanks to Paul Goldberg for his help in setting up interviews.

Brian Curtis—an entertaining, experienced author and established sportscaster—provided consistent and helpful counsel with sensible advice along the way. Thank you!

Thanks to all the old Trojans who were generous with their time—mostly to Craig Fertig, Paul McDonald, Richard Wood, Anthony Davis and Frank Gifford, for their time on the telephone. To Carson Palmer, for participating in the world's longest game of phone tag. To Sam Cunningham and Ambrose Schindler, for having me in their homes. To Mike Garrett, for his availability, hospitality and grace. And to Pete Carroll and Matt Leinart, for setting aside chunks of time amid an unending flurry of activity and demands.

A special thanks to WeAreSC.com's Garry Paskwietz, perhaps the most knowledgeable Trojan historian and one of USC's most passionate fans. He was generous with his time and willing to share his memories.

UCLA's Matt Stevens and Wisconsin's Pat Richter displayed grace and patience in discussing details of losses of long ago. And thanks to the athletic departments at UCLA and Notre Dame; they sure didn't feel like rivals.

I'd like to thank all of my coworkers at Fox Sports Net who provided input, especially Mark Walton, John Hefner and Lindsay Soto.

Thanks to my great wife, Susan, for her undying support and patience, her ideas and direction and mostly for her love. To my precious daughter Jalyn, just three years old at the time, but thrilled to accompany the old man to the library on several research trips. And to her kid sister, Keira, a blessing from above.

And thanks for everything in my life to my parents. An endeavor does not need to be nearly as worthwhile as writing this book for them to hop on board with support and encouragement.

Thank you to my literary agent, Peter Miller, and my editor at New American Library, Brent Howard. It took expertise from both of you to get actual ink on actual paper and make this project a reality.

FOREWORD

When I walked onto the USC campus for the first time in the early sixties, there was no way I could have known what this university would come to mean to me and my life. The school and the people associated with it are a part of me and I am a part of them.

From my early experiences with Coach McKay, through my Heisman Trophy season of 1965, and from taking over as athletic director in 1993, to our back-to-back national championships, much of what I have experienced at USC has helped to make me the man I am today.

I feel the Trojans deep athletic tradition and their history of greatness running through my veins. As hundreds of thousands of USC alumni will attest, the all-encompassing college life the university provides is a beautiful and unique experience that, in many ways, lasts a lifetime.

The current state of Trojan football is the envy of every

collegiate athletic program in the country. From Pete Carroll to his assistant coaches to the last player on the bench, there is an air of excellence surrounding every aspect of the team. The passionate support we receive from alumni and boosters can be felt throughout the athletic program. The Coliseum might be an historic football stadium, but on Saturday afternoons in the fall, it is much more than that. It is home.

In the chapters that follow, you will discover some of the great stories and great games that, in part, make USC football what it is: an unparalleled collegiate athletic program that always has and always will move forward in greatness.

I feel blessed to be tied to the past, the present and hopefully the future of USC football. As athletic director, I feel confident making the promise that the proud men of great character who are associated with this team will continue to strive for excellence on and off the field.

Fight On!

—Mike Garrett

THE TROJAN TEN

INTRODUCTION

There have been more than one thousand football games played in the storied history of the University of Southern California: 1,084 to be exact, as the 2006 season gets under way. The fascinating stories of the great players and fierce competitors who have worn the USC uniform are endless.

Trying to quantify the best of anything—football games, football players, clam chowder or show dogs—is, at best, an inexact science. Identifying the *ten most meaningful games*, the precise battles that were most influential in shaping the course of this prestigious university's football history, is downright impossible.

What follows are the stories of the ten games—fewer than 1 percent of those ever played by USC teams—that make up one person's list. Taken into consideration were the following factors:

* **Thrilling moments:** Some sporting events stand out because of one particular play or one instant of greatness.

There are about 150 plays in the average college football game, and sometimes the execution of a single one means the difference between victory and defeat.

* **Significant games:** While all eleven or twelve games on a team's schedule each season carry equal weight in a final record, there is no denying that some games are more important than others. A win over a highly ranked team at the end of a season is obviously considered more meaningful than your run-of-the-mill early October victory.

* **Rivalry games:** Chapter one of the as yet unwritten book *USC Football For Dummies* will undoubtedly spell out the inherent importance of games against Notre Dame and UCLA. Somehow, another one of those leisurely victories over Oregon State doesn't exactly register very high on the passion meter.

* **Groundwork games:** Sometimes a seemingly innocuous victory can, with the benefit of retrospect, be seen as so much more. No destiny is a straight course. It is often in the unexpected curves and the sharp angles in the time line of our histories that we find our most relevant moments.

* **Life-changers:** It is in the most important games that players perform under the hottest of lights. Reaching a pinnacle can be the ultimate award. Falling a single step short can be haunting. It is greatness in times of scrutiny that is greatness indeed.

Since fielding its first football team in 1888 behind a quarterback named Arthur Carroll (no relation), the Trojans, formerly called the Methodists and Wesleyans, have won 732 games, lost 298, and tied 54.

Scores of players from several decades were extremely gracious with their time as they told their stories from the games detailed in the following chapters. Even though reflections in a rearview mirror can be a bit more distant than they appear, players mostly recalled details of their greatest triumphs with amazing accuracy. All-time great Anthony Davis half jokingly threatened to withhold his participation in this project if the 1974 Notre Dame game was not listed as number one of the ten most significant. Partly to avoid AD's wrath, and partly to logically relate the Trojans' great history, the top ten games are presented here in chronological order. Additionally, there's really no point in choosing one over another, because as far as football games go, the "Trojan Ten" are all pretty damn good.

CHAPTER ONE

USC

VS.

NOTRE DAME, 1931

THE SETUP

The rhythmic metallic click and clack of the wheels on a 1920s locomotive called out commands as the miles between Lincoln, Nebraska, and Chicago disappeared steadily behind. On the train rode Gwynn Wilson, graduate manager of the USC football team, an early-days version of an athletic director, and his wife, Marion. Wilson was a thousand miles from home and on a mission.

He had been sent by USC to set up a series of games with the most prestigious football school in the country, Notre Dame. He was in Lincoln to catch up to legendary coach Knute Rockne, who was in town with his Fighting Irish for a game against the University of Nebraska.

Upon graduation from Notre Dame, Rockne had been offered a job as a graduate assistant in chemistry, and accepted on the condition that he would be allowed to help Jesse Harper coach the football team. When Harper retired after the 1917 season, Rockne was named his successor. What followed were thirteen years of unprecedented college football glory, during which the Irish won six national championships and put together five undefeated seasons. Rockne's lifetime winning percentage of .881 (105–12–5) still rank as the all-time best in both college and professional football.

Wilson and Rockne were not strangers. After the 1924 season, USC fired coach "Gloomy Gus" Henderson despite his sparkling six-season record of 45–7. Speculation is that Henderson's demise, at least in part, was his 0–5 record against intrastate rival Cal. When the Trojans were looking to fill the vacant coaching spot, Rockne, who was at the top of just about every school's wish list, was at the top of theirs. Notre Dame was in Southern California finishing off an undefeated season with a 27–10 win over Stanford in the Rose Bowl when Rockne agreed to a meeting with the USC brass, including Gwynn Wilson. Stories differ as to the extent of the progress made in the discussions, but by some credible accounts, it was significant. A recent *Sports Illustrated* story told of Columbia University's pursuit of Rockne the next season. It read in part: "Earlier in 1925, while in Los Angeles for the Rose Bowl, Rockne had met secretly with Southern Cal officials, but details of that impending deal had leaked, ending the negotiations."

The next time Wilson and Rockne came face-to-face was on the day of the Notre Dame/Nebraska game, November 26, 1925, amid the crush of people in the lobby of the Lincoln Hotel. Wilson told Rockne that he needed to speak with him about something important. Rockne responded by saying that he was too busy to get together before the game, but offered to book Wilson and his wife a reservation on the train that Notre Dame was taking back to Chicago so they could talk. Wilson, focused on his task, accepted, and he and Marion boarded the train after the game as personal guests of Knute and Bonnie Rockne.

The next day, the foursome ate breakfast and lunch together, but Rockne was evasive and noncommittal about a potential USC/Notre Dame matchup, and Wilson became silently frustrated.

Sensing the need for a change of venue, and perhaps looking for a little distance from the wives to turn up the pressure, Wilson suggested that Rockne and he adjourn alone to the observation car. There, Rockne's avoidance of the subject went into overdrive, but Wilson made a point to stay calm and polite, ultimately enjoying an intimate afternoon with one of the nation's great sports heroes. The conversation ranged from football to politics to travel. "He told me so many stories, stories about the Gipper, Jim Thorpe and that kind of thing. It was truly," Wilson said, proving his very point sixty-four years later, "an afternoon to remember."

Finally, faced directly with the question of beginning a series, Rockne answered, "Gwynn, I'm gonna say no, and I'll tell you why. You know what they're calling my team in South Bend . . . all over the country, as a matter of fact? They're calling us Rockne's Ramblers," growled the coach, referring to implications that his team was traveling too much. "And I don't like it. We're gonna play at home more."

As the train made its way toward Inglewood Station just outside of Chicago, Wilson began to feel that it had been a wasted trip. "Maybe in a couple years," Rockne said, "but not now."

The two men exchanged pleasantries, and Wilson began to walk back to his seat. On a literal and figurative train heading in the wrong direction, Wilson's mind wandered westward. The California sunshine was but a warming thought on a chilly trip taking him farther east by the minute.

In an interview decades later, Wilson recalled, "When I told my wife, she thought it was kind of strange that Knute had turned the proposal down flat, because his wife, Bonnie, had seemed so enthusiastic about playing a game in Southern California."

Wilson continued. "You see, while Rockne and I were talking in the observation car, Bonnie and Marion were also talking. Bonnie was shocked at the way the people in Nebraska had treated the fans and team from Notre Dame."

The treatment was so bad, in fact, that Notre Dame dropped Nebraska from its schedule. According to *Sports Illustrated*, "administrators cited anti-Catholic slurs from the stands and a derisive halftime skit by students that depicted the Irish as ruffian brick masons."

"Of course, in those days, we considered visiting teams as guests in Southern California, rather than intruders," Wilson said. "Marion told Bonnie how well we treated the teams. For example, we could get 'em in the Beverly Hills Hotel for six dollars a day, American plan, and they could have all the milk and meat they could eat. Bonnie Rockne had liked the idea of coming out to California and was sure that Knute would too.

"Now there was no way I was going to knock on his door again and start begging, but as it turned out, I didn't have to. I sat in a seat where I could see the door to Rockne's compartment. About fifteen minutes later, he walked out twirling a cigar between his thumb and forefinger. He didn't come down the aisle to me immediately. He stopped and talked to some of his players, like he didn't want to seem too anxious. He was walking down the aisle as if he had no particular destination."

But he was, in reality, walking toward history. Rockne approached, and as Wilson recalls, "He had kind of a silly smile on his face and a gleam in his eye. He bent down slightly, and asked me, 'Gwynn, what was this you were saying about some football games?'"

It was all Wilson could do to stop himself from screaming out with joy. He had finally gotten what he came for.

In 1989, sixty-four years and sixty-three USC/Notre Dame games after that train ride, Wilson reflected, "If these two ladies weren't gossiping on a train from Lincoln to Chicago on an autumn afternoon in 1925, this great series would never have been played."

Longtime USC administrator Arnold Eddy has said, "It's the greatest thing to happen in USC athletic history and maybe in all the history of the University of Southern California."

There they were—on a train kicking out miles beneath its wheels like dirt from a dog digging for a bone. They breezed across a barren plain just northeast of Montezuma, Iowa, two men giving birth to a baby that would grow up to be a superstar.

THE GAME (NOVEMBER 21, 1931)

The sixth USC/Notre Dame was the first one ever played in South Bend, Indiana. The two previous road games for USC had been played at Soldier Field in Chicago with attendance for each topping 99,000.

The 1931 game was also the first one played without Knute Rockne's presence. The legendary Notre Dame coach was tragically killed in a plane crash eight months earlier while flying, coincidentally, to Los Angeles on business.

According to Nick Pappas, a Trojan running back in the mid thirties, even though USC's run at Rockne back in 1925 was unsuccessful, the relationship proved fruitful because, upon turning down USC, Rockne referred the man who would become the Trojans' next coach. "There's a guy out there in Iowa that you ought to get," Rockne told USC administrators. That guy turned out to be the man whose 121 wins trail only John McKay's 127 on USC's all-time list: the great Howard Jones. Jones had gained Rockne's respect in the ultimate fashion—by beating Rockne's team on the football field. Jones' Iowa team snapped

Notre Dame's twenty-game win streak in 1920, etching Jones into Rockne's permanent mental referral list.

The Irish came into the 1931 matchup riding a *twenty-six-*game win streak and recognized, still eight years before the first Associated Press poll, as the top team in the nation.

A capacity crowd of 50,731 packed Notre Dame Stadium, which had just opened the previous season. USC running back Gus Shaver remembers the scene vividly. "We got out on that football field, and the stands came just about right down to the sidelines. It was full of people who were rooting and hollering, and they had their players lined up along their sideline stretching all the way from one goal line to the other to try to intimidate the opposition."

Neither team was able to get on the scoreboard for most of the first half, which was certainly a testament to the immense talents of the respective defenses. USC went into South Bend averaging thirty-eight points per game, while the Irish had been scoring nearly thirty per game. After twenty-nine scoreless minutes, the Irish finally broke through as fullback Steve Banas went up the middle from a yard out to make it 7–0 Notre Dame.

When running back Marchy Schwartz added a short touchdown in the third quarter to give the Irish a seemingly comfortable 14–0 lead, the roar from the stands was a familiar one in the relatively new stadium, which had yet to see a Notre Dame loss.

USC mounted a drive late in the third quarter, starting on Notre Dame's forty-eight yard line following an Irish punt. The Trojans moved the ball downfield with a balanced mixture of passes and runs, and early in the fourth quarter, they were starting at a fourth and goal inside the one yard line.

The problem, other than the Notre Dame defense that had shut out six of its previous seven opponents, was that the ball was as close to the right sideline as it was to the goal line. In

1931, although Scotch tape, the electric razor and the jet engine had already been invented, hash marks had not.

Since running back Gus Shaver, one of four all-Americans on that team, had been tackled within a couple yards of the right sideline, that was where the ball was spotted. The Trojans lined up with just two linemen to the right of the center and four to the left. The snap went not to quarterback Orv Mohler, but instead directly to Shaver in the backfield. He dashed forward and slightly to his right, put his head down and dived to a spot on the goal line about two inches from the sideline.

Shaver, two Notre Dame defenders, the sideline and the goal line came together in an instant like five ball bearings jumping to a suddenly exposed magnet. Grainy black-and-white film shows the referee, dressed completely in white, lunging forward and dropping to one knee to get his eyes within inches of the ball. The back judge rushed in, as did the official positioned behind the offense, who ultimately raised his arms, palms forward, signaling a touchdown.

Had the NFL's system of challenge by instant replay been around at the time, the call would not have been overturned—not necessarily because it was the right call, but because it was so close that there was not the required "conclusive video evidence" to overturn it.

Interviewed in 1987, Tom Mallory, a halfback on that Trojans team, said, "It was tough. We made quite a number of good gains. We should have scored earlier but we just didn't put it together—that was all. Then right there at the last, things started to click."

The Trojans had cut the lead to 14–6, but most of the tension felt by fans in the stadium was relieved when the extra point was blocked. The Trojan sideline, which had been buzzing moments before, was suddenly quiet. With the two-point conversion still twenty-seven years away from conception, USC remained two scores behind with about thirteen minutes to play.

Following the kickoff, Notre Dame went three and out, and punted to give USC possession at its own forty-three. The Trojans offense, which had picked up a much-needed boost from the previous touchdown, rolled downfield again. On a first down at the Notre Dame ten, Shaver took a pitchout and swept around left end, a 1931 version of the Trojans' famed "Student Body Left," which resulted in another touchdown making it 14–13 Irish with eight minutes remaining.

Three possessions later, USC took over with two minutes to play, still down a point and eighty-one yards from the end zone.

As they ran onto the field, the Trojans offense had an entirely different collective feeling than it did earlier in the game. The two late touchdowns had them back in it, and they were as calm as they were confident. The drive took them down the field, at times in large chunks. With under a minute left, USC faced a crucial third down on the Irish sixteen. According to Notre Dame's 1932 football guide, "Time was running out for SC, and the spectre on Howard Jones' shoulder grew heavier. He then sent Homer Griffith into the game with a play, but Mohler, a very clever quarterback, knew exactly what to do. He waved Griffith off the field, and with less than sixty seconds, and Notre Dame expecting a pass on third down, he called a place kick. Big Johnny Baker dropped back to the twenty-three yard line. Captain Stan Williamson snapped the ball, Mohler held . . ."

Baker, who had been playing *left guard* all day, moved toward the ball, drew his leg back and flung his right foot forward. The ball sailed end over end, above the outstretched arms of Notre Dame's leaping down linemen and toward the goalpost, a sturdy white "H" planted at the goal line.

Gus Shaver was undoubtedly USC's most valuable offensive player. He was a speedy, slender back who weighed about 175 pounds with marbles in his pockets. He had sliced up the Irish defense with his running ability for most of the day, but when Baker was called upon to kick, he suddenly became an offensive lineman.

Shaver remembers, "I had to take Baker's place at the line—I had never been in the line before and I didn't know what was gonna happen. I thought I might end up in the backfield, but fortunately nobody hit me."

The ball clearly had the distance, but as it floated toward the goalpost with a hundred thousand eyes upon it, it appeared to be flirting with the left upright. The stadium, which had been flooded with noise to distract the USC kicker just moments earlier, fell almost silent.

The Notre Dame media guide's section on the 1931 season reads:

> For the first time, three Los Angeles radio stations broadcast the game. Since not everyone owned a radio in those days, many public parks set up bleachers accommodating four to five thousand "spectators." An estimated ten million football fans from coast to coast heard that game.

Those ten million heard from an announcer what the fifty thousand in attendance saw for themselves. Johnny Baker's "kick from placement" sailed just inside the left upright giving USC a 16–14 win. The Trojans had miraculously rallied from a fourteen-point deficit, scoring sixteen unanswered points in the fourth quarter to pull out the victory in their first game ever at South Bend. It was USC's second win in six games against the Irish and just the second time in twenty-seven years that Notre Dame had lost at home. And the first time undoubtedly, on a last-minute, third-down field goal.

Gus Shaver, the one-play guard, said years later, "I think it pretty well stunned the South Bend people, but we had a few rooters there who went wild." As did the traveling party on the Trojans sideline. Old film shows men literally dancing on the sidelines, taking off their winter coats and hats and flinging them jubilantly in the air. It was graduation day at Annapolis right there in Notre Dame Stadium.

The next day, the Associated Press game story ran as the top item on the front page of newspapers throughout the Midwest.

Notre Dame's mighty fortress of football, impregnable against 26 assaults in almost three years of gridiron warfare, fell at last today.

Fluttering over its ruins tonight flew the cardinal and gold battle flag of the roaring Trojans from Southern California, who astounded the world of football by ransacking it with one 15-minute rush in the last period of battle today by a score of 16–14.

And the *South Bend Tribune*, hometown newspaper to Notre Dame, was generous in its praise for USC:

TROJANS TOPPLE N.D.
FROM GRIDIRON THRONE

U.S.C. STAGES THRILLING RALLY
TO TAKE 16–14 DECISION

Although the score stood 16–14 in favor of the Trojans when Howard Jones' boys and the Irish finally ceased hostilities, there was no reason for any great weeping and gnashing of teeth on the part of the Notre Dame backers. A victory by a great eleven demanded applause—not alibis.

There was a touch of glory in the defeat of the Fighting Irish even if it was a bit overshadowed by the publicity which the Californians won after such a fighting finish.

Who was to blame for the defeat of the Irish? No one. It was just one of those things. And the Notre Dame backers, after they saw their hopes of a national championship had been blasted, were glad to know that the bunch of brilliant gridders had done it.

When the Notre Dame boys gather around the stove for the discussion in the good old winter time, they can easily come to this conclusion—it was just one of those things.

Years earlier, Rockne had been quoted as saying, "The secret is to work less as individuals and more as a team. As a coach, I play not my eleven best, but my best eleven."

On November 21, 1931, there can be no argument that the best eleven wore the cardinal and gold of Southern California.

	1	2	3	4	F
USC	0	0	0	16	16
Notre Dame	0	7	7	0	14

Scoring:

Second Quarter

Notre Dame: Banas, 1-yard run (Jaskwich kick)

Third Quarter

Notre Dame: Schwartz, 3-yard run (Jaskwich kick)

Fourth Quarter

USC: Baker, 1-yard run (kick blocked)

USC: Shaver, 10-yard run (Baker kick)

USC: Baker, 20-yard field goal

POSTSCRIPT

In the craziness of the locker room celebration following the last-minute victory, Coach Howard Jones was even more reserved than usual. As important as the game was for USC, some of Jones' thoughts were on his old contemporary and coaching adversary Knute Rockne. He spoke with some of the Notre Dame officials to find out where the late coach was buried, and as the Trojans left South Bend, they did not immediately begin the trip back to Los Angeles, but instead they headed to the great Rockne's grave site.

Hours after leaving their blood and sweat on the football field, mentally drained and physically exhausted, they stood in the fading light of a cold Midwest dusk: a team of proud Trojans, hatless and humbled in an Indiana cemetery, paying silent tribute to the fallen leader of their most bitter rival and most respected opponent.

Upon their return to California, it was the Trojans' turn to be honored. Any doubt about the scope and magnitude of their victory over the Irish was put to rest by the masses.

A parade through downtown Los Angeles was, according to headlines of the day, attended by 300,000 people. That would be a good crowd even by today's standards, but consider the population of Los Angeles in 1931 was about 1.25 million people. If the same percentage of the population turned out for a parade today, the attendance would be just short of a million people. That would be some kind of party.

Howard Jones addressed the crowd over a PA system, saying, "The boys played the greatest game of football that any Southern California team has ever played for me."

As the USC band blasted out a joyous rendition of "Conquest," the players rode two per automobile up Broadway to city hall. With ticker tape and emotions flying in the calm

Southern California breeze, Mayor John C. Porter presented the team with the key to the city.

USC president Rufus Von KleinSmid took the microphone at city hall and, perhaps caught up in the excitement of the moment, announced to the crowd, "Ladies and gentlemen, there is no more depression in Southern California."

The win over Notre Dame was the seventh straight for USC, which went on to finish the season with three more victories including a 21–12 defeat of Tulane in the Rose Bowl. With a 10–1 record and only a six-point opening-day loss to St. Mary's keeping them from a perfect season, the Trojans were recognized as national champions by virtue of holding the number one spot in the final Dickinson rankings, the most-respected and comprehensive ranking system of the time.

In 1954, Notre Dame's first sports publicity director, Arch Ward, wrote a series of articles to commemorate the twenty-fifth anniversary of Notre Dame Stadium. One of the most memorable stories remembered the game this way:

> A whirlwind from the University of Southern California blew up at one end of the stadium that afternoon 23 years ago and roared irresistibly down the field. Before it, it swept Notre Dame's three-year reign as monarch of American football.
>
> The mind can be a treacherous thing, especially in reminiscences, but that one, this department can never forget. It was the greatest game we have ever seen in the monument to the memory of a great man and a great sport.
>
> Other games come racing to memory, readily and rapidly, every time this antiquated typewriter goes heavenward to the press roost on the roof, accompanied by a paunch, a bald pate and a creaky back, but none quite as vividly as that afternoon of Nov. 21, 1931.

USC

VS.

TENNESSEE, 1940

THE SETUP

Coming off a 9–2 season in 1938, which was capped by a Rose Bowl victory over Duke and a number seven final ranking, USC was expecting great things in 1939. A season-opening tie with Oregon was followed by seven straight victories. Each win in itself was impressive, but as a whole, the streak was a tribute to the greatness and dominance of Howard Jones' fifteenth Trojan team. Seven up, seven down. 160 points scored, twenty-six allowed. Four of the seven victories were shutouts, and five were by double digits.

The last game standing between USC and an undefeated regular season was a matchup with crosstown rival UCLA, set for December 9. The winner would be crowned conference champion and would play *at* the Rose Bowl, *in* the Rose Bowl, twenty-three days later.

Riding trains to and from games often took days. To keep sharp, teams would stop along the way to practice wherever they could find an adequate patch of grass. On the way back from South Bend, Indiana, after a 20–12 win over Notre Dame, the Trojans got off the train on a late November day, for a workout in Boise, Idaho. Ambrose Schindler, a senior quarterback, fullback and defensive back on that team, recalls, "It was a freezing cold day in Boise, and we were on this windy hill. I caught cold during practice, and by the time we played UCLA, I had a really bad head cold and lots of congestion in my sinuses."

But Schindler, a senior who was heavily counted on, dressed that day and played not only offense and defense, but special teams as well against the Bruins.

"Early in the game, I got hit in the head and suddenly I had double-vision. The rest of the day, I saw two footballs. Instead of getting a pitchout on the run, I had to cheat over and just stand and wait for it. On punt returns, I saw two balls coming down, and I thought to myself, I better catch the one that's darkest."

If the USC team had any questions about the genius of Howard Jones before the UCLA game, they didn't after it. UCLA had a certain fleet-of-foot running back who would go on to great fame as a pioneer on the baseball field. Jackie Robinson had so much speed that the Bruins would run him almost exclusively outside on sweeps, reverses and quick tosses around the line.

Jones, who was a regular off-season golf partner of UCLA head coach Bill Spalding, knew the Spalding philosophy rather well and, more important, knew his tendencies even better. Like Jones and third-ranked USC, Spalding and the Bruins were having a great season, and came into the game ranked ninth in the nation.

Game planning to stop Robinson and his speed, Schindler

says, "Jones came up with the idea of moving the tackle, the end and the defensive halfback to the outside an extra two yards. Howard is up there drawing on the blackboard, and we all noticed this gigantic hole in our defensive front. Coach turned around, smiled at us and said, 'Ya see this hole?' We all nodded. He said, 'They'll never find it.' And they never did."

The proof is in the numbers. USC shut down UCLA's running game, but it was not for lack of effort on the Bruins' part. Despite averaging a paltry 2.3 yards per carry, UCLA continued to test the Trojans defensive front, running the ball thirty-eight times. Robinson, wearing 28 rather than his now-famous 42, rushed for 571 yards that season, averaging sixty-three yards per game on the ground, but managed just twenty-three against the Trojans. It's no wonder UCLA kept running the ball, though, because their passing game wasn't very effective, either. The Bruins completed just seven of eighteen passes for seventy-two yards.

What UCLA lacked in offense, they made up for in defense. Through three quarters, the Trojans couldn't get much going, either, and the teams were deadlocked in a scoreless tie. But with the clock ticking down toward the five-minute mark, and the murmur in the stands growing steadily louder, UCLA mounted the best drive of the day, racking up seventy-five of their 161 total yards, winding up with a first and goal on USC's three yard line. Running plays on first and second down got the Bruins down to the one yard line. Fullback Leo Cantor got the call on third down and was thrown for a two-yard loss back to the three.

Here is where football was a very different game from what it is today. The story goes that UCLA quarterback Ned Matthews actually huddled up the players and called for a vote. Who wants to try a field goal, and who wants to go for the touchdown? Ned Matthews: democracy in shoulder pads.

One has to keep in mind that a field goal from the 3 yard

line wasn't quite the automatic that it is today, and at least some of the thinking had to be that there's just something so much more inherently macho about powering a football over the goal line than kicking it through the uprights.

Not surprisingly, in a game that had been deadlocked all day long, five players voted for the field goal, and five voted to go for the touchdown. The deciding vote was left to Matthews. What kind of QB—what kind of leader—what kind of *man* would decide to kick it?

USC/UCLA. Less than five minutes to play. Fourth down. 0–0 ballgame. A Rose Bowl berth on the line.

Either way, it was going to be one of those plays that shapes a season, and ultimately for USC, it was a play that shaped history.

Matthews called the play in the huddle and started toward the line. He looked over the defense and made sure his team's offensive alignment was exactly as it should be. The crowd was louder than it had been all day, and the anticipation was palpable in the stadium. Matthews took the snap, faded back and locked in on a receiver cutting across the back of the end zone. He fired a tight spiral that looked to be a perfect strike heading for the waiting baby blue–covered arms of end Don MacPherson. But at the last instant, Trojans defensive back Bobby Robertson, using every inch of his reach, stretched desperately, dived and knocked the ball harmlessly to the grass of the Coliseum end zone. A collective groan came from parts of the stadium, while the other half, filled with Trojan backers, rejoiced. Bullet dodged, drive stalled.

The Trojans took over, staring at ninety-seven yards of field on a day when they were unable to do much of anything offensively. Doyle Nave was playing quarterback, and like all quarterbacks in the thirties and forties, he called his own plays. Nave headed out to the field to start the Trojans in the other direction and, in his mind, somehow get the points that would earn USC the victory.

It was Nave who had emerged from the depths of the depth chart the previous January to lead the Trojans to a Rose Bowl win over Duke. A fourth-string quarterback, he was called upon in the fourth quarter, trailing 3–0, to rally a stagnant USC offense. Hitting receiver Al Krueger on four consecutive passes, Nave directed a game-winning drive as the Trojans pulled out a 7–3 victory. One of his teammates later told the story that since Nave played just twenty-eight minutes all year, he was not technically eligible to receive a varsity letter. He and Al Wesson, USC's publicity director, were walking together after the game when Nave asked, "Al, do you suppose I can get a letter now after what happened today?" Wesson responded, "Doyle, after what you did today, they'll give you the whole alphabet!"

With Nave's status on the team (and on campus) substantially changed in that brief but brilliant rally against Duke eleven months earlier, he had proven himself a solid on-field leader over the course of the 1939 season. Now, in the year's final game, with the stakes high, he took the field to lead his team again.

Ambrose Schindler, eighty-seven years old and more than sixty-five years removed from the action, leaned forward in his chair early in 2005, recalling the final minutes of the UCLA game. "First huddle, Doyle calls a pass play. The pass was incomplete, but I'm over on the sideline watching, and Howard Jones grabbed me and says, 'Get in there.' If we got intercepted down near our goal line, we likely would have lost. Howard wanted to play for the *tie*. A tie would get us into the Rose Bowl. Doyle was playing to win the game!"

As good as UCLA was that season, they had what turned out to be the misfortune of an extra Pac-10 game on their schedule. Coming into the game, the Bruins were 5–0–2 in conference. The Trojans were 5–0–1. The extra tie UCLA had was looked at by the conference as a missed opportunity, and a tie on this day would give the Rose Bowl bid to USC.

Schindler pulled on his helmet, steadied his nerves and headed toward the huddle. With single purpose and double vision, he ran the offense, picking up a couple of first downs to keep the clock moving. Minutes later there was nothing but zeros on the scoreboard—in both time and score. It was the Trojans second tie of the season and their second of three ties with UCLA in a six-year span.

Any football player will tell you a tie doesn't do anybody much good, but on that day, it was good enough for USC. The Trojans were going to the Rose Bowl, which had been the goal from the beginning of the season. In those days, the Rose Bowl was *always* the goal.

THE GAME (JANUARY 1, 1940)

As the 1930s became the 1940s, the Allied forces were getting into World War II, *Gone With the Wind* was on its way to a best picture Oscar and a rested-and-ready USC football team prepared to face a talented team preceded by its fierce reputation.

The Tennessee Volunteers of the late thirties didn't exactly make a habit of losing. In fact, they hadn't dropped a game in more than two seasons, but their impressive run of twenty-three straight wins was only part of the intimidating story.

To understand the big picture regarding the 1939 Volunteers, you have to start with the previous year when the Vols stormed to one of the greatest seasons in college football history. The Tennessee team of 1938 went 11–0, finishing with an incredible string of five straight shutouts, including a 17–0 spanking of Oklahoma in the Orange Bowl. They allowed no more than seven points in any one of their eleven games and blistered their opponents by a combined score of 283–16.

The numbers insist they were one of the most dominant teams ever. And then they got even more dominant.

Amazingly the 1939 Volunteers, under coach Bob Neyland, for whom their stadium is currently named, rode the shutout streak of the previous year through the first game of the new season, and then the second, and the third, and they didn't stop stopping every offense they faced until their regular season was over.

Ten wins, no losses and *not a single point* allowed all year.

U. of Tennessee—1939

North Carolina State	13–0
Sewanee	40–0
Chattanooga	28–0
Alabama	21–0
Mercer	17–0
Louisiana State	20–0
The Citadel	34–0
Vanderbilt	13–0
Kentucky	19–0
Auburn	7–0
	212–0

That was what faced the USC team, which had also gone undefeated, but not untied and certainly not unscored upon. After the 0–0 season ender against UCLA, the Trojans entered the game at 7–0–2, having outscored opponents 167–33.

Schindler reflected, "The beauty of it was, we had three weeks between the UCLA game and the Rose Bowl. We were all healed. Believe me, playing both ways, you got pretty beat up and had to play hurt, but we were healthy."

Rose Bowl organizers were thrilled. They had a glamorous matchup between a powerhouse from the East and an intensely popular team from its own backyard. A matchup of undefeated, athletic, well-coached teams, which appeared to make the chances for a competitive game very strong. At the time, the Rose Bowl was extremely sensitive to the possibility of a one-sided game because of a change the Tournament of Roses Association had to make in its early days.

According to the Rose Bowl's official Web site, the association decided to enhance its festivities in 1902 by adding a football game. The site's explanation reads, "Stanford University accepted the invitation to take on the powerhouse University of Michigan, but the West Coast team was flattened 49–0 and gave up in the third quarter. The lopsided score prompted the tournament to give up football in favor of Roman-style chariot races."

The game, though, was reinstated in 1916, and despite the undeniable ongoing popularity of chariot races to this day, football has been the event of choice on New Year's Day ever since.

As the Trojans prepared to face the Volunteers, respected *Los Angeles Times* columnist Paul Zimmerman wrote a December 28, 1939, article about a decidedly spirited USC practice. It was titled "Hard Drill for Jonesmen" and began thus:

> For the information of our Rose Bowl guests from Tennessee, that was not an earthquake they felt yesterday. That rocking motion felt here and there which caused buildings to jiggle, and the populace to hold its breath was the Southern California football team going through contact work.
>
> Seismological experts from Caltech in Pasadena estimated the shake originated some twenty miles away, which would place the epicenter just about at Bovard field. Coach Howard Jones, who is responsible for this disturbance, asked the indulgence of the populace, pointing out that his team was going through a dummy scrimmage for the New Year's Day contest with the Vols and he guessed the boys may have taken their work a bit too seriously.

The colorful writing was standard for the day, as was the inclusion of gambling information, which Zimmerman noted to end his article. By many accounts, the point spread that is commonly used today (for example, USC opened as a three-point favorite over Oklahoma in the 2005 Orange Bowl) had not yet been invented in 1939. According to sportswriter William Barry Furlong, the point spread was invented a few years later—in the early forties—by a mathematical wizard named Charles K. McNeil, who studied at the University of Chicago.

In the days leading up to the Rose Bowl of 1940, bookmakers simply circulated *odds* on sporting events.

Zimmerman addressed the issue in that day's final paragraph:

> The local betting odds were 2 to 3 in favor of the Trojans. However, in Middlewestern and Eastern cities, the odds were 4 to 5, take your choice, with more Tennessee than Trojan money available.

Not only was the gambling aspect of the Rose Bowl and other big-time collegiate sporting events mentioned—it was often highlighted. In fact, following that December 28 article, the betting information was the *headline* to write-ups in the *Los Angeles Times* on three of the next four days. The headlines for December 29 and 30 were:

TROJANS LOOM AS 3–5 GRID FAVORITE

SWITCH IN BETTING ODDS PUTS VOLS ON EVEN TERMS WITH S.C.

And, most tellingly, regarding the prevalence of gambling, the *headline* of Zimmerman's article published the morning of the game, January 1, 1940, read:

TROJANS FAVORED IN ROSE BOWL

The article itself didn't focus on gambling issues, and beautifully whet the appetite for the game later that day.

> Rose fragrance and the pungent odor of arnica filled the air out in Arroyo Seco today. For the hour was drawing near when the drama of the 25th annual Tournament of Roses football classic would be enacted.
>
> The attar of roses was a stage prop, used these many years to tantalize those in a wintry clime. The arnica was there to ease the pain of gridiron warriors who do battle this afternoon on the greensward.
>
> Opponents in this daddy of bowl games were Tennessee, long eager to participate in this traditional intersectional struggle, and Southern California, victorious in five previous appearances.
>
> Favorite by a slender margin was the West's defender—undefeated and twice tied Troy—but a capacity crowd of 90,000 persons who figured the advantage was the figment of someone's imagination were destined to sit in on this grid struggle. And many thousands of others, unsuccessful in their quest for tickets, will be listening to this expected thriller on their radios.

With the first-ever televised football game in Los Angeles still nine years away, a fan's only choices were a game ticket or a radio. The first bit of sunlight of the first day of the first year of the forties brought with it the highly anticipated matchup. On an overcast morning in Southern California, those with and without tickets shook sleep from their eyes and New Year's hangovers from their heads as the countdown to kickoff began.

92,200 fans packed the Rose Bowl, and just like good seats, points were at a premium. The Trojans' season average of 3.5 points per game allowed made their deadly defense seem like Swiss cheese compared to Tennessee's defense, whose next points allowed would be their first.

Not surprisingly, the opening quarter ended in a scoreless tie, but at that point in a football game, an absence of scoring does not necessarily mean that teams are evenly matched. Although the Trojans had not gotten into the end zone, they had been able to move the ball. The same could not be said for Tennessee.

In his game article the next day, *Los Angeles Times* columnist Dick Hyland wrote,

It was apparent early in the game that either Tennessee was not the great ball club it has been hailed, or else the Trojans of Southern California were a real championship team, outclassing a club that has, in turn, outclassed defensively everything it encountered for two straight years.

The vaunted Vol line certainly did not outclass the Trojans.

With the knowledge that they wouldn't need many points to walk away with the roses, the USC offense took the field to begin a drive midway through the second quarter. The Trojans took particular pleasure in running the ball because of several speeches by Coach Jones in the weeks leading up to the game.

Bob Robertson, a versatile two-way player at Troy from 1939 to 1941, remembered forty-five years later, "They had two defensive linemen, guards by the name of (Ed) Molinski and (Bob) Suffridge, that had received all-America recognition. We had Harry Smith, who had received all-America recognition, and this is an illustration of Howard Jones and his coaching— for two weeks prior to that game, he kept saying, 'We'll show 'em who has the all-American guards.' And that's all we heard. And when we played the game, we ran for something like four hundred yards, and I'd say 375 of 'em were through Molinski and Suffridge."

It's funny how the mind works, funny how the memory fails in such a positive way. With decades as a boundless buffer to blur the edges of a long-ago reality, stories become funnier, ex-girlfriends become prettier and athletic accomplishments become greater. For Robertson, the glory days apparently became a bit more glorious over time because, although the Trojans were far more effective than any team had been that season against the Vols, USC didn't actually run for four hundred yards. They ran for 229, which accounted for about 85 percent of their total offense.

As for Tennessee's offense, you can't say much, but you can say they certainly had a nice balance that day. Although seventy yards passing and seventy-one rushing aren't really much to brag about for a team with a twenty-three-game win streak.

Leading the way for USC were a couple of former bitter rivals from San Diego. Quarterback Ambrose Schindler and fullback Joe Shell had each been the big man on their respective high school campuses—Schindler at San Diego High, and Shell at Hoover High. Their battles on the field were legendary, and through the competition, an intense dislike evolved. On the first day of 1940, though, after years together at USC, the pair was the best of friends, roommates and the most respectful of teammates.

Schindler was credited for much of the yardage, both through the air and on the ground, but newspaper accounts acknowledged that Shell's blocking was the key to most of the Trojans' offensive success. Hyland's article stated:

As he did in the UCLA game, Schindler not only played quarterback, but returned punts as well. His 10-yard return to the Tennessee 47 is what got the first scoring drive started. Three plays later, after a run by Schindler and two by Jack Banta, had the Trojans down to the Vols 32.

The next play, as written by Paul Zimmerman, saw "Schindler throw a flat pass to Bobby Robertson and the baby-faced halfback didn't stop until he was chased out of bounds on the 21."

Two plays later, Schindler called his own number again and he went for nine yards down to the eleven, but an unnecessary-roughness penalty netted another ten yards, bringing the Trojans down to the one. Schindler explains, "In those days, we only had three officials on the field, instead of six or seven, like they have today. They weren't calling anything! Their guys were punching me in the ribs after the play was over, hittin' me in the head and everything. One play they tackled me. I was on the ground. The whistle had blown, and as I started to get up, a guy dove on me and hit me with a forearm—knocked my face right into the turf again. They *had to* call that."

From the one, Schindler called his own number again to get within a foot of the goal line, and then the same play capped the march as Schindler, in the words of Zimmerman, "plunged into pay territory."

The Trojans kicked the extra point to take a 7–0 lead to the locker room. The second half started in much the same way that the game had gone previously: a first down here, a moderate gain there, but mostly dominant defenses dictating the action.

For all its failure throughout the afternoon, though, Tennessee's offense put itself in position to tie the game in the fourth quarter. In the final minute of the third, having done almost nothing all day and desperate for a spark, the Volunteers came up with the unthinkable, running a fake punt from their own end zone! It was so unexpected that it was a successful twelve-yard pass play, good for one of only six completions and nine first downs they managed all day. From there, having seen their running game stifled from the opening whistle, they went to the air and mounted their only significant drive of the game. The big play was a twenty-six-yard completion on a pass thrown off a reverse that got them inside USC's forty. A few plays later, they were down to the fifteen and moving toward the game-tying touchdown. "Scared the pee out of us," remembers Schindler.

But eighty-three yards after it started, the Tennessee drive died a sudden yet painful death on the Trojans' fifteen yard line when USC's Roy Engle recovered Fred Newman's fumble.

Seeing the Tennessee offense threaten their lead, the Trojan offense took the field to bulk up the tenuous seven-point lead and began to roll. The Vols defense had lost a couple key players to injury, and was beginning to run out of gas from an afternoon spent getting the bulk of the work.

Schindler ran the ball three times for seventeen yards, and then Jack Banta carried most of the load in the next eight plays, taking it across midfield and down to the Tennessee thirty. Suddenly the Trojans were running wild. Their offensive line was so dominant that Tennessee even went to a *seven*-man defensive front. It didn't matter. Everything was working for USC.

Hyland wrote:

The Trojans were then pulling the stunt of telling the opposition what was coming and then doing it. They warned Tennessee that Banta was going to catch a pass when it was fourth down and 5 yards to go, just prior to the final touchdown. "You better have Molinski cover him," the Vols were warned. The Tennessee All-American who was anything but an All-American the way the Trojans banged him around may have tried, but bounding Banta was too fast, got in the clear, and the touchdown soon followed.

Schindler confirmed the story 6.5 decades later. "As we were making that final drive, I would try to figure out the best play, and then call it in the huddle. These bastards, they would go to the line of scrimmage and say, 'We're coming right over you Molinski. Where's your all-American certificate?' And then we would run right over 'em! I was wasting my time figuring out what to call 'cause my guys were tellin' 'em where we were going, but we did it. We went right down the field, eighty-five yards."

And what they didn't get right the first time, they ultimately got right in the end.

"On one play, Joe Shell missed his block, and we got tackled for a two-yard loss," said Schindler. "He came back to the huddle and said to me, 'Amby, call it again. I can get that guy.' Well, Howard Jones had told us not to do that—not to ask the quarterback to call a certain play, but Joe was our captain and I knew he would do what he was telling me. I called it again. '30 formation, 22 shift. Coach won't like this, but we're gonna run it again.' Joe got his guy. We gained seven yards and picked up the first down."

The drive was an offensive exclamation point at the end of a nearly perfect daylong script written by the USC defense. The Trojans stormed down field in a steady, strong and consistent march. They chewed up just about everything that remained of the clock, the field and Tennessee's collective will. The drive went eighty-five yards in nineteen plays and was capped expertly by Schindler, who took a snap from the two yard line in shotgun formation, lowered his head and faked, as if he was going to run it up the middle. Instead, he stopped after two quick steps forward, looked up and to his left and lofted a perfect pass, which left end Al Krueger pulled in for the game-clinching touchdown. The Rose Bowl crowd embraced the victorious Trojans with a thunderous and unrelenting ovation. 14–0 was the final score. The mighty Volunteers of Tennessee, after twenty-three straight wins, and a season's worth of shutouts, had finally met their match.

"You heard about that defense and you wondered about it," said Schindler sixty-five years later. "We knew that we were good, and we were positive we could do it. All it took was unity and we had it. We had a great spirit and were confident that everybody could do their job. It was the best feeling I ever had with a football team. All year long, we were close-knit and solid. We were buddies, and in our adult lives, we've remained that way."

Paul Zimmerman's *Los Angeles Times* article the next day began,

> Like so many white-shirted specters, Southern California's powerful gridsters slashed their way through the gloom-glutted Rose Bowl yesterday and before the dusk of this dark afternoon had blotted out the playing field entirely the South's mighty Tennessee had been trampled underfoot, 14 to 0.
>
> Chief ghost among these giant ghouls who made a valiant Vol band almost blanch with fear was ambling Ambrose Schindler who stubbornly smashed and slid and scooted through the Southern soldiers so thoroughly that we can might near forget Sherman's march to the sea.
>
> And the massed multitude of 90,000 cheered him to the echo as he scampered off into the darkness of the sidelines in the last minute of play, leaving the wreckage of a great football team behind.
>
> For that defeat of this doughty eleven broke a 23-game winning streak for Tennessee and also terminated a series of 15 games in which the Volunteers permitted nary a score.

Entertaining United Press International writer Henry McLemore, cleverly stating that the game seemed to pit men against boys, put it this way:

> They raise them rugged out here. Perhaps nature sees that they do so in order that they will be able to withstand earthquakes, unusual

weather and the taste of water that comes out of taps. There is a lesson to be learned from this Rose Bowl game. There is no sense in betting on a team that buys its clothes in the boys' department to beat a team that has to shave twice a day and is fitted for suits in the grown-up section.

Leaving no doubt about the dominance of USC, no less an authority than Tennessee coach Bob Neyland was quoted in the *Examiner* as saying, "We were badly beaten by a superior team."

The 1939 Trojans celebrated their victory a few days later on a cool night at the famed Ambassador Hotel, keeping warm with girlfriends, champagne and memories of a well-crafted victory in the season's most important game. They had certainly closed the college football season in style.

The team was the second to last for head coach Howard Jones, who died of a heart attack in the summer of 1941. The Rose Bowl victory was Jones' fifth. The impact he had on his players—thousands of them in his coaching career—is undeniable. Eighty-six-year-old Ambrose Schindler, often emotional when speaking about his days at Troy, actually came to tears when thinking back to his precious moments with the old coach following the 1940 Rose Bowl.

"The previous year, we had beaten Duke in the final minute with those four passes by Doyle to Al Krueger. Throwing wasn't Howard Jones' way. After the game against Tennessee, he came to me in the locker room and put his arm around my shoulder and said, 'Amby, you won that one the way I like to win 'em—with power.'"

After Jones' death, sportswriter Maxwell Stiles summed up the coach's love of the sport, writing, "To Howard Jones, football was the first rays of dawn, the noonday sky, and the stars that shine at night."

And still in 2006, as the Trojans practice, be it under the sun or the stars, they do so smack-dab in the middle of the USC campus on a precious piece of Southern California real estate called Howard Jones Field with the principles, dedication and commitment of the old coach still very much alive.

	1	2	3	4	F
USC	0	7	0	7	14
Tennessee	0	0	0	0	0

SCORING:

Second Quarter

USC: Schindler, 1-yard run (Jones kick)

Fourth Quarter

USC: Schindler, 2-yard pass to Krueger (Gaspar kick)

Passing:

USC: 7–14–43

Tennessee: 6–14–70

Rushing:

USC: Schindler, 19–75; Lansdell, 18–68; Banta, 6–35;
Peoples, 7–29

Tennessee: Butler, 5–40; Coffman, 3–15; Cafego, 7–1

POSTSCRIPT

Thirteen different postseason polls ranked college football teams in 1939, but strangely, all tabulated their final ballots *prior* to the bowl games. Although in existence for just three years, the Associated Press (AP) poll had become the most prestigious and widely accepted of the bunch.

Without the Rose Bowl win over the Vols taken into consideration, the AP rankings had the Trojans finishing third, one spot *below* Tennessee. Texas A&M, which allowed an NCAA record 1.7 yards per play and finished off an undefeated season with a one-point win over Tulane in the Sugar Bowl, was voted number one in the AP as well as in nine other polls.

One poll chose USC as the top team in the land. Relying heavily on strength of schedule, the Dickinson rankings, which prior to the AP poll was the first and last word in polling, gave the Trojans the nod. The remaining two polls had Cornell as their top pick.

The Dickinson, highly respected in its own right, was good enough for USC, and as far as the Trojans were concerned, the Rose Bowl win simply solidified what had already been established—that they were, indeed, national champions.

Like black-and-white pictures on the yellowing pages of a football player's aging scrapbooks, the shine of that 1939 national championship slowly faded. As the importance of the term "national champion" grew over the years, debate raged about the validity of a split national title between two schools, let alone multiple national champions for any one single season. A couple years later, the Dickinson ratings faded into obscurity and then were gone altogether, replaced first by human polls and then by far more comprehensive computer systems. Despite the recognition of the 1939 team by USC as national champions at the time, that acknowledgment too soon faded and eventually disappeared completely. As the years passed, some of the members of that 1939 team began to lose interest in USC football. Some simply walked away, some moved away and others inevitably passed away. A handful of hard-core Trojans, though, remained fixtures at the Coliseum on Saturday afternoons, and took note of something a bit bothersome in the mid-seventies. To pay homage to the great teams of the past, USC began to display large banners around the stadium emblazoned with years of national championship teams in cardinal and gold. All the great ones were there: 1931, 1932, 1962, 1967, 1972 and 1974. A separate banner for each, flying proudly in the autumn breeze. The players from 1939 all wondered the same thing: "Where are we? Why don't we have a banner?" The phone calls began—players calling one another, asking why they had been excluded. Calls went into the administration, as well, but too many years had passed, and too many issues were pressing for anybody to look deeply into the matter.

Years went by, and players lost hope of getting their due recognition until one day in late July 2004, when Athletic Director and USC Heisman Trophy–winning great Mike Garrett righted the wrong. Garrett announced, "It was brought to our attention by various individuals that we should be claiming the 1939 Trojans among our national champions in football. We took this matter seriously, did significant research and determined this to be true. That 1939 team was one of the greatest in our history. In fact, its coach, the legendary Howard Jones, acknowledged as much when at the team banquet that year he said this squad was his finest ever at USC, at least in terms of depth."

Knowing there would be criticism, USC released a carefully worded statement that made a strong case for its decision:

USC now recognizes its football team of 1939 as national champions. There were five other years (1929, 1933, 1976, 1979 and 2002) in which the Trojans finished atop at least one poll, but USC does not consider the selectors in those years as being all-encompassing enough at the time to claim a national championship.

The NCAA does not conduct a national championship in Division I football and is not involved in the selection process. Over the years, there have been nearly 30 selectors of national champions using polls, historical research and mathematical rating systems. It is up to individual schools to determine whether a No. 1 selection in any of these systems merits a national championship claim. It is not unusual for more than one school to claim a football national championship in the same year (as USC and LSU did in 2003).

Stanford (in 1926), Michigan (in 1932) and SMU (in 1935) claim a football national championship after being selected almost solely by the Dickinson System.

To make it official, the remaining members of the 1939 team were invited back to USC in 2004 to be honored at halftime of the October 16 game against Arizona State. On a calm, sun-splashed afternoon, a dozen old Trojans walked proudly onto a field they knew well, which was seemingly unchanged by time. They received an ovation from a crowd made up mostly of fans who weren't even born in 1939.

The applause they took home in their memories. They received commemorative rings, which they took home on their fingers. And they treasured their long-awaited recognition for being the best, which they took home in their hearts.

Of course taking credit so many years later for something as prestigious as a college football national championship *did* bring USC a great deal of criticism outside of Los Angeles.

When asked how the 1939 team had come to claim a national championship sixty-five years after the fact, Ambrose Schindler perks up. "No! That didn't happen *this* year. That happened in 1939. Everyone now thinks that SC waited sixty-five years to do this. No. We *were* national champions. I can show you my certificate." And he did.

"What happened this year was a climax—and it's taken a long time for this. But back then, we were all called into the athletic department and got these certificates. My yearbook has a team picture—look at the headline."

Schindler flips to the middle fold of his 1940 *El Rodeo*. In the picture stretching across two pages stands a team of young men, each with a full head of hair, a tight belly and a blank canvas as his future. A thousand words, indeed.

But this squad is best summed up by just two words, and there they are—big face, bold type across the top of the page: NATIONAL CHAMPIONS.

CHAPTER THREE

USC

VS.

WISCONSIN, 1963

THE SETUP

To USC, losing Howard Jones was like losing its soul. After a one-year stint under Sam Barry in which the Trojans went 2–6–1, the school hired three consecutive alumni to lead the football team. Jeff Cravath, Jess Hill and Don Clark ran the show in the forties and fifties, and although there were several good years and a couple very good years, the Trojans, who had gotten a taste of national championships under Jones, rarely even got a spot at the table of college football's elite in the two decades that followed. There were one top five and three top ten finishes in the national rankings between 1940 and 1959, and six conference championships yielded a 3–3 Rose Bowl record, with one of the losses coming at the hands of Michigan, 49–0, in 1948.

1960 was a year of change in America. John F. Kennedy

was elected president, Elvis returned from the army and a bouncing baby boy was born into the Allen family of San Diego. They named him Marcus.

At USC, the Trojans needed a coach. School president Norman Topping set out to replace the capable Don Clark, who had stepped down after three seasons on the job. Head coaches make hundreds, if not thousands, of decisions every season, but the second-best one Clark ever made for USC's long-term success was his hiring, in 1959, of an assistant coach from the University of Oregon named John McKay. Clark's best decision was recommending his new assistant as his own replacement upon retiring from coaching after the 1959 season.

Years later, Clark reflected, "I liked McKay as an individual—he had a great sense of humor, and he was relaxed and great with our athletes. He was a very important addition to our staff that year, and I was pleased to be able to recommend his replacing me at the university."

Dr. Norman Topping, who was named USC president in 1958, took the recommendation into consideration, but at first glance, McKay might not have appeared to have what it took to be a force in Division 1 coaching. Consider the successful coaches of the time: Bear Bryant, who had gone from Texas A&M to Alabama in 1958; Bud Wilkinson at Oklahoma; Bobby Dodd at Georgia Tech; Frank Broyles at Arkansas, et cetera. They were all tough, serious, no-nonsense men who ran college football programs like military training units. McKay's approach was a bit different.

All-American tackle Ron Mix was entering his senior season at USC when McKay arrived as a defensive line coach. The six foot three, 215 pounder out of Inglewood went on to a brilliant pro career with the Chargers and Raiders in which he was called for holding just twice in eleven seasons, and named to the all-AFL team nine straight years. Even though they worked on different sides of the ball, Mix and McKay got to know each other rather well. The lineman's impressions of the first-year assistant wouldn't exactly qualify as a hard sell for McKay becoming a head coach. Said Mix in 1985, "I didn't think he'd go anywhere in his career. He was a happy-go-lucky kind of guy. Other coaches would be walking around. They'd always be frowning. They'd never smile, never have a kind word. John would laugh, crack jokes, build a personal relationship with the players, and I thought he'd be history. Of course, he is history—but in a much different vein."

There was something about McKay that appealed to Topping—a lot of things actually. And after giving the situation serious thought, the school president made a decision of his own. One fateful afternoon on the USC campus, a dozen years before Heritage Hall was built, Topping summoned the thirty-six-year-old assistant coach from Everettsville, West Virginia, to his office. Topping remembers, "He showed up at my door smoking a cigar. I looked him over and said, 'John—how would you like to be the head football coach?' He said, 'Hmmm—I gotta think about that. Maybe I oughta talk to [wife] Corky. I really have to give this some thought. . . . OK. I've thought about it. I'd love to!' " And in typical McKay fashion, a new era in USC football had begun.

John McKay was an all-state high school running back in West Virginia. Upon graduation, he worked for a year in the coal mines and then served in the air force in World War II. He started at defensive back for Purdue in 1946 as a freshman, then transferred to Oregon where he was a two-way starter in 1948, earning all-America honorable mention and all-coast first team honors while setting a school record averaging 6.4 yards per carry.

It would make a great story to say that McKay hit the field as a head coach for the first time, whipped a team into shape and led them to new heights, but it didn't happen that way. In 1960, several factors worked against the new coach as the

Trojans lost all-conference players to graduation, lost starters to injury and lost games to their first three opponents, scoring just six points in the process. They did salvage a meaningful slice of the season with a homecoming win over eleventh-ranked UCLA in the penultimate game of the year. And the momentum from that win? It lasted all of six days. Then they dropped the season finale to Notre Dame, finishing the season at a disappointing 4–6.

Record-wise, 1961 wasn't much better, and in many ways was much worse. After a 30–0 whipping at the hands of the Irish, the Trojans were a dismal 1–3, and rumblings about the head coach could be heard both on and off campus. The relatively unknown McKay had won just five of his first fourteen games, and during a midseason meeting with alumni and boosters, President Topping was bombarded with anti-McKay sentiment.

"They were most vociferous," he recalled. "They were saying that I have to get rid of John, that he was a failure, and I was a failure for hiring him. I listened to it, and listened to it— finally I clapped my hands and said, 'All right, you listen to me now!' I stood up on the chair and said, 'We oughta wait for one more year until John has his team together with the kids *he* recruited, because I have seen them and they are going to do well.'"

McKay remembered, "We started with a one-year contract, and I almost didn't make it through the first year. All I wondered was whether I was gonna get enough time to get the kind of players I believed in. I thought the 1960 and sixty-one teams overall were the two *slowest* teams I'd been around. We had very little speed, and I vowed if I had time, I would recruit players that could run." In fact, McKay was so staunch in his beliefs that he felt speed on a college football field cured almost all ills and overcame almost all obstacles. He was once asked about the intensity of his team and answered, "Intensity is a lot of guys who run fast."

McKay held strong to his theories about football. He took over as head coach, identified the problems with his team and then went out and recruited his ass off. He held the reins of a once-proud football program and he was determined to ride it to glory.

Hal Bedsole, an all-American left end in 1962, said of that year's team, "It was a tribute to the coaching staff. They found the best athletes and put 'em on the field simultaneously. The typical thing is to say, 'I want the ball. I want the ball.' Everybody wants the ball, and we all got it enough to do what we needed to do and to feel like we had participated in the game. But I tell ya one thing—ya better do good when they get it to ya because there were a lot of guys who could do something with it!"

In 1962, all of those guys did do something with it. Something special.

THE GAME (JANUARY 1, 1963)

The 1962 USC team was the first made up mostly—which is to say *almost entirely*—of John McKay's recruits. The season started in impressive fashion, with the unranked Trojans pulling off a 14–7 upset over the highly touted eighth-ranked Duke Blue Devils. The following week, USC made its debut in the polls at number nine. A subsequent win over Southern Methodist landed them at sixth, and a shutout of Iowa vaulted them to third. Number three with a bullet. The eighth game of the season brought the Midshipmen of Navy to Southern California, and as the Trojans walked off the field with a 13–6 win, and a sparkling 8–0 record, they were hours away from becoming proud owners of the number one national ranking, with only UCLA and Notre Dame standing in the way of an un-defeated regular season. UCLA and Notre Dame—in 1962, that sounded like a job for the Trojan defense.

The Trojans had held their eight opponents to just fifty-two points, surrendering an average of 6.5 per game. Only two foes had scored in double digits. The other six didn't register more than a touchdown, and two teams failed to score completely. With the games gaining importance, and the defensive unit gaining confidence, their two chief rivals didn't stand a chance. UCLA was pushed aside 14–3, and Notre Dame was blown out 25–0. The McKay era had unofficially become an era, indeed. A USC career that had gotten off to a very shaky start was sud-denly on extremely solid ground. The Trojans were undefeated, ranked number one in the nation and on the way to their first Rose Bowl in eight years. The final regular season scoring totals were 219 for and fifty-five against. Craig Fertig, a sophomore on the 1962 squad who would go on to star a couple years later, said, looking back, "There was amazing chemistry on that team, and it might have been coach McKay's best job of coach-ing." USC great Marv Goux, the Trojan captain in 1955, who twice won the Davis-Teschke Award, given annually to the team's most inspirational player, was an assistant coach on McKay's staff. He said in 1987, "That team was so dedicated and so intelligent, and they knew how to play the game."

The coaching staff knew a thing or two, as well, and had a full month to prepare for the Rose Bowl. The focus of the entire country would be on Pasadena come January 1, as top-ranked USC was pitted against number two Wisconsin, the once beaten, high-scoring Big 10 champion. Practices began as light workouts in mid-December and gained in intensity and physi-cality as game day drew nearer. As heavily as the Trojans had relied on their defense for most of the season, much of the coaching staff's worries were in regard to that very unit. The

Wisconsin offense busted through everything that stood in its way like an armored tank smashing balsa wood barricades. The Badger players were imposing in stature, but they were midgets compared to the very numbers they had amassed during the course of the season, going off for more than 362 yards and thirty-two points per game. In the sixties, there was an agreement between major colleges that each would send films from its previous games to future opponents. So impressive was Wisconsin, that at the Jonathan Club's seventeenth annual gridiron breakfast on the Friday before the game, featured speaker John McKay quipped, "They sent us their game films. We shipped 'em back. They made us sick!"

The day before the game, McKay, whose team came in as a three-point underdog, was a bit more serious. He said, "We have to stop the greatest offensive team in collegiate football. We have stopped some great running teams and some great passing teams, but not both on the same day as we must now."

The big concern was an unpredictable quarterback named Ronald VanderKelen, a deceivingly quick right hander who played the game like an Old West gunslinger with an itchy trigger finger. He had a reputation for throwing in any direction, any distance at any time, regardless of down and distance or game situation. When he was back in the pocket, he avoided trouble like a nun on parole.

VanderKelen had come from seemingly nowhere to bring the Badgers to national prominence in 1962 despite playing all of ninety seconds in a decidedly unspectacular college career prior to his senior season. In fact, the Wisconsin coaching staff itself had major doubts about VanderKelen's ability before reluctantly handing him the starting job that summer. Clark Van Galder, a Badgers assistant, was quoted as saying, "It isn't that Ron can't throw, rather it's the way he throws. Ron throws the ball from down here." He demonstrated a sidearm motion below shoulder level with his palm facing up. The coach continued in a rather politically incorrect vein, saying, "You might say he throws like a woman, but he gets the ball to the receiver and that's what you want, isn't it?"

Yeah. That's what you want, unlike a coach stating that his starting quarterback throws like a woman. Can you imagine a coach speaking like that these days? Pete Carroll: Hey, that Matt Leinart sure can elude the rush, but he runs like a girl, doesn't he?

Unthinkable.

Kickoff came at about two twenty p.m., under mostly cloudy skies on a calm afternoon at the Rose Bowl. The stadium in Pasadena was jam-packed and it didn't take long for the capacity crowd to see USC flex its offensive muscle. Just more than 5.5 minutes into the game, quarterback Pete Beathard found, of all people, left tackle Ron Butcher for a thirteen-yard touchdown on fourth and goal. Wisconsin, though, roared back with a score of its own, and the first quarter ended tied at seven. The Badgers had a chance to take the lead early in the second, but all-American linebacker Damon Bame intercepted VanderKelen in Trojans territory and USC cashed in on the turnover to go up 14–7. After the Trojans made a defensive stop, they took possession again on their own twenty, where Bill Nelsen, who shared the quarterbacking duties with Beathard, fumbled. The ball was recovered by Wisconsin on the USC twenty-two, but the refs ruled that the play had been blown dead prior to the fumble. USC retained possession and capitalized on the break, marching the rest of the way, seventy-two yards for the touchdown that made it 21–7 at halftime.

Newspaper reports the next day said that when the whistle blew to end the second quarter, usually mild-mannered Badgers coach Milt Bruhn, along with two of his assistant coaches, "Rushed across the gridiron and wildly berated the officials." Bruhn was quoted after the game, saying, "I thought they were all wrong on the play where we recovered the fumble. It was too fast a whistle."

The call was questionable enough to get the attention of those watching from the press box, including Notre Dame coach Joe Kuharich, who claimed that "a quick whistle" deprived the Badgers of a chance to go in for a tying touchdown.

Whether it was by benefit of a referee's call, superior game planning or any of the other hundreds of variables that make up thirty minutes of football, the first half was a smashing success for USC. The Trojans worked Wisconsin's defense from all angles, ultimately capping second quarter scoring drives with a one-yard touchdown plunge by Ben Wilson and a twenty-five-yard scoring jaunt by Ron Heller, who played despite ligament damage to his right knee.

By the time the band hit the field at halftime, the huge Trojan contingent in the crowd had turned the Rose Bowl stands into a spill-over New Year's Eve party—a joyous celebration in which all was well in Trojan Nation. This team the fans had watched all season long and had come to trust with any lead— let alone a 21–7 edge at halftime—was thirty minutes away from its first Rose Bowl victory in ten years.

Meantime, in the Wisconsin locker room, it was deathly quiet. Star receiver Pat Richter, a future Wisconsin athletic director who went on to be inducted in both the college football and Rose Bowl halls of fame, remembered in 2006, "We were down so far, I don't recall any screaming or hollering. It was more of a kind of quiet embarrassment. We were in shock. It was a situation where we were just trying to get back to some kind of respectability."

The Trojans took the ball to start the second half, and before most of the 98,698 in attendance had returned to their seats, USC was in the end zone again. Hal Bedsole, the all-American receiver who averaged an astounding twenty-five yards per catch that season, took a pass from Beathard and went fifty-seven yards for the touchdown. Wisconsin's defense, which had to be thinking that it needed a stop to give the Badgers any chance, held up for less than a minute. Just fifty seconds into the second half it was 28–7, and the rout was on, or so it seemed. Less than five minutes later, Wisconsin answered on a seventeen-yard run by VanderKelen, cutting the Wisconsin deficit back to a manageable fourteen points. A roar went up from the traveling party of about 5,500 red-clad Badger fans escaping the brutal cold of the Midwest, but until that moment chilled by the mostly one-sided action playing out in the warmth of Southern California. USC increased the lead to twenty-one again later in the third quarter on a twenty-three-yard hookup from Beathard to Bedsole, who made a sweet grab, reaching high above his head to haul in a frozen rope in the back of the end zone on a third and nine play. Then, on the first play of the fourth quarter, Beathard brought receiver Fred Hill into the act with a thirteen-yard touchdown strike, making it 42–14. The rout was on again, or so it seemed.

The Trojans sideline took on the same kind of atmosphere that was in the stands. It was New Year's Day, the lead was gaudy and their big men on campus stature was getting bigger by the minute.

"We were ahead forty-two–fourteen," recalled Bill Nelsen. "I'm down there, saying, 'Listen guys—the parties are down the street—let's just figure out which ones we're going to!'"

The party to which they were actually going has been raging since the beginning of organized sports. Typically, a team with a big lead late in a game starts to relax, and the team that is trailing becomes desperate. The combination of those two factors is a volatile mix that can blow up at any moment. The morning after one of those parties, there is usually a hangover made up of equal parts heartbreak and regret.

While the Trojans were in party mode, the Wisconsin offense

made a subtle but extremely effective change at the beginning of the fourth quarter, and the game took on an entirely new personality. For three quarters, the Badgers had been splitting one of their ends wide, and leaving the receiver on the other side close to the linemen the way a tight end would be used in today's game. Needing points, and a lot of them, the Badgers came out in more of a pro-set offensive alignment, using two wide receivers, and suddenly a stagnant offense came alive.

"When we split the guys out wide," recalls Richter, "we also started doing a lot of against-the-grain-type things. VanderKelen would roll toward the right side and I would come back to the left, getting some misdirection." And it was working.

Another factor in Wisconsin's impending comeback was USC's defensive approach. With each tick of the clock working in their favor, the Trojan linebackers and defensive backs were receding like the Pacific at low tide. They were in the "no big plays" mind-set, so Wisconsin settled for numerous midrange gains, eating up chunks of the field fifteen to twenty yards at a time.

Their first touchdown of the fourth quarter came 3:12 after USC scored, and their second came 3:11 after that. In the blink of an eye, a 42–14 Trojans laugher became a 42–28 Rose Bowl on the brink of becoming a classic.

Damon Bame remembers, "It was almost as if when the sun went down, we went down with it."

The grand old stadium did not yet have lights in 1963, and midway through the fourth quarter, the Pasadena dusk arrived and brought with it the final half hour of daylight on a New Year's Day to remember. The Trojans lead wasn't entirely gone, but like a marathon runner whose every stride feels like a beating in itself in the final mile, the finish line couldn't come soon enough. The lead, once a hefty twenty-eight points, had been cut in half. Worse yet, 8:42—in this game, a lifetime—remained.

Wisconsin was a team on the move. They ran motion out of

the backfield, sent ends wide during the snap count and slith-
ered through the Trojans' defense like a slippery snake through
tall wet grass. The Badgers' next possession appeared to be
headed for another seven, but their drive died when two-way
player Willie Brown intercepted VanderKelen in the end zone.
Brown was all over the field, and was undoubtedly USC's most
productive player in the Rose Bowl. In addition to the fourth
quarter interception, he racked up 267 all-purpose yards *and*
was in on nine tackles.

The USC offense that was so strong for three quarters did
nothing with the ball after the turnover, and as Wisconsin took
possession, there was an overriding sense of doom among the
cardinal-clad spectators despite the fourteen-point lead.

The consolation for the fans, whose New Year's Day was
suddenly made up more of consternation than celebration, was
that the scoring was being done in sevens, and even two more
Wisconsin touchdowns would only tie the game. But on this
day—at least toward the end of it—whatever could go wrong
did for USC.

Wisconsin's possession didn't yield any points, but the Badgers' punt managed to pin USC deep in its own territory, and
the Wisconsin defense forced the Trojans to give up the ball
once again.

Punter Ernie Jones, who was suddenly getting a pretty good
workout, was back near his own goal line when the snap came
sizzling toward him, gaining altitude with each yard. It sailed
clear over his head into the end zone, and when he raced back
to cover the ball, Wisconsin's Ernie Von Heimburg covered
him, resulting in a safety. The two points cut the dwindling
lead down to twelve with 2:40 remaining, as the Trojans special
teams unit stayed on the field to kick off in the quickly fading
light.

Wisconsin took over and kept right on cruising. VanderKelen was suddenly Johnny Unitas, Bart Starr and Joe Namath all

rolled into one. He was a mad man. The fifth-year senior, who had been eligible for the NFL draft the previous spring but was unchosen through all twenty rounds, was looking not only like a draft choice, but a first rounder. It took all of three pass plays and 1:21 for the Badgers to find the end zone again. VanderKelen, uncannily scrambling out of trouble on almost every play, hit Richter for nineteen yards and another touchdown. It was the quarterback's eighteenth completion in twenty-two fourth quarter attempts, and amazingly the Badgers were within five at 42–37 with 1:19 remaining.

An onside kick was coming. The Badgers knew it, the Trojans knew it and everybody in the stadium knew it. Whether they could see it or not was another story. On a field lit as much by the rising moon as by the setting sun, USC managed to cover a bounding ball that had seemed to bounce against them for most of the longest second half they ever played.

The Trojans offense then took the field, and according to a January 2, 1963, article in the *New York Times*, "The game ended with the thankful Trojans running backward deliberately to kill the clock and then punting on the final play."

The punt, inches or maybe millimeters from being blocked, emerged from the darkened sky and bounced harmlessly on the Badgers side of the fifty as the final seconds ticked off the scoreboard.

The final score read USC 42, Wisconsin 37.

Winston Churchill once said, "Without victory there is no survival." On this day, victory *was* survival for USC. Quarterback Pete Beathard, looking back in the eighties, said, "It was an exciting football game, but boy, it was nerve-racking down at the end. VanderKelen did a great job but we eked it out. It really was a very memorable game and, without a doubt, in my mind, the greatest Rose Bowl ever."

A few years after the game was played, John McKay was a

guest on the old sports television show *The Way It Was.* He said, "It was one of the greatest games of all time and one that I will never forget."

Players participate in most college football games for a few hours on a Saturday afternoon. This one, they seem to play for a lifetime. Forty-three years later, Richter says that somebody mentions the game to him at least once a week. He recalled an incident from 1994 when, as athletic director for the Badgers, he was back in Pasadena for that year's Rose Bowl. Richter was sitting in a hotel lobby, talking with Wisconsin coach Barry Alvarez, who said, "You're never gonna believe this, but Tommy Lasorda just walked in."

Richter continues. "So we walked up to him, and Barry says, 'Hi, Tommy. I'm Wisconsin's coach Barry Alvarez.' Tommy said hello to Barry, and then I said 'Hi. I'm the athletic director, Pat Richter.' Tommy says, 'You're Pat Richter! Jeez, that was a hell of a game you played!' And there's Coach Alvarez standing there like, *What the* hell *is goin' on? How does everybody remember that game?*

"Another time," Richter remembers, "a guy came up to me to talk about the game, saying he'd never forget it. I thought that was nice, but it wasn't because he was a Wisconsin fan. It was because his dad was watching on TV and wouldn't let the family eat dinner until it was over, and that was almost ten o'clock Eastern time."

In 2004, Collegefootballnews.com ranked the hundred greatest games in the history of college football, and the 1963 Rose Bowl was listed at number thirteen.

Richter, who went on to play seven years for the Washington Redskins, had the day of his life, catching eleven passes for 163 yards. VanderKelen, who shared the game's most valuable player award with Pete Beathard, set a Rose Bowl record with 401 yards passing on thirty-three completions. The seventy-nine total points scored was a Rose Bowl record that stood for twenty-eight years.

VanderKelen said, years later, "When the gun went off, all I could do is stand there. I desperately wanted one more chance, but then I guess that's what makes this game so great. You could speculate throughout history what would have been if Wisconsin had one more chance."

As it was, the Badgers scored the game's final twenty-three points, outgained the Trojans 486 yards to 367 and had thirty-two first downs to just fifteen for USC.

It was a tough ending for USC fans to watch. The Trojans were like a finely tuned race car blowing away the field for the first ninety-five laps of a hundred-lap race. Then the carburetor blows, the fan belt snaps, the engine leaks oil, the gas gauge hits empty and the driver has a splitting headache. Somehow, though, they made it to the finish line. They managed to work some black checkers onto the white surrender flag and sputter to the victory. Ultimately, out from under the mountain of garish numbers and lopsided statistics, crawled a battered, but not beaten, bunch of Trojans. They were an undefeated team who withstood a furious rally to walk from the darkness that had fallen upon the Rose Bowl into the light of the school's first national championship in twenty-three years.

	1	2	3	4	F
Wisconsin	7	0	7	23	37
USC	7	14	14	7	42

Scoring:

First Quarter

USC: Butcher, 15-yard pass from Beathard (Lupo kick)

Wisconsin: Kurek, 1-yard run (Kroner kick)

Second Quarter

USC: Wilson, 1-yard run (Lupo kick)

USC: Heller, 25-yard run (Lupo kick)

Third Quarter

USC: Bedsole, 57-yard pass from Beathard (Lupo kick)

Wisconsin: VanderKelen, 17-yard run (Kroner kick)

USC: Bedsole, 23-yard pass from Beathard (Lupo kick)

Fourth Quarter

USC: F. Hill, 13-yard pass from Beathard (Lupo kick)

Wisconsin: Holland, 18-yard run (Kroner kick)

Wisconsin: Kroner, 4-yard pass from VanderKelen (Kroner kick)

Wisconsin: safety (Jones tackled in end zone)

Wisconsin: Richter, 19-yard pass from VanderKelen (Kroner kick)

Passing:

Wisconsin: VanderKelen, 33–48–401, 3 interceptions, 2 touchdowns

USC: Beathard, 8–12–190, 4 touchdowns

Nelson, 2–6–63

Rushing:

Wisconsin: Holland, 4–27; Kurek, 11–26

USC: Wilson, 17–57; Heller, 4–32; Beathard, 8–23

Receiving:

Wisconsin: Richter, 11–163; Holland, 8–72; Kroner, 5–64

USC: Bedsole, 4–101; Brown, 3–108; Heller, 1–18

POSTSCRIPT

The day after the game, Jim Murray's column in the *Los Angeles Times* summed up the craziness and excitement of a most unforgettable day in Pasadena.

The game lasted only slightly less long than the War of 1812. It started out in broad daylight, but ended in conditions so dark that a man would bump into an elephant. The official timer needed a calendar. If the game lasted one more quarter, they would have run into next year's Rose Parade traffic.

There were so many points scored, the Dow Jones ticker was running behind at the three o'clock close.

The game was like Russian roulette with all barrels loaded or a tennis game in which neither side could hold its serve. I have seen drunks put up a better defense falling off a stool.

There were 79 points scored, 69 passes attempted. Anybody caught carrying the ball was a sissy. USC won, but they were like the kid who comes home with his nose bleeding, his ear torn, his clothes ripped and both eyes black and he says, "But you oughta see the other fellow."

I know some schools that shouldn't schedule Ron VanderKelen. He completed more passes than a sailor on leave in Tahiti. USC had a 42–14 lead at the start of the final quarter before they discovered the hole in their pocket. They ran out of their earnings quicker than a guy who starts letting his wife sign.

I won't say VanderKelen had plenty of time back there, but have you ever heard of a guy reading the Kinsey Report while waiting to throw a touchdown pass?

The officials had a lively day. They gained more yards on the ground than both teams put together.

Coach John McKay won his first Rose Bowl game, but the press acted more as if he had just stolen his grandmother's crutches.

It was alas, for VanderKelen, true. He was 14 into the Trojans in the fourth quarter and on his way to what would have been Wisconsin's fifth touchdown when he completed one pass too many. Willie Brown of USC caught it.

Four coronaries later, the game came to a merciful halt.

No one went up to Coach McKay to ask, "When did you know you had it won, coach?" He still isn't sure.

At least there's one good thing: the University of VanderKelen can't come to the Rose Bowl two years in a row.

A few days after the game, McKay joked, "I got ready to go dancing when we were up forty-two to fourteen. I left the stadium and left my assistants in charge. I was surprised the next day to find out they got that many points on us."

That was John McKay.

In retrospect, it is almost humorous to think that boosters and alumni were calling for the coach's head midway through the 1961 season. His status at USC was solidified soon thereafter, and his place in college football is now legendary.

In sixteen seasons in Troy, McKay's teams went undefeated three times, won four national titles, five Rose Bowls and nine conference championships. He won national coach of the year honors in 1962 and 1972, and compiled a 127–40–8 record (.749) while finishing in the top ten in the polls nine times.

But the stats and the records tell just a minor part of the John McKay story. His legacy is cemented by the relationships he forged and the people he touched. His sense of humor and quick wit were such a large part of his legend that the fact that he was a major innovator and creative force in the offensive design in college football is often overlooked.

Some of McKay's greatest hits:

* After the undefeated 1962 season: "Isn't it wonderful how much smarter I am this year."

* On pressure from the fans: "I'll never be hung in effigy. Before every season, I send my men out to buy up all the rope in Los Angeles."

* 1965, versus Notre Dame, when USC's Mike Hunter fell flat on his face returning the opening kickoff: "My God, they shot him!"

* 1966, in the locker room after a 51–0 loss to Notre Dame: "Gentlemen, those of you who need showers, take them."

* In 1968, when asked why OJ Simpson had been carrying the ball so much: "Why not? It isn't very heavy. Besides, he doesn't belong to a union."

* 1970, after a twenty-five-point loss to UCLA: "Today our offense could not run, block or throw the ball. But our defense made up for it by not tackling!"

* On recruiting his son, J.K.: "I had a rather distinct advantage. I was sleeping with his mother."

* When told by recruits J.K and Pat Haden that they were thinking of going to Stanford: "If it was between Stanford and Red China, I would pay your way to Peking."

* In 1976, when asked about his team's execution after a lopsided defeat while coaching the Tampa Bay Buccaneers: "I'm in favor of it."

* In 1977, after his Tampa Bay team broke its twenty-six-game losing streak: "Now just three or four plane crashes and we're in the playoffs."

McKay served USC in a dual role during his final four seasons, running the Trojan sports programs as athletic director as well as serving as head football coach. He was inducted into the College Football Hall of Fame in 1988 and the Rose Bowl Hall of Fame in 1991, and was a member of 1994's inaugural class of USC's Athletic Hall of Fame.

Craig Fertig, one of the star players of McKay's early years, said of the coach, "He was probably the smartest person I've ever been around as far as football goes. He had a knack of reading a situation. He could tell you exactly what a team was doing on defense and come up with 'well, if they're doing that, we should be doing this.'"

Pat Haden, former USC and Los Angeles Rams quarterback, actually lived at the McKays' house during high school so he could keep his eligibility at Bishop Amat High School after his parents moved away. "I think he was the best evaluator of talent that I've ever seen," Haden says. "He would have some high school kid who was an all-American linebacker, and the first day he'd watch him practice, he'd say, 'You're a tight end.' Two years later, that kid was an all-American tight end. I think he had a great skill for piecing an entire team together. You may have come in as one kind of player, but you would have left a different player, playing a different position, much more successfully."

McKay made a bold move in 1975, resigning at USC to become the first head coach of the NFL's expansion Tampa Bay Buccaneers. Although McKay's Bucs lost their first twenty-six games, they eventually emerged as contenders. Tampa Bay made the playoffs three times under McKay, including a run in 1979 that culminated with an appearance in the NFC championship game. The team was the first expansion club to reach a conference title game within its first four seasons. McKay retired in 1984 at the conclusion of his ninth season in Tampa Bay with a 44–88–1 record.

Jim Perry, a former assistant athletic director at USC and author of *McKay: A Coach's Story*, said, "McKay was the most unforgettable person I've ever met. To say he was a strong personality is an all-time understatement. When he spoke, everyone listened. When the team went to see the movie *Patton*, with George C. Scott, there was an instant flash of recognition among his coaching staff. 'My God,' they said, 'that's Coach!' And on the field, John McKay *was* General Patton."

JOHN McKAY'S USC COACHING RECORD

Yr	W	L	T	Bowl Result	Top-10 AP Ranking
1960	4	6	0		
1961	4	5	1		
1962	11	0	0	Rose—USC 42, Wisconsin 37	1
1963	7	3	0		
1964	7	3	0		10
1965	7	2	1		10
1966	7	4	0	Rose—Purdue 14, USC 13	
1967	10	1	0	Rose—USC 14, Indiana 3	1
1968	9	1	1	Rose—Ohio State 27, USC 16	4
1969	10	0	1	Rose—USC 10, Michigan 3	3
1970	6	4	1		
1971	6	4	1		
1972	12	0	0	Rose—USC 42, Ohio State 17	1
1973	9	2	1	Rose—Ohio State 42, USC 21	8
1974	10	1	1	Rose—USC 18, Ohio State 17	2
1975	8	4	0	Liberty—USC 20, Texas A&M 0	
Totals	127	40	8		

CHAPTER FOUR

USC

VS.

NOTRE DAME, 1964

THE SETUP

It is not far geographically from East Los Angeles to Westwood, but in so many ways, the two cities are worlds apart. Growing up in the fifties, an East Los Angeles kid named Mike Garrett was a hard-core UCLA football fan who watched his heroes play on Saturday afternoons.

While the Bruins were stringing together three straight top-five finishes, Garrett was having some early success of his own on the athletic fields of his community. When he entered Roosevelt High School in the early sixties, a sports star began to take shape, and his college of choice began to take note. In his junior year, UCLA was first in contact and then in close contact. The interest was unmistakable.

And then it was gone.

"UCLA recruited me really hard my eleventh grade year,

and then they just went cold on me," he says, looking back with nearly half a century of retrospect. "Many years later, one of the UCLA guys told me that they had backed off because they thought I was too small."

Not all schools were about to make the same mistake. USC's new coach, John McKay, felt strongly that there was enough talent in Southern California alone that he could put together a winning team made up mostly of local players. His focus turned to Roosevelt High and the blossoming five-foot-nine prep all-American.

"McKay and USC always recruited late," Garrett remembers. "My senior year in high school, they came in and said, 'We want you,' and I said, 'OK. Let's do it.'" And just like that, colors changed, allegiances shifted and USC secured a spectacular superstar in the making who would lead them to new levels of greatness.

A member of the 1962 freshman team, Garrett caught wind of the troubles McKay had during the new coach's first two seasons at USC, and very early on, Garrett understood what lay ahead. One day, early in spring practice, McKay wanted there to be no misunderstanding. Garrett explains, "He had the entire team together and said, 'You sons of bitches are *not* gonna get me fired.'"

Some players were taken aback, but not the bright-eyed freshman. He says, "You have no idea how hard we worked. And that made our history. McKay *made* modern USC football. We always left everything on the field. I loved John McKay. I just *loved* him. He was the first guy I ever met that matched my tenacity in gettin' after it. McKay was a tough guy. Our workouts were very much like Pete Carroll's. We scrimmaged *so* much. That's when we had 120 guys. Man, it was a meat grinder. If you were faint of heart or you couldn't play with pain or soreness, you couldn't play here."

Former USC coach John Robinson says, "Mike was the fiercest. He was like a bulldog."

Anybody who ever played with him, or even saw him play, speaks glowingly of Mike Garrett's talent.

OJ Simpson: "He was almost kinetic in the way he moved, in his ability to juke guys."

Marcus Allen: "Total scat-back. Moves, speed, strength—the guy had everything."

Anthony Davis: "He was the forefather of the great runners at USC."

Rod Sherman: "He had tremendous balance and tremendous explosion. He also had an enormous amount of enthusiasm. He approached every day in practice like it was game day."

Craig Fertig: "He owes all of his success to me."

Fertig, of course, is known for his sense of humor, and he points out that the only way for a running back to get the ball is for a quarterback to either hand it to him or throw it to him. By that logic, though, Fertig owes all of *his* success to the centers he played with throughout his career. A bit more seriously, Fertig says, "If I was in a street fight and I could have one guy on my side, I'm takin' Mike Garrett."

Steve Brady, a tailback at USC in 1966 and 1967, says that Garrett is "the shiftiest runner I have ever seen in football. He could fake you out in a hallway."

As USC returned for the 1963 season as national champions and Rose Bowl winners, Mike Garrett was a sophomore determined to play a large role in the Trojans' success in the years ahead, and he got off to a great start. The 1963 Trojans went 7–3, with Garrett establishing himself as an offensive force. He ran for 833 yards, averaging a whopping 6.5 yards per carry.

The following year was even more impressive as the slippery tailback started to garner national recognition as one of the best runners in the country. Garrett's rushing total increased to 948 yards, and he was heavily relied on as USC made a run at another Rose Bowl.

In four conference games, including a late-season win over UCLA, the Trojans went 3–1, losing only a homecoming heart-breaker to Washington, 14–13. Also 3–1, and tied for first, was Oregon State, a team USC had not played. To determine whether it would be USC or Oregon State representing the conference in the Rose Bowl, a vote would be taken among the other six schools in the conference, which at the time was called the Athletic Association of Western Universities (AAWU). Each school would send its vote by telegraph after the completion of the following Saturday's action. The announcement of the procedure came on November 26, 1964, as USC was neck-deep in preparation for what would turn out to be one of the most memorable games in the history of college football.

THE GAME (NOVEMBER 28, 1964)

A *Los Angeles Times* article the day before the game explained the Rose Bowl scenario. It read in part, "Presumably, should Southern California beat No. 1 ranked Notre Dame, the Trojans would stand a good chance of winning the bid. Should the Irish beat USC, as expected, Oregon State is anticipated to be the Western representative."

Yes, Notre Dame was *expected* to beat USC. The Irish hadn't lost all season, and brought with them to California the nation's number one ranking. It was a remarkable turnaround for Notre Dame after winning just two games the previous season. The difference, many thought, was first-year coach Ara Parseghian, who had taken South Bend by storm, running off nine straight wins to start his Notre Dame career, and had been eliciting comparisons to the great Knute Rockne.

The Irish were dominant on both sides of the ball. They averaged thirty points per game from an offense powered by a pair of kids out of Southern California: Heisman Trophy–winning quarterback John Huarte and future NFL star receiver Jack Snow. A massive defensive line weighed in at an average of 230 pounds (huge by 1960s standards) and led a unit that gave up an average of just sixty-one rushing yards per game and had allowed a mere eight touchdowns all season. So impressive was the Irish defensive front, *Los Angeles Times* columnist John Hall wrote an article that was printed on the day of the game with some advice for John McKay.

With the Trojans about to wrap it all up with Notre Dame today comes a really serious suggestion on how to combat the Irish.

Having visited South Bend with UCLA on Oct. 17, the memory of the ordeal of watching the Irish work out the day before the battle is still vivid. Not to mention alarming, stunning and frightening.

Bruin coach Bill Barnes and aide Sam Boghosian were standing around with several others in front of the stadium as the Irish players began to arrive for their drill.

"What's that?" swooned Billy in the tone of the first caveman to discover the dinosaur.

"It's just one of the kids from the freshman team," answered a South Bender flatly.

Little sophomore tackle Kevin Hardy (262) and soph defensive end Alan Page (230) strolled by.

"Since when did the Chicago Bears start working out here?" asked Boghosian. He got no answer, just a look of pity.

From there, it got worse as the juniors and seniors began to check in. "Gosh," said Barnes. "Gee," said Sam, and the damage was done.

Larry Zeno even sneaked back to the equipment room later that night and hid his own jersey so he wouldn't have to play the next day. Unluckily, they borrowed one for Larry from the home team, and, of course, it was too big.

If McKay hasn't gotten the point yet, it is this: Don't let the Trojans watch Notre Dame take the field or warm up. Blindfold 'em at least until the kickoff. And no peeking.

The Irish are human. They just don't look like it.

That was what awaited USC on the season's final Saturday at the Coliseum. A twelve-point underdog, the Trojans went in simply looking for a shot at the Rose Bowl. The mighty Irish had crossed the country in search of so much more, determined to cap off a perfect season, which would bring them the undisputed national championship.

Kickoff came at one thirty on a picture perfect seventy-degree day in Los Angeles. Notre Dame got on the board early with a first quarter field goal and, with the score 3–0, struck again. This time, it was a long, sustained drive that took them through the Trojan defense with relative ease. Despite racking up thirty yards in penalties, Notre Dame went seventy-three yards on ten plays with Huarte (pronounced *Hewart*) finding Snow in the end zone on a twenty-one-yard strike to make it 10–0 just three plays into the second quarter.

USC moved deep into Notre Dame territory on the following drive, but McKay eschewed the field goal, trying to pick up a first down on a fourth and four from the Irish sixteen. A well-designed play sprung receiver Dave Moton loose in the right front corner of the end zone, but Craig Fertig's pass sailed just out of his reach. Notre Dame took over on downs, the zero remained in the home team's column on the big scoreboard in the Coliseum and, aside from the groans, fans in the stands remained mostly quiet.

Two possessions later, the Irish were on the move again.

They put together a drive that was one play longer and one yard shorter than their previous touchdown march, but it ended in the end zone just the same. Notre Dame, top ranked and undefeated, was simply doing what it had done all year: scoring touchdowns on offense, making stops on defense and looking altogether dominant as they headed into halftime leading 17–0.

The Trojans' locker room wasn't nearly as dour as one might think because McKay's approach was never to portend doom. Instead, he insisted that if not for a costly fumble, a missed scoring opportunity and some bad luck, the score would be close. Several Trojans recount the story of how McKay pretended to be deep in thought, and then, as if making a very insightful observation, said, "Gentlemen, we are down seventeen to zero. If we don't score at least seventeen points in the second half, we are going to lose this football game."

Fertig says, "We had some math majors in the room, and after a little figuring, they confirmed that the coach was correct."

Minutes later, McKay got a bit more serious, telling his team that all they needed to do was score on the opening drive of the second half and they would come back to win.

Four decades later, Fertig explains that during the week of practice, McKay stopped drills one day and brought the entire offense over near the outfield wall of Bovard Stadium, where the Trojan baseball team played. "We didn't have a blackboard out there, so coach takes out a marker and starts drawing on the wall! 'Here's what we're gonna do,' he said. 'Notre Dame has thrown the quarterback for 748 yards in losses,' or whatever the number was—a tremendous amount of losses. 'We're gonna keep eight guys in and block for Craig.'"

"I thought that was a hell of an idea," cracks Fertig, "and I said 'What are we gonna call this coach?' He was a very innovative guy, so he says, 'Notre Dame Pass.'"

Whether they believed McKay's halftime declaration or not, there was a bounce in the Trojans' steps as they hit the field to a lukewarm reception from the hometown crowd. Garrett, the most dangerous return man in the nation in 1964, took the second half kick and weaved his way out to the USC thirty-four.

Trailing by seventeen, it was time to go to "Notre Dame Pass," the blocking scheme that McKay had designed. Fertig had more time to throw the ball and began to slowly pick apart the Irish secondary. When the passing game got going, the running game followed, and just as McKay had insisted, the Trojans took the ball straight down the field on the first possession of the third quarter, powered by the passing game, a rare Fertig scramble, which went for nineteen yards ("Might have been the longest run of my career," he says), and the running of Garrett and fullback Ron Heller.

What was thought to be an impenetrable defensive front of Notre Dame was being handled at the line of scrimmage. USC went sixty-six yards in ten plays with Garrett finishing it off on a four-yard run down to the one, and a one-yard burst into the end zone through a gaping hole off left guard. The drive took 4:04, and with the score 17–7, the 83,840 at the Coliseum came to life.

Each of Notre Dame's next two drives could have stretched the margin back to seventeen, but the renowned luck of the Irish was nowhere to be found. Following the Trojan touchdown, they drove down to USC's nine yard line before an errant pitchout by Huarte hit the turf and was recovered by the Trojans. The following possession, Notre Dame worked its way sixty-five yards down to the USC one yard line, and Joe Kantor's burst into the end zone was nullified by a holding call, which in the sixties was a fifteen-yard penalty. The next three downs didn't yield much, and still early in the fourth quarter with the Irish up ten points and looking at a fourth and goal from the twelve, Parseghian decided against a field goal try. A fourth down pass fell incomplete and USC took over, still down 17–7.

Fertig led the team out to the huddle, and with a renewed

sense of purpose, he brashly took over the game. He threw to Fred Hill for twenty-eight yards. He hit Rod Sherman for thirteen, then found Hill again a couple plays later for fourteen. The stadium perked up a bit more with each completion, and with the noise at a level it hadn't reached all day, Fertig whipped the stadium into a frenzy zipping a BB to Hill in the right side of the end zone. It was a twenty-three-yard touchdown pass that made the score 17–13.

As the Trojans lined up for the PAT, many who knew John McKay wondered what he had up his sleeve. Kicking an extra point would make it a three-point game and USC would merely *tie* with a field goal. There were few things in football John McKay disdained as much as playing for a tie. He would not do it in an exhibition game, and he certainly wouldn't do it against the number one team in the country with his team's Rose Bowl hopes left to a vote among conference rivals an hour later.

With USC in kicking formation, Ron Heller came scampering frantically onto the field with instructions from McKay to go for a two-point conversion. Just as Heller was about to get to Fertig, who was the holder on kicks, the ball was snapped. Penalty flags flew as kicker Dick Brownell, stunned by the intruder, booted it wide. The Irish, of course, declined the twelve men on the field penalty, and the score stood 17–13 with about five minutes to play.

With the lead cut to four and the Coliseum alive, the Trojans kicked off. They desperately needed a stop from their defense, and they got it. Notre Dame ran three plays, ran some clock and had to give up the ball. Jack Snow, who would go on to make his NFL home in Los Angeles with the Rams, had a fantastic game, catching ten passes for 158 yards; he was also Notre Dame's punter. With the crowd roaring and the Irish in serious need of a good punt, Snow uncorked a high spiraling beauty allowing his coverage team to get down field and nail Garrett on USC's twenty-three. It was a clutch kick and great special teams work by Notre Dame, but a lineman was called for holding and USC readily accepted the penalty sending Snow back fifteen yards.

The next punt wasn't nearly as good. Garrett, one of the most slippery and elusive return men ever, caught it at his own forty-six, took a few steps to his left, dodged two men and headed back to his right, where he broke three more tackles. He powered his way through the second wave of defenders, sped across midfield and was hit at the Notre Dame forty-two. He lost the football but USC recovered it at the forty. Luck of the Trojans.

Fertig wasted no time getting the gang moving. On the first play from scrimmage, he hit Hill for twenty-three yards, and as the clock ticked down under two minutes, USC was seventeen yards away from the end zone and an enormously unlikely comeback. After a two-yard pickup on first down, Fertig broke the huddle, looking at second and eight. He took the snap and backpedaled while surveying the field. With the Irish defensive line breaking through into the backfield, Fertig spotted Fred Hill on a flag pattern to the front left corner of the end zone. Having faded back beyond his twenty-five, Fertig uncorked a soft pass to lead Hill to his spot. As the ball was thrown, the defensive back fell down, leaving the receiver all alone. The pass, though, was thrown when the defender was in perfect position, so Hill had to extend into an all-out dive to get to the ball. He made a spectacular catch, snatching the ball as he was parallel to the ground about two yards deep in the end zone. He brought it in to his chest as if he were cradling a newborn baby as his body crashed to the turf within a quarter inch of the sideline. The referee hesitated as the frenzied crowd fell silent for an instant. The ref gestured "no catch." He ruled that Hill came down on the sideline in the end zone.

Fertig to this day insists that Hill's catch was made inbounds, and black-and-white film seems to support the claim.

The crowd groaned and the USC sideline barked. The Notre Dame defense breathed a sigh of relief and got in position to line up again, potentially two plays from victory.

That "Notre Dame Pass" alignment that McKay designed didn't do much good on the third down play. Fertig was in trouble from the beginning. As he scrambled to his left, sophomore Alan Page, who went on to greatness in the NFL and beyond, had the quarterback in the crosshairs. Page had shed a couple offensive linemen like lint on his sweater, and made a beeline for Fertig. He gobbled Fertig up, and as he was throwing the quarterback to the grass at about the thirty yard line, Fertig somehow managed to get rid of the ball. With the viciously strong defensive end wrapping up the quarterback just above his rib cage, Fertig could manage nothing more than a sidearm push with his arm moving only at the elbow from his chest outward, palm down. Thinking it was a fumble, players from both teams scrambled for the ball and a Notre Dame defender came up with it. The refs, though, ruled it a forward pass and USC retained possession.

Still haunted by the play a few years later, Parseghian pointed out that there were three ways it could have been called. Two of them—intentional grounding and a fumble—would have been good for Notre Dame with USC either losing possession or being pushed back to about the thirty-five yard line.

Decades later, knowing in his heart of hearts that he actually faked an attempt at a forward pass, and that the play probably *should* have been ruled intentional grounding, Fertig says, "I *did* have my Screen Actors Guild card at the time."

The call, though, went the way of the Trojans, but still they had just one more shot: a fourth down from the fifteen. What to do?

McKay's first thought that season was always Garrett. That day, as most days, he was the best athlete on the field, racking

up nearly 200 all-purpose yards, but only seventy-nine had
come on the ground against Notre Dame's vaunted run defense. USC needed eight yards for a first down, and since the
linebackers had been lining up within five yards of the line of
scrimmage, a run wasn't a viable option.

Pass play choices were swirling in McKay's head when receiver Rod Sherman hurried toward the coach with a suggestion. Sherman—a sophomore, for crying out loud, who had
once enrolled at UCLA—insisted that he could get open.

He was quoted in the next day's newspaper saying, "I told
coach on the sidelines that I thought I could get a step on #1
[cornerback Tony Carey], and he told me to take it to the huddle." Years later, Sherman saw his bold move in an interesting
new light. "Perhaps it was sophomoric enthusiasm—or stupid-
ity."

Whatever it was, on a team stacked with offensive talent,
the kid had just called a play for himself! Sherman took
McKay's OK and ran with it. Literally. He sprinted toward the
huddle knowing that, if all worked as planned, within seconds
a football would be flying his way with the game in the balance. The play was called "84-Z Delay" and as the Trojans
headed to the line of scrimmage, the Coliseum crowd was
howling. Several in the stands urged on the Trojans, waving red
roses, as if dangling a slab of raw beef in front of a hungry alli-
gator.

Notre Dame set up with five down linemen and three linebackers a step behind. They had eight men within three yards
of the ball, and as Fertig placed his hands under center, he had
three offensive linemen to his left and two to his right, a single
receiver split wide to each side and two backs in an I formation
behind him. He knew the Irish were going to bring heavy pressure.

Just before the snap, Garrett, the deeper of the two backs,
took off in motion to his left, and at the snap continued at full

speed but began a slight arc toward the line of scrimmage, drawing the attention of both an outside linebacker and the free safety.

As Fertig faded back and slightly to his left, Page, the middle linebacker, burst through on a blitz, ripping through the spot between the center and the right guard. The linebacker on the far side shifted toward the center of the field to occupy the space left vacant by Page, but he did not drop back in coverage. Instead, he moved parallel to the line of scrimmage a couple yards on the defensive side of the ball, leaving a gaping hole down the middle of the field.

Sherman, lined up wide on the left, took a few steps forward and faked an outside move to the flag. His man bit ever so slightly, and when the receiver turned his shoulders inward to make his cut toward the goalpost, he established inside position on his man in the open field. Fertig, a right-hander moving backward and to his left, was again under intense pressure from Page. The instant before the future all-pro hit him, with his momentum taking him backward and throwing off the wrong foot, Fertig unloaded.

Sherman, streaking on an angle toward the end zone, caught the perfect strike in stride at the three with Carey first flailing at the ball in a futile attempt to knock it down and then diving desperately to grab a piece of Sherman's jersey. Instead, he ended up with a fistful of air, a face full of dirt and a long, lonely walk back to the Notre Dame sideline.

As Sherman sped across the goal line, the USC sideline exploded. The Coliseum erupted.

The Trojans took the lead, the fans were in a frenzy and Fertig was flat on his back. "I didn't see it," he said. "I heard it. When I heard those 83,000 people, I knew something good happened—and thank God for Rod—he caught it."

McKay said, years later, "A great play by everybody. Rod did the right thing, Garrett went in motion to the left pulling the defender out of the man-to-man on that side, we made the play and [with a sly smile] we were heroes."

Recalled Garrett, "It was a great moment—and I'll never forget it—the *sound* of that stadium lifted you. It was like walking on sound."

Sherman, a three-year letterman, pointed out, "The only difference between Fred's catch [on third down, which was ruled out of bounds] and mine is that he made his in front of a Catholic official, and I didn't!"

Fertig, who jokingly takes credit for all of Garrett's accomplishments, says a bit more seriously, "Mike was the key to the whole play and he never gets any mention. He went in motion, and their strong safety and strong linebacker both went after him. So now, before the ball even hits my hands, there are two guys chasing Garrett, who is running sideways and there's nobody in the middle of the field lurking and I had an open shot."

Reminded in 2006 that even though it might have been what he described as "an open shot," it still took a perfect pass to get the ball to Sherman, Fertig says, "Well, according to me it was a perfect pass, but according to Sherman, he had to climb a ladder to get it. Come on. It hit him right between the one and the two." Sherman, wearing 12, could have told his quarterback any story he wanted at the time because Fertig didn't see a thing. Page flattened him the split second he released the ball. The quarterback got up slowly, and on the way toward the sideline celebration, he shook the cobwebs from his head. With the clock frozen at 1:33, the scoreboard operator changed the score to 20–17 USC.

Notre Dame didn't even threaten on the final possession. Amazingly the Trojans had done it. In one of the most unlikely comebacks in college football history, USC scored twenty second half points on a team that hadn't given up as many as sixteen in any full game all year. The Irish were minutes away from an undefeated season and a national championship, but instead finished 10–1 and ranked third in the final poll. Depending on your perspective, there was plenty of praise to go around on the USC side or a ton of blame on the Notre Dame side.

The great Jim Murray of the *Los Angeles Times* expressed his opinion in his column the following day.

Anybody want a good deal in used shamrocks? How about a fleet rate on green balloons?

A little bit of heaven didn't fall from out of the skies, a little bit of football did. When it nestled in the arms of Rod Sherman once again the Irish jig was up.

They came into this town No. 1 on all the better polls. They got about as much chance of winning the next election as Slippery Rock. They'll fall so fast they'll think they hit a cake of soap.

The game had all the rock-ribbed defense of a saloon fight in the dark. USC can move the ball on the German army but they can't resist a pass any better than Mamie Stover. . . .

[In the second half] the Irish looked like a guy trying to hold on to a top hat in a snowball fight. For one thing, they were so afraid of USC's Mike Garrett that five of them dove at him if he changed his seat on the bench.

Murray's harshest lines, though, were reserved for Ara Parseghian. The old-school writer was miffed at the mere idea that there were comparisons being made between the new coach and the legendary Knute Rockne.

They told us Ara Parseghian was "another Rockne." The nerve of them!

Why, would you believe it? Parseghian didn't even get himself wheeled in on a stretcher at halftime. Rockne would have. He would have pointed to his leg, artfully bandaged, and sobbed, "Boys, if you let the Trojans beat you, my doctor says I might lose that."

I have it on good authority Notre Dame wasn't even crying when they came back on the field for the second half. This is a team that performs best when it needs a Kleenex more than a first down.

Rockne's attack, a foe once grumbled, consisted of "five Hail Mary's and 11 All-Americans—a punt, pass and prayer, and 10 minutes of loud sobbing in the dressing room between the halves."

You can bet Rock wouldn't have let them come back on that field dry-eyed. Not with the national championship at stake. Rockne offered blood, sweat and tears years before Churchill made that famous halftime speech.

You know what I'll bet Parseghian did? Adjust his defense. Diagram plays on the blackboard. Switch blocking assignments. Another Rockne? *I ask you.*

Know what they had on the blackboard? Besides the plays, that is? The words "Just 30 Minutes More." Can you believe it? Now, what kind of attitude is that? Why, this team was listening for footsteps in the dark. Rockne would have had them crashing out there disappointed because there was only 30 minutes more. He would have got them fired up if he had to fake pneumonia. He would have won by Gipp or by gyp.

Ara's handicapped by the fact no one broke his nose with a baseball bat and that he never got dandruff as a kid. With a puss like Rock's you'd start to cry even before he opened his mouth. You just knew you couldn't let a loveable old codger like that down—him tied to a stretcher and all. I'm starting a collection forthwith to send Ara a stretcher, arm splint, an eye patch and a box of onions to sneak in his handkerchief.

We'll get that national championship yet, keep the beer iced. We won't die trying, we'll try crying.

The next day's *South Bend Tribune*, in a column entitled "After Loss, Tears Fill Irish Eyes," aptly described the Trojan locker room as "a scene of utter pandemonium."

McKay and his assistant coaches were all thrown fully

clothed into the showers. The Trojan celebration had become as wet as it was loud.

John Hall's *Los Angeles Times* article painted the picture, invoking a visual of the most popular music group of the era.

In the locker room, it looked like 51 Beatles suddenly turned loose in cardinal-and-gold uniforms.

"Yeah, yeah, yeah, yeah," they chanted and danced as they sprayed soft drinks on the ceiling and the blackboard that spelled out "BEAT MICHIGAN" and "WE UPSET THE WORLD!"

"Let's have the showers!" somebody screamed, and the coaching staff was dragged happily off for a clothes bath.

Assistant coach Marv Goux grabbed John McKay around the waist and twisted him into the air, somebody ripped the shirt off of coach Mike Giddings. The walls were rocking.

Garrett was caught in a stampede down the hallway, was shoved and started to fall, taking a newsman's coat button with him as he grabbed for support.

"Sorry, sorry," Mike apologized as he tried to recover the button from under the feet of 10 teammates.

"We never gave up," Garrett said. "We still thought we could win at halftime."

Fertig agreed. "Coach McKay told us we could do it, to go out there and take the second half kickoff to a touchdown and that would be all we needed.

"We were moving the ball all along. Notre Dame is great but we were confident," said Craig.

Almost lost in the craziness and emotion of the moment was the big picture. The vote. Remember the vote? The teams of the conference were minutes away from choosing a representative for the Rose Bowl. The common thinking was that deciding against USC in the wake of the incredible win over the number one team in the nation would be like picking

against the Allied forces as the echoes of D-day were still ring-
ing out.

Reminded about the impending decision in the joyous
locker room as they began to dress for a celebration dinner,
Trojan players and coaches were asked about their fate.

Rod Sherman, who had played his high school ball in
Pasadena, offered to show everybody around the city as they
got ready for the Rose Bowl.

Fertig embraced his father, the police chief of Huntington
Park. "I told you we could do it," said the quarterback. "We've
got plans for New Year's Day!"

McKay, dressed in a gray sweat outfit and still wringing out
his clothes from the unplanned shower, said, "I'm not going to
worry about it. I'm going out to enjoy the evening and forget
about the vote."

Fred Hill was beaming. "This was the greatest moment in
USC's football history. There's never been a comeback like this.
It'd be a disgrace if they kept us out of the Rose Bowl now, but
you never know. Strange things happen."

	1	2	3	4	F
USC	0	0	7	13	20
Notre Dame	3	14	0	0	17

SCORING:

First Quarter

Notre Dame: Ivan, 25-yard field goal

Second Quarter

Notre Dame: Huarte, 21-yard pass to Snow (Ivan kick)
Notre Dame: Wolski, 5-yard run (Ivan kick)

Third Quarter

USC: Garrett, 1-yard run (Brownell kick)

Fourth Quarter

USC: Fertig, 21-yard pass to Hill (kick failed)
USC: Fertig, 15-yard pass to Sherman (Brownell kick)

Passing:
USC: Fertig, 15–23–225
Notre Dame: Huarte, 18–29–272

Rushing:
USC: Garrett, 21–79; Heller, 14–44; Williams, 3–19
Notre Dame: Wolski, 16–76; Eddy, 10–39; Kantor, 14–45

Receiving:
USC: Sherman, 7–109; Hill, 4–88; Garrett, 4–28
Notre Dame: Snow, 10–158; Sheridan, 5–63; Eddy, 2–37

POSTSCRIPT

Craig Fertig and Bill Fisk had exercised their rights as team captains and chose the spot for the celebration. Like good soldiers following marching orders, players rolled out, and the parking lot at Enoch's Steakhouse in South Gate began filling up quickly. Cars pulled in with horns honking and players leaning out windows. One by one, they arrived from the Coliseum and filed into the restaurant, embracing as if they hadn't seen each other for years, although it had actually been minutes.

They settled in for a night of good laughs and great food. Fertig remembers, "We're havin' a Gatorade or two and somebody says, 'Put on the TV and let's hear about us goin' to the Rose Bowl.' I'll never forget it. Fred Hessler was the voice of the Bruins; he was the Tom Kelly of UCLA. We turn on the TV and Fred says—and really, I'll *never* forget it—he says, 'This is the most disgraceful thing I have ever seen. Oregon State is going to the Rose Bowl.'"

The Trojans sat there in stunned silence, all dressed up with no place to bowl. Hurry up, somebody take away their steak knives. Fertig remembers, "You should have seen the air go out of that party."

Like Fred Hill said, strange things happen.

Oregon State had won the conference vote. They had an overall record of 8–2 and, like the Trojans, were 3–1 in conference. Offensively, the Beavers weren't very impressive, scoring more than fourteen points only three times in their ten games. USC, on the other hand, scored more than fourteen seven times and *averaged* more than twenty points per game.

The headline in the Sunday *Los Angeles Times* delivered the news, first the good, then the bad.

USC SHOCKS #1 IRISH, 20–17, BUT
OREGON STATE COMES UP SMELLING LIKE A "ROSE"

Columnist Sid Ziff—who might have temporarily lost a bit of credibility the previous day with his pregame story stating, "The first half should be close. The second half—who knows? The Trojans have been running out of steam. Probably their only chance is to grab an early lead"—was furious, and he expressed his anger.

His postgame column was about the conference vote, which Ziff seemed to take personally. The story read in part,

I DON'T BELIEVE IT

If they were going to do that, why did they string us along? Why did they make us wait for a week and let us cling to the belief that if the Trojans won it would put them in the Rose Bowl?

It isn't fair to the Trojans who overcame hopeless odds to score their greatest football victory of all time. People here want USC now more than ever. Do you think Oregon State will do a better job against Michigan? Why did they have to spoil USC's finest hour?

The injustice wasn't lost on any of the Trojans, particularly Fertig, who wittily said, years later, "Here we just beat Notre Dame, and Oregon State, God bless 'em, they had knocked the devil out of Idaho seven to six. We beat the number one team in the country, they beat Idaho and they go to the Rose Bowl. You think that still doesn't bother me? Yes, it does."

Truth be told, Oregon State's win over Idaho came earlier in the season, and it was by the score of 10–7. The 7–6 victory in the season finale actually came against Oregon, but Fertig's point is still valid.

Athletic Director Jess Hill, who seemed to strike a chord of caution in his postgame comments, warning that the vote could go either way, might have been preparing others for the worst. Apparently he didn't prepare himself. In yet another *Los Angeles Times* article about the Trojans' misfortune, the headline read,

"IT'S RANKEST INJUSTICE"—HILL VOICES USC'S SHOCK

In the article, Hill expressed that shock.

"It's the rankest injustice that ever occurred in the field of intercollegiate athletics."

These words, voiced by USC Athletic Director Jess Hill, expressed the shock and disappointment of all Trojan fans Saturday after their team was shunned in favor of Oregon State as a Rose Bowl representative despite the thrilling 20–17 victory over No. 1 ranked Notre Dame.

Coach John McKay, who had been carried off the field by his conquering warriors, showed his deep disappointment, but would only say:

"I hope Oregon State does a real fine job. It is a well-coached team and I hope it justifies the conference decision that they are better than we are."

Oregon State Athletic Director A. T. (Slats) Gill was hardly surprised. "I'm quite happy, but I had thought we would get it," he said.

Trojan players, who had shed tears of happiness in their dressing quarters at game's end, were a disconsolate lot two hours later when they gathered at a restaurant with wives and girlfriends to celebrate what they had hoped would be their invitation to the Rose Bowl.

Instead, the dinner was more like a funeral than a celebration.

Craig Fertig's wife, Nancy, broke into tears. "The only fair thing would be to have a playoff," she sobbed.

"Yeah, let's play 'em tomorrow," said field goal kicker Dick Brownell.

"I'm in favor of going out and burning a big USC in the Rose Bowl lawn," defensive halfback Ed Blecksmith said angrily.

USC didn't get a crack at Oregon State the next day, but they did face them the next season. In a game that had been scheduled previous to the Rose Bowl controversy, the Beavers came to Los Angeles on a cool night in early October of 1965, and left a loser, 26–12.

As for Mike Garrett, one of USC's all-time greats, he never did get to smell the roses. The Trojans had earned a ticket to Pasadena in 1962, the year prior to Garrett's participation on the varsity team, and again in 1966, the year after his departure.

"That was my best shot to go to the Rose Bowl," Garrett said of 1964. "We thought if we beat Notre Dame we were going. We weren't, but we knew we could beat Oregon State."

No less an authority than John McKay said, after his retirement, "The biggest regret I have is that Mike Garrett never got a chance to play in the Rose Bowl. I'm still ticked off that they voted that way."

For some, time heals all wounds. For others, the scars from those wounds make the individual stronger. Speaking in 2005, in the afterglow of back-to-back national championships, and about a month removed from a glorious Orange Bowl whipping of Oklahoma, Garrett reflected on that season forty-one years before.

"I've learned in my life that some of the great moments were things that I *didn't* achieve after working so hard for them. I don't have any regrets and I don't feel terribly sad about it—I know it gave me great character and great fortitude and perseverance."

The next season, 1965, brought another vote, which was significant to Garrett and USC. This one, though, was not among six schools with perhaps their own agendas and jealousies. It was a vote of the national media, which decides the winner of the Heisman Trophy.

The Trojans finished 7–2–1, and in the top ten, but were in the national spotlight throughout the season mostly because of the dazzling brilliance of their senior tailback. Garrett ran for 1,440 yards, averaged a whopping eighteen yards per punt return and scored thirteen touchdowns.

As the Heisman voting deadline approached, Garrett was considered the favorite but had notable competition in Floyd Little of Syracuse, Purdue's Bob Griese and Florida's Steve Spurrier.

On December 3, 1965, one week after USC's season-ending 56–6 romp over Wyoming, Garrett became the first Heisman Trophy winner in the history of Trojan football.

He finished with 179 first place votes, seventy-eight more than runner-up Howard Twilley of Tulsa, and his 926 total points gave him a comfortable 398-point margin of victory. Reflecting in 2005, just a couple months after watching Matt Leinart win USC's sixth Heisman, Garrett said, "I thought about the award when I was in junior high school in 1955. Ohio State came out to California with a running back named Howard 'Hopalong' Cassidy. I used to see him on that Big 10 highlight film they had on television. I said I'd love to win that award.

"I didn't know what it took to get there, but I was interested in getting to know. When I got to school, I saw how tough it was, how grueling the scrimmages were. I said, 'OK, so you have to do these kinds of things to be an All-American, to be a Heisman Trophy winner. . . . I can do that.'"

But Garrett added, "Individuals get awards. Teams win." His Trojans of the mid-sixties did both. "I counted on the fullback and the O-line play. I counted on the quarterback to get me the ball deep so I could have the proper vision. We all orchestrated those plays together. Every time I ran the ball, there were ten other guys with me. I always ran the ball like it was the last play of the game and I couldn't let the other guys down."

While being interviewed in 2005 about his Heisman-winning season, Garrett was read a quote and was told only that it came from one of the Heisman Trophy winners. The quote read, "If you're successful in life, you misconstrue the whole thing if you walk away with your head in the clouds. I felt more humble and more insignificant when I won because I just remember in the dressing room over the course of the year guys taping their knees, taping their shoulders, going through the whirlpool to help a team win and I was part of that team."

He nodded his head in agreement. The sentiment was that of a team-oriented star. Asked if he knew which of the seventy members of the elite Heisman club had spoken the words, he quietly nodded again. The words had been spoken by Mike Garrett himself, decades earlier.

In an era in which players were only eligible for three seasons and a thousand-yard season was a rarity, Garrett racked up 3,221 rushing yards in his college career, an NCAA record. He also set thirteen other school, conference and national records and was the first Trojan to run for a thousand yards in thirty-eight years. He starred on the baseball field, as well, hitting .309 in 1965 as an all-league outfielder at USC. He was later drafted by the Pirates and Dodgers, but stuck with football and became the first thousand-yard rusher in the history of both the San Diego Chargers and Kansas City Chiefs. He was named all-pro and played in two Super Bowls.

Those who played with and against Garrett speak unanimously of his toughness, determination and resolve. Asked about those very qualities, Mike points to his older brother, John Sherman, for whom he named one of his newborn twins in 2004, and John McKay.

"Under McKay, we scrimmaged and we scrimmaged. Then we scrimmaged and scrimmaged some more, and I made a vow that I would not break. I learned a lesson there. You can hit me, you can talk badly about me, but I don't care what you do or say. To beat me you'll have to kill me."

Schools around the nation are still trying, in vain, to beat Garrett and USC to this day. Once upon a time, a Rose Bowl vote went against him and his teammates, but forty years later, with Garrett still an integral part of the Trojan family, USC made sure there was no vote necessary as they cruised to a national championship.

And by the way, regarding that 1965 Rose Bowl, McKay must have had an inkling of what lay ahead for Oregon State when he commented that he hoped they justified the vote with their performance on New Year's Day. The Beavers represented the conference in Pasadena by getting blown out by Michigan, 34–7.

CHAPTER FIVE

UCLA

VS.

USC, 1967

THE SETUP

If Notre Dame is USC's most respected rival, UCLA is its most insufferable. Having to deal with the thought of the Irish for one week every year, and with the Irish themselves for a few hours each season, is tolerable. Having to share a city with UCLA is downright maddening. Generally, USC students and players wish that UCLA's students and players would just go away, and the feeling is unmistakably mutual.

It is, however, what can be called a natural rivalry. Anyone, on any day, anywhere in Los Angeles could come face-to-face with somebody from the opposing school. The city is vast, but at times the quarters are close. Trojans 1967 consensus all-American linebacker Adrian Young says simply, "Cardinal and gold does not go with baby blue—in any spectrum whatsoever." On the palette of college football, the colors clash like a purple sofa on an orange carpet. Longtime UCLA coach Red Sanders once said of the rivalry, "It's not a matter of life and death. It's more important than that."

Of course, in the early years, UCLA calling the annual game with USC a "rivalry" was kind of like a couple mice speaking of their "rivalry" with the local pythons. It has been a decidedly one-sided affair for several stretches throughout the teams' competitive histories. In fact, if the beginning of the rivalry was the beginning of the football game, UCLA would have fumbled the opening kickoff and USC would have returned it for a touchdown.

The schools first met on the football field in 1929, with USC squeaking by UCLA 76–0. The next year, the Trojans won 52–0. After a four-year layoff, presumably for the Bruins to recover from the beatings, the teams got together again in 1936 and have met every season since.

Each year, in anticipation of the game, USC holds a huge pep rally in which a three-story bonfire is lit, the band plays, cheerleaders dance and players fire up the student body with exaggerated predictions of just how badly the Trojans are going to beat the Bruins. Back in 1940, a couple UCLA fraternity pledges worked their way toward the waiting pile of wood and set it ablaze hours before the scheduled start time of USC's pep rally. With the flames climbing and the smoke billowing, several USC students hunted down and caught their UCLA counterparts. Minutes later, the frat boys were sporting jagged new crew cuts and found themselves wearing enemy colors: USC painted on their bare chests in cardinal and gold. The prank might have lit a flame under the Trojan football team as well because, come Saturday, they went out and smothered UCLA 28–12 at the Coliseum.

It took nine tries for UCLA to beat USC, which they finally did in 1942. Future Hall of Fame quarterback Bob Waterfield led the Bruins to a 14–7 victory, snapping UCLA's winless streak. On campus, the Trojan faithful took the loss pretty hard, but the staff of the school newspaper, *The Daily Trojan*, made light of the end of the streak in its next edition.

A full page was devoted to a sarcastic look at the loss in which a picture of a UCLA player diving across the goal line was printed underneath the words *In Memoriam*. Below the picture, the caption read,

TROY'S DOMINATION OVER UCLA
Born Sept. 29, 1929   Died Dec. 12, 1942

The streak was indeed dead, but USC got its revenge in double time. Wartime travel restrictions forced the schoolyard enemies into multiple playdates with the teams meeting twice in each of the 1943, 1944 and 1945 seasons. They faced each other in the first and last games of their respective seasons in those years, with USC going 5–0–1.

Prior to the game in 1947, the UCLA frat boys were at it again. They dognapped USC's canine mascot, which was known by the name of George Tire-biter, and sheared the letters UCLA into the dog's coat before returning him to the outskirts of the USC campus. With the game just days away, there was no chance that the hair would grow back, so a couple USC sorority girls jumped into action. Sparks flew from their knitting needles as they feverishly whipped up a handsome new doggie sweater, which George sported on the Coliseum sideline on Saturday. The Trojans beat the Bruins yet again, 6–0, earning a trip to the Rose Bowl.

In 1957, Trojan pranksters turned the tide. Word is, a USC spy infiltrated the UCLA rally committee and was put in charge of those flip cards fans hold up in the stands to portray an image or spell out a message. The cards were left on each seat between the thirty yard lines of the Bruins' side of the Coliseum (all games between the rivals were played at the Coliseum until 1981). When directed, the fans held up their cards, and although the big message read out UCLA, there was an SC logo prominently displayed as well. Angry UCLA rally organizers ran into the stands to kick out the people holding the SC section of the cards, but discovered that they all had UCLA student IDs and had no idea what they were holding. They'd been had. The stunt got the attention of the *Los Angeles Times*, which ran a sidebar next to its game story on the following day, entitled "SC Stacks Deck in UCLA Card Section."

The following season, USC students produced a bogus edition of UCLA's newspaper, *The Daily Bruin*. They reportedly hijacked the delivery truck that carried the papers to the UCLA campus and exchanged their version of the newspaper for the real one. The headline read, *Highly Spirited SC Rates Wide Choice*.

The story below said the Trojans were being picked unanimously to win the game. Other stories in the fake newspaper made mention of the "facts" that USC was a forty-point favorite and that UCLA coach Bill Barnes said his team had no chance and shouldn't even bother showing up; several allusions were made to Bruin players who had run afoul of the law. One UCLA player was quoted as saying, "I'd feel a lot better about our chances against those terrific Trojans if we had a couple of players who understood the game." As it turned out, that fake newspaper was about as reliable as *The National Enquirer*; the game ended in a 15–15 tie.

Just like old habits, apparently old pranks also die hard. A new generation of Trojans, perhaps inspired by stories of their long-since graduated brethren, pulled off the same newspaper scam on the Thursday before the game in 1988. That day, with the help of some creative USC students, *The Daily Bruin* ran the headline *Presidential Candidates Dukakis, Paul Agree: UCLA Is for Losers*. Inside, an article named *Hustler* publisher Larry Flynt the "UCLA Media Man of the Year."

With the tie in 1958, UCLA retained possession of the victory bell, one of college football's most famous trophies, a symbolic prize that goes to the winner of the USC/UCLA game every year. Since UCLA had won the year before, they simply kept it. The 295-pound bell came from a Southern Pacific locomotive. In 1939, right around the time USC was fighting its way toward that Rose Bowl win over Tennessee, it was given to UCLA by its alumni association. For the next two years, it was a constant presence on the Bruins' sideline, where UCLA cheerleaders rang the bell once for every point the Bruins scored. In 1941, six Sigma Phi Epsilon fraternity members from USC made their way into UCLA's ranks during an early-season game at the Rose Bowl. After the game, they helped Bruin students pack the bell in a truck for the trip back to Westwood. Just before they were ready to go, one of the USC kids took the key to the truck and hid it in his pocket. When the others went to hunt down a replacement key, the Trojans cranked up the truck and left with the bell.

After more than a year of hiding it at various sites around the city, the USC crew got a bit careless and allowed the bell to appear in a photograph, which was printed in a USC magazine, *The Wampus*. The sight of the bell in the magazine brought about a wave of mean-spirited pranks by UCLA students. USC students retaliated in kind, and the stunts got so out of hand that USC president Dr. Rufus B. Von KleinSmid threatened to cancel the USC/UCLA football matchup.

Enough was enough. The student body presidents of both schools agreed to a meeting, which took place at Tommy Trojan on the USC campus on November 12, 1942. Keep in mind that this was not Arafat and Rabin on the White House lawn in 1993, but it was a significant meeting in the world of Trojan/Bruin relations. It was resolved that the bell would be used as a trophy for the victor in the annual football game between the two schools and would reside at the winner's campus until the other team won it back.

Heading into the 1985 game, UCLA had won three straight and was looking to make the streak an all-time Bruins best four in a row. UCLA seniors who hadn't redshirted had the unique opportunity of finishing their college careers 4–0 against USC. One such player was fiery guard Jim McCullough, who was the dynamic and vocal heart and soul of the Bruins solid offensive line. He played under Terry Donahue, the UCLA coach who would tell his teams that each year is actually three seasons— the preseason, the Pac-10 season, and the game against USC— insisting he actually didn't care whether they won any of the games in the first two of their seasons. A 1–10 season would be fine, provided the win came in the right game. That was how much the USC game mattered to the coach and, in turn, to his players.

McCullough, the reigning state heavyweight wrestling champion of California, was so fired up to meet the Trojans in his final collegiate conference game, he didn't know what to do with himself. The passionate and dynamic Bruin was in his final weeks at UCLA and couldn't wait until game day. He was so focused on the idea that his team was facing the hated rivals from across town, the fact that a win would vault eighth-ranked UCLA into the Rose Bowl was almost incidental.

The Bruins were favored over the struggling Trojans, who were 4–5 and limping to the finish line under coach Ted Tollner. USC had gotten blown out at Notre Dame earlier in the year, 37–3, and viewed the UCLA game as a chance to salvage the season.

It was a game that saw UCLA blow several prime chances. It was as if fortune's sweet kiss puckered up her luscious lips just to repeatedly turn her cheek on the Bruins at the moment of truth. They fumbled the ball on a first-and-goal opportunity, fumbled again later inside the red zone and opted for a field goal on another red zone possession. USC hung around, capitalized on the Bruins mistakes and made few of their own, en route to a 17–13 victory.

Matt Stevens, who went on to a solid career as a television analyst, was the quarterback of that UCLA team. He tells the story of how frustrated McCullough was after the game. The Bruins were having a great year and, in sixty minutes of sloppy football, made it all disappear: the game, the Rose Bowl, their season.

Walking off the field, McCullough was beside himself. As he headed toward the tunnel, he heard the taunts of the USC fans in the Coliseum's lower level and quickly veered off course and headed for an entrance into the seats to take out his frustrations. Stevens, McCullough's best friend, says he ran down the heated lineman just before he got into the stands, and began pushing him toward the tunnel. The USC fans, seeing the UCLA quarterback physically dragging one of his teammates away, took the taunting to a new level. McCullough started making R-rated hand gestures and screaming wildly toward the stands. Stevens finally got his frustrated friend into the tunnel and held on to him until they were through the door of the locker room. McCullough was out of his mind! Once in the locker room, he picked up anything he could get his hands on, throwing chairs and equipment all over the room, steamrolling through anything in his way and leaving a trail of destruction in his wake. Finally, in front of his own stall, he took off his helmet and smashed it repeatedly into the side of his locker. Stevens calmed him a bit, suggesting McCullough take a shower and cool off. Once under the water, the big lineman began to sob uncontrollably. Says Stevens, "He really looked like he needed a hug. We were best friends and all, but there are certain lines you have to draw."

Out of the shower, McCullough dressed without toweling off and walked in his damp clothes with Stevens, through the stadium tunnel and into the Coliseum parking lot, where his parents waited. Matt says, "He was still so angry that he refused to speak. I kind of handed him over to his father, telling him that Jim is really upset, but at that point, I was happy to pass him off. My babysitting duties were over."

McCullough's father gave Stevens a wink and said, "I've got him from here." But really, he didn't. McCullough refused to get in the car; instead he turned his back and walked through the parking lot and out the gate of the Coliseum. "At this point it was getting dark and his parents are concerned about their son angrily walking the streets of South Central Los Angeles," Stevens recalled. McCullough's father drove slowly behind, following his son at walking speed for about five miles. Finally the elder McCullough had had enough. Right around the intersection of La Cienega and Robertson, he pulled the car up next to Jim and said, "Son, this is your last chance to get in the car, or I'm leaving." Still about seven miles from Westwood, and discretion being the better part of insanity, McCullough got in and completed the trip in silence, chauffeured home by a compassionate and understanding father. Once on the UCLA campus, he walked into his dorm room and shut the door—a table for one and a broken heart to go.

The following year, with UCLA out for revenge, and the game at the Rose Bowl, there was no sloppiness and there were no fumbles in the red zone. There was, however, a major butt kicking. Behind Stevens' passing and Gaston Green's running, UCLA broke out to a 24–0 lead. During a time-out, with five seconds left in the first half and the ball on USC's forty-two, Stevens says receiver Karl Dorrell (yes, the same one) told him to go over to Coach Donahue and tell him they should run Right Hail Mary, a play designed specifically for situations like this.

Matt went over and passed the word on to Donahue, who shot back, "Matt, I'll do the play calling, OK? Hold on a second." Donahue then turned his back and got on the headset with offensive coordinator Homer Smith. A few seconds later, the coach said, "Look, Matt, this is what we're going to do. We're gonna run Right Hail Mary." Stevens ran back in, called the play in the huddle, took the snap from center, faded back and let it fly. The ball was tipped by Flipper Anderson on the right side of the end zone, and into the waiting arms of . . . Karl Dorrell. 31–0.

As the teams came out for the second half, Stevens says the Rose Bowl was about half full. All the USC fans who had made the trip to Pasadena had seen enough, and left. On the first possession of the third quarter, the pounding continued as UCLA drove about seventy-five yards for a touchdown with lit-tle resistance. 38–0. When Stevens got back to the sideline, he says that Donahue told him Homer Smith wanted to speak with him. Matt put on the headset and said, "What's up, Coach?" Smith answered, "I don't want you calling any audibles or changing any plays. We're going to run fullback dive, fullback dive, fullback dive. The rivalry is in jeopardy. Great game." Hard to imagine as the teams get ready to meet in the 2006 season, given the recent domination of USC, but the UCLA coaches were actually worried about embarrassing the Trojans! Regardless of which team is on top during any given period, each game is significant because it is played at the end of the season, often as the final game on each team's schedule. If one or both are at or near the top of the Pac-10 standings, the only path to Pasadena on New Year's Day goes right through the other team.

Each school has had its runs of success and domination in the series, but perhaps the most evenly matched stretch between the Bruins and Trojans came from the mid-sixties to the mid-seventies, when eight times in an eleven-year span, both teams' Rose Bowl hopes hinged on the game between the teams. That is USC/UCLA at its finest: when both schools are having great seasons and the inner-city rivalry takes on significance beyond the city limits. Some seasons it affects the whole Pac-10, and other times, the game has national ramifications and draws the attention of the entire football world.

THE GAME (NOVEMBER 18, 1967)

For the fourth consecutive season, the 1967 game had Rose Bowl implications for both the Trojans and Bruins. USC started the year as the seventh-ranked team in the country. There was not a very long way to go to number one, nor did it take them long to get there. A season-opening 49–0 demolition of Washington State vaulted them to number four, and back-to-back wins over number five Texas and Michigan State put them at the top of the rankings, and a 30–0 shutout of Stanford solidified their spot.

The following week, though, trouble awaited. And it was wearing gold helmets. Notre Dame was ranked fifth in the country, and was feeling pretty good about itself as USC week approached. The previous year in Los Angeles, the Irish put a whipping on the Trojans that neither team could forget. As the number one team in the country, the visitors stormed into the Coliseum and beat the snot out of the home team from opening whistle to closing gun. The final was 51–0 and USC looked like little more than an annoying speed bump on Notre Dame's joyride to the national championship.

To remind the Trojans of just how dangerous Notre Dame was, John McKay had put on the team bulletin board a poster that had been circulating around the Notre Dame campus. The poster was headlined *Fall of Troy*, and it ran down the weekend's events in South Bend. For October 14 at one thirty (game time), it simply said, *Troy Annihilation*. In a section beneath the scheduled events, there were headlines taken from the previous year's *Los Angeles Herald Examiner* that read *Troy Suffers Worst Beating in History* and *USC Votes Irish #1.*

As if the printed material staring at them wasn't motivation enough for the USC players, there was also the fact that they came into the game with the rather unlikely combination of being both the top-ranked team in the nation *and* significant underdogs! A *South Bend Tribune* article two days before the game read:

IRISH FAVORED OVER USC, ODDSMAKER NUTS, SAYS ARA

The poll takers and oddsmakers seem to be at considerable odds over just who has the No. 1 college football team in the land this week; but by the time Notre Dame and Southern Cal get through with each other Saturday, both the raters and the bettors should be looking at the world of football thru a clearer crystal ball.

"We are favored by WHAT?" shouted Notre Dame's Ara Parseghian when the Chicago football writers told him he was listed as a 12.5 point favorite. "You can tell whoever made that up that he's nuts."

One skeptical bookie said, "I can't ever recall the No. 1 team being a two-touchdown underdog. Sure, I've known the top team being the 'dog' by a point or two or even a touchdown when they're on the road [the game will be at Notre Dame]. Two touchdowns? Never. But that's the line and that's what we have to go by. Who you want to bet on?"

Regardless of which team should have been favored, there was one certainty surrounding the game. John McKay was insistent that his Trojans would not take the field until the Notre Dame players did. You could get the best of McKay once, but not twice. Not in the same way. The last time USC played in South Bend, two years earlier, the Trojans took the field and waited for the Irish. And they waited. And waited some more.

For fifteen minutes, they stood there: a soggy group of acci-
dental tourists in a miserable mess of an Indiana afternoon. It
was 39 degrees and raining, and as McKay stewed, Parseghian
was undoubtedly enjoying a cup of hot coffee, nice and snug in
his office, laughing with his assistants. "We won't show up on
the field until they show up," warned McKay on the Thursday
before the game, having learned his lesson. "I don't care if it
takes until midnight. I guess the 59,000 people are going to feel
mighty foolish sitting in that stadium if they don't get to see a
game."

As kickoff approached on this Saturday, there was no rain
falling and there were no Trojans on the field. One of the game
officials went back to the USC locker room and told McKay it
was time to head through the tunnel. McKay told him that as
long as Notre Dame wasn't on the field, his team would stay
exactly where it was. Five minutes later, the same official came
back and again knocked on the dressing room door. They had
essentially the same conversation. The official then threatened
to rule the game a forfeit. "And how would the final score be
recorded?" asked the coach. "Two to zero," said the official.
McKay responded, "I'll take it. That would be the best friggin'
deal I've ever gotten in this place," and he slammed the door.
Minutes later, one of the Trojan assistant coaches got word to
McKay that the Irish had just taken the field. USC soon followed.

Ara Parseghian didn't make many of the right calls that day,
but he was correct about one thing: whoever made his team a
12.5 point favorite was nuts!

The Trojans' speed and skill were far more effective than
Notre Dame's size and strength. USC's defense dominated,
making a joke out of the Irish passing game by intercepting
seven passes. Cocaptain Adrian Young, who coincidentally was
born in Dublin, Ireland, led the way with four of the pickoffs

and twelve tackles. The Irish offense was stifled all afternoon with three quarterbacks combining to complete just fifteen of forty passes, averaging little more than four yards per attempt. Offensively, USC did most of its damage on the ground, rushing for 219 yards, 150 of which came from emerging star OJ Simpson, who scored all three of the Trojans' touchdowns en route to a 24–7 thumping. Not bad for a double-digit dog.

After the game players from both sides offered up explanations for the relatively easy USC victory, but McKay simplified it as only he could, saying, "We had more speed, better running backs and just better football players in there than Ara did—and that's why we won."

USC held on to its number one ranking for the next four weeks, but then shockingly saw it disappear in the slop of the great Northwest. Oregon State, which had stolen a Rose Bowl appearance from the Trojans in that vote three years earlier, beat them on the field in the penultimate game of 1967. Field conditions did what defenses could not do that year: slowed down a lightning-quick USC attack that boasted half of the world-record-holding 440-relay team in Simpson and receiver Earl McCullough. Flanker Jim Lawrence also could fly and most of the Trojans' skill position players were faster than their opposing counterparts. A muddy track on a rainy day in Corvallis slowed USC enough for a strong Beavers team to pull out a 3–0 victory and knock the Trojans out of the top spot in the rankings. That 1967 Oregon State squad had an appetite for the upset and ultimately became known as the "Giant Killers." In addition to beating number one USC, it had also beaten number two Purdue and tied UCLA when the Bruins were number two.

The loss was a potential killer for USC, given the fact that it came so late in the season. At 8–1, the Trojans had fallen to number four in the rankings with just one regular-season game remaining: the one against UCLA. The Bruins were unbeaten, coming off a 48–0 win over Washington, and number one with a bullet after taking USC's spot at the top of the charts.

The USC/UCLA crosstown rivalry made for an intense matchup every season, but this year the teams could have been complete strangers instead of the very familiar foes that they were, and the game would still have been full of meaning and implications. At stake were the Pac-8 championship, the Rose Bowl trip that went with it and the inside track to the national title. Each team also had a superstar vying for the Heisman Trophy: Simpson for USC and quarterback Gary Beban for UCLA.

Looking back, Simpson said, "The fact that we had a shot to go to the Rose Bowl, and had a shot at the national championship—that was beyond anything I had hoped for when the season started."

Beban vividly recalls the moments before the game. "The place was packed. I came out of the tunnel, and over the entire track around the field, there were cables from the media, and I remember looking around at that stadium and thinking, 'This is gonna be one heck of a day.'"

Linebacker Adrian Young was a bit more direct: "What more could you ask for? Inner-city rivalry, inner-state rivalry, and national championship. And I never liked UCLA. Still don't."

Kickoff came as scheduled on one of those spectacular, why-would-you-live-anywhere-else? kind of Southern California afternoons. There was a slight breeze blowing and a packed stadium rocking under a deep blue sky that went on forever. A few fluffy white clouds gave the proper depth perception to the striking view of the mountains from the upper deck. The perfect 70-degree game time temperature was the final touch on the kind of conditions that go into a chamber of commerce brochure.

More than ninety thousand at the Coliseum watched as top-ranked UCLA struck early in the first quarter, scoring on a twelve-yard run by halfback Greg Jones. The Bruins were looking to extend the lead later in the quarter when Beban faked a handoff to the right halfback cutting left in the backfield. Beban faded back and slightly to his right while looking to his right. Suddenly, he snapped his head around and fired back to his left to the same halfback, who had circled out. Beban's throw was accurate but didn't have quite enough zip. Cornerback Pat Cashman, a senior out of Long Beach, had read the play perfectly and was streaking in from the secondary. Cashman bolted in front of the intended receiver, snatched the ball out of midair and headed the other way. There was nothing in front of him but a little bit of green and a whole lot of glory. While the Coliseum crowd went from zero to sixty decibels in nothing flat, Cashman rode the wave of cheers fifty-five yards for the game-tying touchdown. With the game still tied midway through the second quarter, USC put together a long drive. Earl McCullough did most of the work with an agile fifty-eight-yard pickup on a sweep around left end. While they had moved the ball steadily most of the season, on this day the Trojans were doing so without much production from Simpson. Their star running back averaged more than 154 rushing yards per game, but was held to just ten yards on his first eleven carries against a UCLA defense focused primarily on stopping the Trojans' Heisman candidate. Then, on a second down from the UCLA thirteen, Simpson took a pitchout to the left side, got a great block in the backfield from Outland Trophy–winning tackle Ron Yary and then almost single-handedly made a joke out of the Bruins defense. In regular speed the run is spectacular. In slow motion it defies both logic and physics. Literally ten of the eleven UCLA players on the field hit Simpson, got a hand on him or were at some point within a yard of him.

Longtime *Los Angeles Times* sportswriter Mal Florence was interviewed years later and said UCLA coach Tommy Prothro, a man who spent a lifetime in the game of football, insisted the thirteen-yard excursion by Simpson was the greatest run he ever saw. Yary, an all-American tackle, said, "I cut my guy off, but there were still about five more guys who hit OJ. He went through 'em, around 'em, underneath 'em and over the top of 'em and somehow got into the end zone."

Simpson himself attributed the run to "good training at SC. We always had to run these drills where they were throwing things at your feet, and Coach Fertig was always grabbing at the ball when you were running through all of these heavy bags. The key to the drill was to keep your knees going through all the traffic. I just turned up and tried to keep my legs churning and get upfield. Guys were coming at me, and I was busting through a lot of arms and legs, and finally, when one guy wrapped me up, I could see the goal line and I just kind of lunged into the end zone." The place went nuts. USC took a 14–7 lead to the locker room and OJ was just warming up.

UCLA hit the field for the second half and, just like at the beginning of the game, didn't take long to find the end zone. On the opening drive of the third quarter, the Bruins quickly made their way near midfield where Beban ran play-action and fired deep downfield to receiver George Farmer, who took the pass in stride and finished off the fifty-three-yard bomb, cruising into the end zone five yards ahead of two USC defenders. Just like that it was tied again, 14–14.

Fans at the Coliseum rode a wild pendulum of emotions for most of the day and watched as neither team did much offensively for the rest of the third quarter. Early in the fourth, UCLA marched down inside the USC thirty. Beban, who had gotten great protection most of the day, took a snap from the twenty-three, faded back and stood in the pocket surveying the field. He fired over the middle and hit Dave Nuttall in a soft spot of the defense. Nuttall took the ball at the seven, broke a few tackles and dived into the end zone for a touchdown, which reclaimed the lead for UCLA. The extra point, though, sailed slightly right, leaving the Bruins with a tenuous 20–14 lead.

The missed PAT was the continuation of a nightmarish day for Bruins kicker Zenon Andrusyshyn. He was even less accurate kicking the football than the announcers were in pronouncing his name. In addition to the blocked extra point, he had also missed three field goal attempts: a thirty-two yarder that sailed wide, and two from the mid-forty-yard range that were blocked. Andrusyshyn had kicked a field goal of fifty-two yards early in the season, so he was certainly no stiff, but McKay had noticed that the soccer-style kicker would drill a ball with a low trajectory if he was, say, forty yards away or more. McKay decided to stack the center of the line on field goal attempts, getting a better push up the middle and allowing the hands of some strategically placed taller players to get up and block kicks. As Jim Murray wrote the next day, Andrusyshyn kicks "like a golfer trying to keep the ball under a tree branch with a punched 2-iron."

Despite the missed extra point, UCLA still had the lead. Although the Trojans were down just six, they felt it would likely take two more scores to win it because there was almost a full quarter of football to play. USC was looking for a productive retaliation and got a good start as Simpson fielded the kickoff on the goal line and returned it to the thirty-four. On first and ten, it was Simpson again. There wasn't much there, but he popped through the middle for three yards. It seemed that either OJ was getting a feel for the defense or the Bruins were tiring. Simpson was getting visibly and statistically more productive as the game wore on.

The next play, a second and seven from the thirty-seven, was a designed pass, but quarterback Toby Page found himself in trouble as the pocket collapsed. He made a good play to scramble out of the congestion and headed to his left. He saved about five yards of potential loss with his mobility, but still was a yard behind the line of scrimmage as he was pushed across the left sideline, bringing up a third and eight from the thirty-six.

There are snapshots that tell stories of generations: the sailor kissing the woman in Times Square on VJ day, Marilyn Monroe trying (in vain, thankfully) to hold down her dress in *The Seven Year Itch*, USC grad Neil Armstrong on the bottom rung of the ladder leading from *Apollo 11* to the moon. As photographers stood ready on the Coliseum sidelines, Page led his crew to the line of scrimmage. The ball was on the left hash. Three down linemen took their spots on the right side of the center, two on the left. Receivers split wide to both sides, and in the backfield, OJ Simpson stood five yards directly behind the quarterback, and about eighteen inches behind a blocking back.

McKay sent in a pass play designed to go to left end Ron Drake to pick up around ten yards and a first down. Page, though, saw that the Bruins were double covering Drake, so naturally he changed the play.

Said Simpson after the game, "We called a pass play in the huddle. Then I'm lined up and I hear, 'Red!' which means an audible. Toby yells out, 'Red! Red! 23!' I almost had a backfield in motion penalty because I was behind him about to get his attention and say, 'Toby, not only am I tired, but that's a *horrible* call on third and eight.' But before I could say anything the ball was snapped."

That snap was Simpson's cue to infiltrate the permanent region of the sports fan's memory bank. He took the ball through the middle and was hit and slowed around the line of scrimmage. Remember those pumping legs he described on the earlier touchdown? Same deal here. He shrugged off two would-be tacklers and picked up speed as he crossed the forty. He strode a couple steps forward and then cut sharply to his left nine yards beyond the line at the Trojans' forty-five. He dashed about twenty more yards up the sideline to the UCLA thirty-five and made a slashing move to his right.

The still clear snapshot on the aging pages of the recap of this game, this season, is that of Simpson in midstride as he cut back from the left sideline on the defining play of a brilliant college career. The final thirty-plus yards were no problem. Like a victory lap after winning a race, Simpson cruised in to finish a dazzling sixty-four-yard touchdown run for the ages. The crowd was either buzzing or roaring, depending on interpretation of such things, but the place was undoubtedly electric.

Game announcer Chris Schenkel, not exactly known for a colorful style at the microphone, made the call on ABC as Simpson crossed the goal line. "Sixty-four thrilling, captivating collegiate football yards . . . Wow!"

Color commentator Bud Wilkinson followed, "I don't recall ever seeing anybody who can turn it on like this boy, Chris."

Mike Garrett remembers, "In those days, they taught us when we were running the ball, you could not fall down if they didn't wrap you up. There was no excuse. If you kept your legs moving and kept a forward lean to your run, they cannot take you down if they don't wrap you. OJ ran that play and they never wrapped him. He just went to his left, then crossed back. It was a typical SC running play, and as talented as OJ was— forget it."

Sophomore Rikki Aldridge banged the extra point through, and USC had regained the lead, 21–20 with 10:38 to play.

On UCLA's second possession after the touchdown, they faced a second and twelve at their own twenty. Beban, who was in and out of the game much of the day with a rib injury, faded back and was swarmed by the USC pass rush. Beban left the pocket heading backward and to his right, but three Trojans were closing fast. By the time they caught him, the quarterback was inside his own five yard line, and a couple steps later, he was dropped on the one.

Jim Gunn got credit for the sack, a nineteen-yard death blow to the Bruins' drive as the clock ticked down toward four minutes left. Two plays later, the Bruins punted from their own three.

Taking possession on UCLA's side of the field, the Trojans strung together two first downs and faced a third and two as the clock moved under the two-minute mark. Strangely, UCLA did not use one of its final two time-outs as the Trojans picked up another first down on the UCLA twenty-one, and time kept ticking away. (The clock did not yet stop on a first down in 1967.)

With a new set of downs and 1:15 left, all USC had to do was protect the football, but on a first and ten from the twenty-one, Page fumbled the snap. UCLA recovered, gaining new life. The Bruins trailed by a single point with 1:10 remaining, and fewer than fifty yards from field goal range.

They did manage one good play—an eighteen-yard completion from Beban to Ron Copeland on third and seven, which got them out to their forty-three—but ultimately UCLA simply had too far to go and not enough time to get there.

The clock ran out and USC had won it, 21–20. All was right at Troy. A Rose Bowl berth was theirs, as was the victory bell and, in a way, the city. Simpson had racked up 177 rushing yards and made a nationally televised case for the Heisman Trophy. The Trojans staked their claim for a move back to number one, and they certainly had to be considered for the national title.

In the next day's *Los Angeles Times*, Jim Murray once again captured the moment brilliantly.

Whew!

I'm glad I didn't go to the opera Saturday afternoon, after all. This was the first time in a long time where the advance ballyhoo didn't live up to the game.

The USC-UCLA matchup had so much pregame buildup that, if I was betting, it had to be the biggest stinker since the last Anna Sten [Think Jennifer Lopez] movie. A 0–0 tie, I told myself. A game they could play at night with the lights out.

It was a four heart attack feature. More fun than watching Sophia Loren getting ready for bed with the shades up. A total of 41 points was scored. One more and UCLA is in the Rose Bowl.

Everything was at stake but French Equatorial Africa in this one. The Heisman Trophy, the Rose Bowl, the conference championship, the national championship and probably the Republican nomination.

OJ Simpson plays the game like a pool hall hustler. He runs a few losing tables at the start, and just when you're sending home for fresh money or orders to hock the car and bring the check, he starts looking like Willie Hoppe [Think Minnesota Fats].

If Gary Beban gets the Heisman Trophy, I hope they fill it with aspirin first. To give you an idea, Beban was disappearing under two tons of beef all afternoon when it hurt him to turn over in bed. The cartilage is torn away from his ribs but it only hurts when he breathes.

	1	2	3	4	F
UCLA	7	0	7	6	20
USC	7	7	0	7	21

Scoring:

First Quarter

UCLA: Jones, 12-yard run (Andrusyshyn kick)

USC: Cashman, 55-yard interception return (Aldridge kick)

Second Quarter

USC: Simpson, 13-yard run (Aldridge kick)

Third Quarter

UCLA: Beban, 53-yard pass to Farmer (Andrusyshyn kick)

Fourth Quarter

UCLA: Beban, 20-yard pass to Nuttall (PAT no good)

USC: Simpson, 64-yard run (Aldridge kick)

Passing:
USC: Sogge, 1–5–13; Page, 0–1

UCLA: Beban, 16–24–301, 2 touchdowns; Bolden, 0–3

Rushing:
USC: Simpson, 30–177; McCullough, 2–56; Scott, 4–37

UCLA: Jones, 13–74; Purdy, 9–28

Receiving:
USC: McCullough, 1–13

UCLA: Nuttall, 7–152; Farmer, 3–81; Spindler, 3–45

POSTSCRIPT

The win over UCLA was enough to return USC to the top of the polls, and the Trojans went into the Rose Bowl as the top-ranked team in the country. Representing the Big 10 on January 1, 1968, was an Indiana team that finished its season at 9–1, but had scored an average of only five points per game more than its opponents in a year of winning dangerously.

The Trojans went in to the game pretty banged up, missing five regulars and losing two more during the course of the game. With a capacity crowd of nearly 103,000 looking on, USC never trailed, scoring on two short Simpson runs, en route to a 14–3 victory.

The win culminated one of the greatest seasons ever at Troy and ended in number one rankings from both the Associated Press and United Press International. The national championship was USC's second under John McKay and sixth overall (including 1939).

Simpson ran for 128 yards and was named the Rose Bowl's player of the game. His season total ballooned to 1,543 rushing yards with a 5.3 yards per carry average and thirteen touchdowns. The numbers were impressive, but only good enough for second in the Heisman Trophy balloting. UCLA's Gary Beban, who fell short on the field against USC, was a very deserving winner of the award, which was presented after the loss to the Trojans, but before the Rose Bowl.

The next season was even better for Simpson as he rushed for 1,880 yards and scored twenty-three touchdowns on his way to what was, at the time, the biggest landslide win in Heisman history (an honor now held by Reggie Bush, who got more than 84 percent of the vote in 2005). The Trojans went through the regular season undefeated and would have been perfect if not for a season-ending 21–21 tie with Notre Dame.

Another national title was at stake in the Rose Bowl, but despite 171 yards from Simpson and a 10–0 second quarter lead, the second-ranked Trojans lost to Ohio State 27–16. The Buckeyes came into the game atop the rankings and won the game in large part as a result of five USC turnovers.

OJ of course went on to great things in the NFL, and not so great things in the years that followed. It was unimaginable during Simpson's celebrated reign at USC that his golden status in the Trojan community would ever be questioned, let alone diminished to almost nothing.

Most impressive about the Trojans 1967–1968 run, as a whole, is the fact they were seemingly unaffected by the loss of several significant players between the two seasons. Incredibly, although ten of the players from the 1967 team were drafted by NFL teams, the overall level of performance at USC did not decline.

Five of the ten Trojans drafted were chosen in the first round. Ron Yary, the top overall pick by the Vikings, was joined in the first round by teammates Mike Taylor, Tim Rossovich, Mike Hull and Earl McCullough.

USC had undoubtedly reestablished itself as a powerhouse in college football. The success of the 1967 season didn't come out of the blue like that of the 1962 season, but it did further solidify McKay as the Trojans' undisputed leader. Like every school, USC had its ups and downs, but at Troy, the range of the extremes had been established at the high end of the success spectrum. Down years were ending at 7–3 or even 8–2. Up years were finished off in the sport's most prestigious bowl game and at times with the national championship. College football success has always been and always will be cyclical, but in the 1960s, the cycles at USC were concentric with victories in the center.

USC

VS.

ARKANSAS, 1972

THE SETUP

The Rose Bowl loss to Ohio State following the 1968 season was little more than a hiccup in an incredible run by USC. 1969 was strikingly similar to the previous year in the sense that the Trojans rolled through the regular season undefeated, and again missed out on a perfect season only because of a tie with Notre Dame.

The Trojans welcomed in a new decade on January 1, 1970, with a 10–3 win over Michigan in the Rose Bowl to complete a fantastic 10–0–1 season. It was undeniably a great year, but the bigger picture was that the season extended one of the finest stretches in the history of college football. From the first game of the 1967 season to the Rose Bowl after the 1969 season, the Trojans compiled an astonishing record of 29–2–2. During the run, they outscored opponents by an aggregate score of 774–383, an average score of about 24–12.

1970 blasted the country in its collective face like a freezing cold burst of winter air. War raged in Vietnam, Muhammad Ali fought a legal battle with the U.S. government and Willis Reed willed the Knicks to a game-seven win over Wilt Chamberlain's Lakers in the NBA finals.

A country divided saw some progress being made in race relations, at least on the athletic fields. While the sports world was ready to embrace the talented African-American stars of the day, like Reed and Chamberlain, Bob Gibson and Ernie Banks, and Bob Hayes and Deacon Jones, the real world was not. The United States was still, in many ways, racially volatile. Jimmy Carter, who would move into the White House six years later, declared an end to segregation in 1970, as he was sworn in as the governor of Georgia. *Time* magazine later ran a story on the softening of the South and put the future president's picture on its cover and proclaimed "Dixie Whistles a Different Tune."

The words from the mouth of a politician and a banner headline on the cover of a prestigious national magazine are one thing. Daily life in the Deep South was entirely another, and as the season began, the USC players were about to get an up-close glimpse of the ugliness and ignorance still pervasive in that region. The opener was scheduled for September 12, 1970, under the lights, at Legion Field in Birmingham, Alabama. Concerned on many levels, John McKay had assurances from legendary 'Bama coach Bear Bryant that the Trojans, an integrated team, would be safe in Alabama, with police escorts to and from their hotel and the stadium. The Crimson Tide was all one color and it wasn't crimson. The way it was is the way it had always been at Alabama; the football was brown, but most everything else—the players, coaches and fans—was white.

On the same night that Phyllis George was crowned Miss America, the Trojans ran through the tunnel to a chorus of boos as they prepared to meet the sixteenth-ranked Crimson Tide. There was plenty of color coming out of that tunnel, including the three most high-profile players in USC's offensive backfield: quarterback Jimmy Jones, running back Clarence Davis and fullback Sam "Bam" Cunningham.

Cunningham had grown up about as far as an American could, both geographically and ideologically, from Birmingham, Alabama. His mother was from Tennessee, and his father from Texas, but they had raised their family in Santa Barbara, California.

"Once we were playing, it was just a football game," Cunningham remembers. "We were intent on winning and doing as well as we possibly could. That game was my first varsity game. I was excited on that level more so than as an integrated team playing an all-white football team. I was aware of that, but more focused on the fact that it was my first game. Playing time was so scarce that when you got your shot you wanted to make an impression."

That night, the two-hundred-pound fullback did both: got a shot and made an impression. The Trojans' first possession of the game started at their own forty. They marched down the field with relative ease behind the passing of quarterback Jim Jones, who kept the drive alive on a third and five from midfield with a seventeen-yard strike to tight end Gerry Mullins. The running game was also working as Cunningham, who had just turned twenty years old the previous month, blew through the Alabama defense with little trouble. A couple plays after gaining seventeen yards up the middle, he finished the drive with a twenty-two-yard wrecking ball of a run over the left tackle, which gave the Trojans a lead they would not relinquish. He blasted through a couple of would-be tacklers near the line, but it was smooth sailing from there.

Running through a major Division I defense was never exactly easy, but Cunningham was shocked at the lack of resistance from sixteenth-ranked Alabama. After the game, he said, "I really didn't think the holes would open up this well, but those guys were not all that big. They were quick and they hit hard—that's all. Next week [against Nebraska], I may have to run *around* whoever is in front of me."

Thirty-five years later, he explained the reason for his surprise at Alabama's defense, or lack thereof. "I had just been through my first spring practice," he says. "I was imagining *that* is what this game was going to be like. Spring practice at USC was pretty brutal. They took all labels off everybody and just let you compete. We went at it hard. But when I got in the game, it wasn't like that. It was kinda like . . . It was weird. It was like"—and he measures his words carefully, tilting his head slightly from side to side as if he's breaking through the line all over again—" 'Hey, here's a big hole. . . . Where are they?' " He laughs at the memory of the gaps in the Alabama defense. "And I'd just run through the hole and score."

Later in the quarter, they did it again after a Tyrone Hudson punt return set the Trojans up at the Alabama thirty-four. Three plays later, it was Cunningham taking it in from the four, further quieting the already stunned crowd. The game was never in question. USC went on to a 42–21 win that was only that close because of a late Tide touchdown. Three hours after Cunningham ran onto the field with the usual questions and doubts of a kid who was about to play his first collegiate game, he strolled off of it with all questions answered and all doubts erased. He torched the Alabama defense for 135 yards and did it on a mere twelve carries. His average run went for more than eleven yards, and he scored two touchdowns.

It was a happy Trojan locker room, but coming off a Rose Bowl victory in the final game of the previous year, most of the players were pretty reserved. Being a newcomer and humble by nature, Cunningham was quietly removing his pads at his locker when a coach's assistant approached, telling him that Bear Bryant wanted to see him.

Cunningham vividly remembered the story in 2006, as if it

had happened the previous day. "They asked me to go over to their locker room. With Coach McKay's blessing, I went. I got over there and Coach Bryant and his team are all there. He has me stand on this bench and says to his team, 'Gentlemen, this is what a football player looks like.' And [putting his head down into his hands] I was like *ohhh*.

"I didn't know why I was going to their locker room, but I didn't want to go there for this. We had just beat them down, and they weren't a bad football team. They were smaller than us, but you could see they had ability. I was real uncomfortable because I could only imagine how this kind of thing would fly in *our* locker room."

Whether he fully understood what was happening at the moment isn't clear to Cunningham, even to this day. But with the benefit of retrospect, he has a full grasp and appreciation of the moment. "I believe what Coach Bryant was doing was expressing to them, 'There's a change coming and this is an example of the kind of player you're going to be playing with, that are going to come in here and compete.'"

Some feel that Bear Bryant scheduled USC for the very purpose of implementing change. He knew that making a verbal case for opening minds and doors to minorities would be far less effective than demonstrating the need for such action on the football field. In professional sports, there's a saying that goes "Winning cures all ills." At Alabama, that phrase could have been "Some ills are the cause of losing." There were two choices for the Crimson Tide: recruit black athletes or fall behind in athletics. Strange to think, of all the good and decent reasons for old-school Southerners to reassess their beliefs, it took the prospect of losing in football to actually bring about change.

As great a writer as Jim Murray of the *Los Angeles Times* might have been, his powers of perception were even better. While so many in attendance that night simply saw a football game, Murray saw the makings of a revolution. In part, his article the next day read:

> OK, you can put another star in the Flag. On a warm and sultry night when you could hear train whistles hooting through the piney woods half a county away, the state of Alabama joined the Union. They ratified the Constitution, signed the Bill of Rights. They have struck the Stars and Bars. They now hold these truths to be self-evident, that all men are created equal in the eyes of the creator.
>
> Our newest state took the field against a hostile bag of black and white American citizens without police dogs, tear gas, rubber hoses or fire hoses. They struggled fairly without the aid of their formidable ally, Jim Crow.
>
> Bigotry wasn't suited up for a change. Prejudice got cut from the squad. Will you all please stand and welcome the sovereign state of Alabama to the United States of America? It was a long time coming, but we always knew we'd be 50 states strong some day, didn't we? Let's hear it for American brotherhood. Tell Uncle Fud to put that sheet back on the bed. Cut out the crud about supremacy. There ain't no Santa Claus, either. Get out of our way. We're trying to build a country to form a democracy. The game? Shucks, it was just a game. You've seen one, you've seen 'em all. The guys in red won it. Hatred got shut out, that's the point. Ignorance fumbled on the goal line. Stupidity never got to the line of scrimmage. The big lie got tackled in the end zone.
>
> Nine years ago, I came down to this same field for a game. The only black guy in the place was carrying towels. Football was as foreign to the citizens of Shantytown as banking. You ran against white folks only when you heard the sound of dogs baying.
>
> There was a man named Martin Luther King and he thought that if a guy paid for a seat in the bus, he ought to be able to sit in it. But the establishment thought this was a quaint idea and went around shouting, "War-r-rr E-a-gle" and "Roll, Tide, Roll," and concentrated

on the important issues like beating Georgia Tech or winning the INS poll.

Alabama wanted to come to the Rose Bowl then. The Bluebonnet Bowl gets to be a drag after awhile. They thought all they had to beat was Georgia Tech. What they had to beat was 100 years of history. The word from Integration USA was, "You can play us in Pasadena when we can play you in Tuscaloosa or Birmingham."

Well, Alabama can come to the Rose Bowl now. They're as welcome as Harvard. And, if I know football coaches, you won't be able to tell Alabama by the color of its skin much longer. You'll need a program just like the Big 10. Grambling may be in for a helluva recruitment fight any year now.

On this night, so oppressively warm that coach John McKay substituted like a hockey team, the USC color scheme prevailed. The Trojans turned the Crimson Tide into a pink puddle. They unwrapped a fullback so big and unstoppable that if he carried cannon he'd be registered in Jane's Fighting Ships. Sam Cunningham scattered tacklers around like confetti all night. He gained more yards on the ground than Alabama.

At the end, the two coaches walked off the field with their arms about each other. That was the first time all night anybody from Alabama had his arms around anybody from USC. Alabama racked up 32 yards on the ground. USC had five backs who outgained them. But why cavil? It was less a defeat for Alabama than it was a victory for America. Birmingham will never be the same. And brother, that's a good thing.

They should give the game ball to that little old lady who, tired out from her day's work, refused to move back in the bus eight years ago instead of giving it to some guy who can just run fast. They wouldn't have been running here Saturday night if it weren't for her. And now, if you'll excuse me, I think I'll go downtown and see if the statue of General Johnston has toppled from its pedestal.

Murray, of course, was right. 1971 saw the first black players, Wilbur Jackson and John Mitchell, letter in football at Alabama. In the years and decades that followed, larger percentages of the Crimson Tide, and other SEC teams, were made up of minorities. In 2004, thirty-four years after Sam Cunningham burst through a team of players, centuries of hatred and a nation's consciousness, a proud and talented African-American man named Sylvester Croom was named head coach at Mississippi State. Croom, a center who went on to garner all-America honors, was one of three black players in Alabama's recruiting class of 1971. To this day, the University of Alabama presents the Sylvester Croom Commitment to Excellence Award to one of its players every season.

Sam Cunningham, still living in Los Angeles just a few miles from the Coliseum, runs his own landscaping business. He remains a romantic about the game he loves, saying, "To me there's only three great places to play college football. There's the Coliseum, there's the Rose Bowl and there's South Bend. Other people have other ideas about what is a great atmosphere, but those are people who never played at those three places."

Cunningham went on to a stellar career at USC and, in 2001, was inducted into the Trojans' athletic hall of fame. Coming out of school, he was a first-round draft choice of the New England Patriots and went on to play nine productive seasons in the NFL. He retired and then watched his younger brother, Randall, become a star quarterback with the Eagles.

In 2005, when asked about the great fullback, no less an authority than Mike Garrett said, "Sam was a great runner. You have to remember, he gave up most of his career in college, blocking. If they ran him like they ran Benson at Texas, or Earl Campbell, if you ran Sam like that, you would have really seen something! Sam was a team player. He gave up running the ball to block. In the NFL, that son of a bitch ran the ball. You saw him. Nowadays with these kids, you think someone's gonna give up that part of his game to block? It's unheard of. When you start talking about Sam Cunningham, you're talking about the ultimate character, the ultimate person. He's a pretty special human being."

The praise flowed from the lips of his coach, as well. Years after Cunningham's playing career ended, John McKay called him "the least selfish man I know" and the "best blocking back I have ever seen."

Pressed a bit on Cunningham and the fact that his talent as a runner might have gone partially untapped at USC, McKay acknowledged, "Yeah, he's really the best running back I ever ruined!"

The man who earned the nickname Sam Bam keeps an eye on football these days and is fully aware of the countless lives he and his teammates touched that fateful night across the country in 1970. Thirty-six years removed from the game against Alabama, Cunningham says, "A friend recently told me how I had done a lot of great things and had an effect on a lot of different people by some of the things that I had done. I said all that was all purely by coincidence and accident. I was fortunate to be with a bunch of cats that were talented enough to make a mark in that game. It didn't have so much to do with me—it was just being at the right place at the right time and having the right people around me and being blessed.

"I tell kids that all the time. If you just go play, the chances are better that great things happen than if you start manufacturing how things are gonna be. If you write a script and life doesn't come out that way, then you're disappointed. But if you just go play like you are supposed to, to the best of your ability, and great things happen, then it's all even more gratifying."

The Trojans went on to a 6–4–1 mark in Cunningham's first year, losing to UCLA and beating Notre Dame. The game in Birmingham very well could have been the highlight of the season as the Trojans dominated, rolling up 559 yards in total offense to Alabama's 264, but the statistics are not what lives on from the night of September 12, 1970.

"Over the course of time, the Alabama game has become significant in history and more meaningful to me," says Cunningham. "I didn't really dwell upon it that much when it happened. I just did it, and of course, all the older cats told me at the time, 'Oh, so you think you're a star?' And I said, 'No, no, no, I'm not a star.' I was just a sophomore and I knew they would keep me in my place.

"Coach Bryant said I did more for civil rights that evening than Martin Luther King had, which is a really, *really* out-there statement. I would never put myself in the same class as Dr. King, but we as a team, on a field of competition where whatever you see you have to believe, effected a change that evening.

"I was invited to go with the 2003 team to [the season opener at] Auburn and I got a chance to feel the effects of what happened thirty some odd years ago. People, black and white both, would come up to me in restaurants, hotels, wherever, to comment. That in itself was humbling and it let me know that a whole lot of people were paying attention. The effect that game had on everybody that evening was more than we knew, because after the game, we just got on the bus and headed for the airport to come back to California. We were gone, but that whole situation was something that remained to be talked about for a long time to come because from that point on, college football in the Southeast was not ever going to be the same."

THE GAME (SEPTEMBER 9, 1972)

In 1972, there was no easing into the season for the Trojans. It was as if they were given a final exam on the first day of a new

semester. As they had in Sam Cunningham's first game, two
years earlier, USC opened on the road in a hostile environment,
christening the new season under the lights against Arkansas in
Little Rock. Cunningham was beginning his senior year at USC,
and making his first start since a serious knee injury had side-
lined him for the final part of the previous season.

The Trojans ended 1971 ranked twentieth in the nation, but
because of a solid collection of returning talent, a strong core of
first year players and Cunningham's impending return, they entered 1972 with the number eight preseason ranking. The Razorbacks squad that awaited was listed at number four, but
thought they were even better than that.

Cunningham remembers, "In the hotel that evening, we
were watching TV, and their quarterback, Joe Ferguson, comes
on and says that they were looking at this game, against us, as
a stepping-stone to the national championship. I kinda went
'Whaaat!?!' I'm thinking, like, 'Dog, wait a minute. You aren't
just gonna punk us like that!' "

The Alabama experience two years prior, although somewhat intimidating, was nothing like the trip to the stadium in
Arkansas. One of those first-year players who had the Trojans
so optimistic about the new season was a sophomore inside
linebacker named Richard Wood, whose career turned out to
be three years of controlled fury and unbridled excellence, in
which USC went 31–2–2. For a school known so well for its offense, Wood made his mark on defense, becoming the first and,
to this day, the only USC player to be named first-team all-
America three times.

Even thirty-four years after the fact, Wood remembers
opening day 1972 vividly. "Going to the stadium, we saw the
crowd out the window of the bus, and it was a pretty ram-
bunctious crowd. I flashed a peace sign to the people, and although it was intended as a peace sign, I also realized that I
was flashing the 'V' sign for victory."

Inside, under the lights, a hostile capacity crowd packed War Memorial Stadium. Wood remembers emerging from the tunnel, looking up and seeing a stadium jammed to the top row, full of fans wearing nothing but red and white. The usual sounds of a capacity crowd were audible, but above the din came loud and spirited yells of "Suuueeey!" One after another the hog calls rang out; it was as if the Trojans were caught in an unrelenting storm of redneck without an umbrella. "Man, it was so intense," remembers Wood. "It really got me fired up."

The Trojans started the week as a six-point underdog, but the betting public wasn't buying it. So much money came in on USC early in the week, the line steadily fell, first down to five, then to four, then to 3.5. The action was still so one-sided that the bookies were forced to make the most significant move in the point spread world of football, bringing the number down to three, a half-point tick that usually starts to swing the action to the other side. In this case, though, it wasn't enough, because even more USC money poured in, forcing the spread down to 2.5 and then finally to two, where it settled the day before the game and remained until kickoff.

With a record crowd of 54,461 crammed into the place, War Memorial Stadium was going wild for the kickoff at eight p.m. local time. The Trojans' Manfred Moore received the kick at the five and made his way toward the Arkansas special teams heading toward him like a wild herd of . . . well, of razorbacks.

Moore made his move around the twenty-five, was hit and fumbled. As the ball popped out, a roar went up from the crowd. Arkansas freshman Doug Yoder jumped on the loose ball, giving the Razorbacks possession at the Trojan twenty-eight, and thus began USC's 1972 season in eminently forgettable fashion.

Arkansas moved the ball down to the ten yard line, but the drive stalled there and the home team settled for Andy Bolton's twenty-seven-yard field goal to make it 3–0.

The next kickoff was taken by USC's Allen Carter, and as McKay and his staff watched incredulously and helplessly from the sideline, he fumbled, as well. McKay must have been thinking that if his players wanted to give the Razorbacks a gift, they should have brought something from home: a bag of California oranges perhaps, or something—anything—that money could buy. Coughing up the ball the first two times they touched it was a bit generous. This time, though, Moore, who had fumbled the first one, made a huge play by recovering Carter's fumble to give the Trojans their first actual possession of the game. They didn't score on their opening drive, or the next, or the next. Very little of note developed the rest of the way through the opening quarter. In fact, the entire first half was kind of a feeling-out period, with the only other scoring coming on a twenty-six-yard second quarter field goal by Mike Rae, who was moonlighting from his regular gig as the USC quarterback. Rae generally handled the shorter kicks with soccer-styler Chris Limahelu taking the longer tries.

The Trojans did have one significant drive late in the second quarter in which they went fifty-eight yards in ten plays, setting themselves up with a first and goal from the two. Cunningham, who was coming off that knee injury and had not taken a single hit in preseason practices, carried the ball on first and second downs, gaining just one yard. On third down from the one, Rae recovered his own fumble but was stopped for no gain. On fourth down, tailback Rod McNeill was stacked up short of the goal line, giving Arkansas possession. The much-anticipated battle between two highly touted offensive football powers went to halftime tied 3–3.

There was calm in the Trojan locker room. Wood, a future team captain, remembers, "Our captains that year were Sam Cunningham and John Grant. Those are some stoic men, guys you could look up to, good leaders and great human beings. They led by example, by the way they practiced, the way they played and the way they carried themselves off the field. Those are the type of guys that inspire you."

If the captains were calm, everybody was calm, and really, there was little reason for the Trojans to be concerned. They had practically handed Arkansas the only three points the Razorbacks scored, and had outgained them 186 yards to 125. The Trojans had already racked up more than a hundred rushing yards and, despite scoring just three points of their own, were starting to feel pretty comfortable on offense. Their final three drives of the half had gone for fifty-nine yards down to the one, a field goal on a short field, and fifty-six yards and a missed field goal attempt. There was little question that they could move the ball consistently; they just needed to make the yardage count, and in the second half, they did.

USC started their second drive of the third quarter on their own forty-one and began effectively moving the football. They had begun six of their previous seven possessions with a running play on first down, and started the other with a short pass. This time, though, Rae went deep, hitting split end Ed Garrison between two defenders at the Arkansas twenty with a perfectly thrown ball, which Garrison took down to the sixteen.

On third and one, Cunningham, who was an outstanding all-around athlete with a substantial vertical leap, went not through the line, but over it. His explosive leaping ability was a deadly short-yardage weapon, which would become one of USC's go-to plays throughout all of 1972, and twenty-four hours beyond. Cunningham over the top was good for two yards and a first down. The next play, Mike Rae called his own number, capping a fifty-nine-yard drive with a five-yard touchdown run. Rae then kicked the extra point to give the Trojans their first lead of the season, 10–3.

The defense headed back out to the field with growing confidence. Arkansas hadn't done much, and on the previous series, Joe Ferguson was temporarily knocked out of the game when he was smashed headfirst into the turf on a quarterback keeper. Ferguson returned to the game and on his first pass was intercepted by Wood, who made a leaping grab around midfield and returned the ball to the Arkansas thirty-five.

One of the hallmarks of the 1972 Trojans was their penchant for capitalizing on opportunities. McNeill, the sleek six-foot-three tailback out of Baldwin Park, cashed in this one almost single-handedly. He ran for five yards on first down, caught a swing pass for fourteen yards on second down, and finished it off four plays later with a burst from the three. A game that was tied at the half was suddenly turning one-sided, as the Trojans led 17–3 and appeared to be getting stronger on both sides of the ball.

They had scored on their final two drives of the third quarter, and cranked it right back up to start the fourth. Future all-American Lynn Swann made his presence felt, hauling in a fifty-yard pass from Rae on a third and thirteen from USC's seventeen yard line. A face mask penalty added on to the end of the play made it good for sixty-five yards and placed the ball on the Arkansas eighteen. McNeill did the rest, taking a first down handoff and darting through the demoralized Razorbacks defense for the Trojans third consecutive touchdown and a steadily increasing lead. The PAT made the score 24–3, and with 12:58 remaining, the Trojans were feeling pretty comfortable.

Remember, though, Arkansas was ranked fourth in the country and had designs on a national championship. They were desperate for a response and made one emphatically, embarking on their best drive of the night. They came out firing and marched sixty-five yards in just five plays while taking a mere thirty-seven seconds off of the clock. Ferguson hit on three of his four passes for sixty-four of the yards, and when they punched it over from the one, the Razorbacks had new life, trailing 24–10 with still more than twelve minutes to go.

The USC answer to the Arkansas touchdown was impressive if not productive. Starting on its own eight, USC moved eighty yards, all the way to the Arkansas twelve before losing fifteen yards on an offensive pass interference penalty, which pushed them back to the twenty-seven. McKay was reminded why he used Limahelu on the longer field goal attempts when Rae came up short on a forty-four yarder. True, the Trojans didn't get any points out of the drive, but by running thirteen plays, they took the clock down to near the six-minute mark. Then, after the Razorbacks took over, fate stepped in. Or rather, Fate stepped in. On Arkansas' second play, Steve Fate, who is listed on the Trojans' all-time roster as a "rover" out of Anaheim, intercepted Ferguson's pass, prompting a mass exodus from the once-raucous stadium. Five plays later, USC made it 31–10, as Cunningham finished off the scoring with a muscle-flexing seventeen-yard romp.

The game was a function of the new math of college football. Preseason polls are as much a guess as anything else, and number eight exposed the pollsters by rolling convincingly, on the road, over number four. In the postgame press conference, McKay's comments weren't directed toward anything in particular, but instead were more of a stream of consciousness.

"Our defense played an excellent game," he said. "That guy Ferguson is a heck of a thrower. He did a great job. Wood is a pretty good sophomore linebacker—in fact, the best prospect I've had at linebacker since I've been at SC. He can run as fast as most backs. I think our tackles played well defensively. We got to Ferguson several times, and he's not the easiest to rush.

"Rae did what we wanted him to do. He did an excellent job. If he continues to play like this, he could be a number one pick in the pros. [He was actually an eighth rounder, going to the Raiders in 1973, eventually reuniting with McKay and Wood in Tampa in 1978.] I'm very excited about this team. I think it has more talent than the Beathard-Brown group back in the early sixties."

The opposing coach, Frank Broyles, was a bit more focused in his comments. Transcripts of his postgame press conference read like a USC fan club meeting. "They are a pretty darn good football team," he insisted. "We never could slow them. They kept us off balance all night, run or pass. Their offense was as strong physically as any we've faced. We couldn't get to Rae, at all. He had oodles of time picking out his receivers and did a great job picking them out. They wore us down, kept constant pressure on us to the point where we were getting blocked a little more each time. All of them were tough to block."

It was one down and an eternity to go for USC, but the first one was huge as they pounded what was perceived to be one of the country's best defenses for 477 yards. McNeill ran it twenty-eight times for 117, and Rae completed eighteen of his twenty-four passes for 269.

The best seat in the house, or worst actually, was occupied by Joe Ferguson, a future teammate of OJ Simpson in Buffalo. Ferguson, who had boldly and callously made that "stepping-stone" comment prior to the game, was under intense pressure most of the night. When asked about the Trojans after the game, he said simply, "If they don't go undefeated this year, something is wrong."

	1	2	3	4	F
USC	0	3	14	14	31
Arkansas	3	0	0	7	10

SCORING:

First Quarter

Arkansas: Bolton, 27-yard field goal

Second Quarter

USC: Rae, 26-yard field goal

Third Quarter

USC: Rae, 5-yard run (Rae kick)

USC: McNeill, 4-yard run (Rae kick)

Fourth Quarter

USC: McNeill, 18-yard run (Rae kick)

Arkansas: Richardson, 1-yard run (Bolton kick)

USC: Cunningham, 17-yard run (Rae kick)

Passing:
USC: Rae, 18–24–269; Haden, 0–1

Arkansas: Ferguson, 19–36–223, 2 interceptions; Nelson, 0–1

Rushing:
USC: McNeill, 28–117; Cunningham, 12–50; Rae, 6–23;
Davis, 6–18

Arkansas: Saint, 12–63; Morton, 9–52; Richardson, 9–25

Receiving:

USC: Swann, 3–79; Young, 3–51; McNeill, 3–20

Arkansas: Hodge, 7–127; Reppond, 7–59; Morrison, 3–37

POSTSCRIPT

You can say this for Joe Ferguson: he knows a good football team when he sees one. So impressive were the Trojans in their win over Arkansas, the voters immediately jumped aboard the bandwagon as it pulled out of Little Rock. The next poll had the Trojans at number one, and that was where they stayed, as they blasted through one opponent after the other. In the following three weeks, Oregon State, Illinois and Michigan State found out firsthand about the destructive power of the top-ranked team in college football. USC scored more than fifty points in each of the three games, beating both the Beavers and Wolverines 51–6, and routing the Illini 55–20.

Five consecutive conference games came and went with the Trojans dominant in all of them, improving to 9–0 with fourteenth-ranked UCLA up next. The Bruins put up little resistance, falling 24–7, and all that stood between USC and a perfect regular season was, of course, Notre Dame.

The Irish were having a pretty good season of their own, winning eight of their first nine games. Seven of the eight wins came by double digits, and their only loss was a four-point defeat in the rain against Missouri. Notre Dame circles the USC game on the calendar every year, but this season, the circle was in red ink. The previous year, the Irish had run off five straight wins to start their season before the Trojans drilled 'em 28–14 in South Bend. The year before that, it was a streak of nine straight Irish wins that was on the line at the Coliseum, and the Trojans took care of that one too, wiping out Notre Dame's perfect season and denying them a national championship.

In 1972, there was the potential for revenge of the highest degree. Everything precious to college football greatness that USC had denied Notre Dame the past two seasons was right

there for the Irish to take from the Trojans. USC was undefeated, ranked number one and seemed to be on a collision
course with Big 10 powerhouse Ohio State for the national title.
The old rivals got together on December 2 in Los Angeles, in
front of more than 75,000 at the Coliseum.

The Trojans jumped out to the lead but Notre Dame refused
to go away, closing to within two points at 25–23 with a touchdown late in the third quarter. Awaiting the ensuing kickoff was
Anthony Davis, a sophomore dynamo out of San Fernando,
who had come into his own around the middle of the season.
Earlier in the game, he had returned a kick ninety-seven yards
for a touchdown and said afterward that, each time he got a
taste of the end zone, he enjoyed it more and more.

The kick was a high end-over-end job that was coming
down short of the goal line. Davis settled under it and caught it
at the four. The mere sight of Davis fielding the kick got the
crowd going, but with each step he took, every fake he made,
and each Notre Dame player he eluded, the fans got louder. He
scampered through the first wave of tacklers around the twenty,
made a few moves and bolted into the open field as the collective
roar in the Coliseum seemed to slingshot him forward. By the
time he got to midfield, the only player left with a shot to take
him down was the kicker, but a place kicker trying to chase down
Anthony Davis is like a greyhound trying to chase down that
mechanical rabbit at the dog track. It's just not going to happen.
AD had done it again. Another kickoff return for a touchdown.
This one, ninety-six glorious yards and a dagger in Irish hearts
from Los Angeles to South Bend.

It was a day to remember for everybody at USC, but a day
that Anthony Davis will never forget. When they totaled up the
damage, he had scored six touchdowns to lead the way in a
45–23 romp. The next day the Trojans were voted number one
again; a week later, they were studying for final exams and a

month later they met third-ranked Ohio State in the Rose Bowl, where a win would virtually guarantee a national championship.

On January 1, 1973, more than 106,000 packed the old building in Pasadena as the Trojans and Buckeyes rang in the new year. The game was tied at seven at the half, but as was the case with so many games that were close at halftime, the Trojans took control in the third quarter and never let go. Part of the equation of the late-game dominance was USC's great conditioning. The other part was McKay's uncanny knack for making halftime adjustments. As Pete Carroll would demonstrate decades later, a subtle tweak in offensive strategy or defensive alignment goes a long way on the football field, and there was nobody better at identifying and exploiting an opponent's weaknesses during a game than John McKay.

The Trojans owned the second half, scoring twenty-one points in the third quarter, and fourteen in the fourth. USC mounted several long drives, and four times found themselves at the one or two yard line, where they always turned to the same guy. Sam Cunningham had been used primarily as a blocker for most of the season, but was unquestionably a unique and deadly short-yardage weapon. His strong legs and outstanding athletic ability gave him a powerful burst off the ground and an amazing vertical leap. Late in the game, having already scored three touchdowns by going up and over the line into the end zone, Cunningham was standing on the sidelines next to McKay as the Trojans got down to the one. McKay looked across the field and got the attention of Ohio State coach Woody Hayes.

McKay then gestured toward Cunningham and visually demonstrated to Hayes what was coming next. He pointed to Sam with his left hand, and started his right hand at shoulder level, brought it straight up and around the top of his head and made an arc back down to his other shoulder, repeating the movement several times. The message was unmistakable, and as Cunningham headed into the game, Woody Hayes *knew* what most who were watching the game suspected: Sam Bam was going up and over the top for the fourth time. And he did. It wasn't exactly Babe Ruth calling his shot, but it was a great football coach expressing supreme confidence in an unstoppable force.

The touchdown cemented the game and the national championship for USC in undeniable fashion. The Trojans won it 42–17, outscoring Ohio State 35–10 in the second half. AD rushed for 157 yards and a touchdown, Mike Rae threw for 229 yards and Sam Cunningham took player of the game honors with his four touchdowns.

They still talk reverently about the 1972 team at Troy, but for those who weren't around to witness the greatness of the squad, the facts tell the nuts and bolts of the story. The Trojans were the first unanimous choice as the number one team in the history of college football, taking every first-place vote in both the AP and UPI polls. They went 12–0 while scoring 467 points, and didn't trail for a single second of a second half all season. The defense intercepted twenty-eight passes and held opponents to an average of 2.5 yards per rush, never giving up a run of longer than twenty-nine yards. They boasted five all-Americans and the national coach of the year and won by an average margin of twenty-eight points per game. To those who saw them play, their dominance and prominence will never be forgotten.

CHAPTER SEVEN

NOTRE DAME

VS.

USC, 1974

THE SETUP

As players from both USC and Arkansas finished their warm-ups on a late November evening in Little Rock, longtime Trojan supporter Joe Essy was a human tornado whirling around his kitchen in the Silver Lake area of Los Angeles. Essy, or "SC" as he's been known to pronounce it, had his traditional game day shirt on and was whipping up a daiquiri and dinner as he got ready for opening night 1974. It was a warm night in Los Angeles and Essy had a date with his radio. The soothing sounds of Trojans broadcasting great Tom Kelly would be Joe's company for the evening as USC took what many hoped would be step one toward a national championship.

Hopes were high indeed for 1974, as the solid group of sophomores who had contributed to the 1972 title returned for a final season. Of course, 1972 had started the same way, or at least on the same field. In fact, Joe Essy had been in attendance on opening night two years earlier when the Trojans went in to War Memorial Stadium as underdogs and came out as winners. The fact that he was there was one thing; how he got there was something else entirely.

Joe couldn't afford to drive and certainly couldn't afford to fly, but insisting years later, "I just had to be there," Essy hit the road. He didn't have much money but he did have a fully operational thumb along with significant hitchhiking experience, so off he went.

With a sleeping bag in his arms, a ticket to the game in his pocket and a mental compass with an unwavering needle pointing eastward, Essy took to the streets on Monday of game week and began the trip from Los Angeles to Little Rock. There were various rides along the way, some enjoyable, some not so enjoyable. One in particular did a good deal of the damage, driving him from Barstow, near the California–Nevada border, to Oklahoma City. It was a straight shot eastward up I-40, and the conversation wasn't very stimulating or noteworthy. "I might have considered it interesting," he says, "if I hadn't had so many memorable experiences earlier that year when I spent the three months of the summer hitchhiking around the country.

"The people who picked me up on the way to Little Rock were fascinated by what I was doing. When I told them I was thumbing it all the way to Arkansas for a football game, they thought I was absolutely out of my mind."

The entire journey, about a twenty-five-hour trip if driven straight through, went very smoothly, and Essy was not without a ride for long. He arrived in about 2.5 days, pulling in to Little Rock early on Thursday, with time to burn before Saturday's game.

"The key to successful hitchhiking is eye contact," he says. "Make eye contact with the drivers. Your arm doesn't have to be completely straight. It can be bent a little bit at the elbow, but that thumb has to be up. You need to stand upright, have clean clothes on and be clean shaven."

Essy has nothing but fond memories of the trip, which was made all the more enjoyable and worthwhile by the Trojans' performance on the field in the relatively easy 31–10 victory.

"It's one of those things that you are always so thrilled that you did. But I didn't want to hitchhike home. I wanted to sneak under somebody's jacket and get on a plane, but the ride home actually turned out to be quicker than the one going there. The whole experience in Little Rock was great even though I stayed at the YMCA, which didn't have any air-conditioning, and if you've ever been in Arkansas in early September, you know how it is!"

Two years later, in the cool comfort of his Southern California home, with the play by play emanating from his radio like a bad odor, Joe suffered through a miserable rematch in which Arkansas whipped the favored Trojans 22–7. Led by Pat Haden, who turned in the worst performance of his college career, the offense did essentially nothing. The senior quarterback threw four interceptions and didn't register the first of his six completions until the final play of the third quarter. USC's only touchdown came on a 106-yard kickoff return by Anthony Davis.

In typical John McKay fashion, the coach said after the game, "They kicked the hell out of us. We played like a junior high team. We threw poorly, tackled poorly and coached poorly. Otherwise, it was a perfect night."

"I didn't think Arkansas beat the Trojans that badly," Essy says thirty-one years after the fact. "Sure, the score was twenty-two to seven, and it was disappointing, but not many people knew that Haden had a sprained pinkie on his throwing hand. That affected him and he threw those interceptions, but it was just the first game of the season. Even back then people knew, if you're gonna lose in college football, lose early in the season."

In the next day's *Los Angeles Times*, Mal Florence expressed his thoughts on the big picture for USC. He wasn't certain where the season was headed, but he was pretty sure where it wasn't. "So the Trojans, ranked fourth and fifth in the wire service rankings," he wrote, "have dropped out of national consideration."

The next week's rankings had USC down to number eighteen, but with a game under its collective belt and a season-opening road trip out of the way, things started falling into place. After beating eighth-ranked Pitt on the road, USC demolished Iowa and Washington State on back-to-back Saturdays by a combined score of 95–10. Victories over the Oregon schools followed and the Trojans were suddenly a solid 5–1 and back up to number six in the rankings.

The next week, an unranked Cal team came into the Coliseum and derailed the speeding Trojan train, playing to a 15–15 tie, and knocking USC back to number eleven. Wins over Stanford, Washington and UCLA followed, lifting the Trojans back up to number five in the UPI poll with just one regular season game left.

Yes, *them* again.

THE GAME (NOVEMBER 30, 1974)

The most prestigious annual matchup in college football once again had national championship implications. Oklahoma, Michigan, Ohio State and Alabama were all highly ranked and had a shot at the final number one ranking, but the mere fact that either the Trojans or Irish would have a victory over the other to close out the regular season would be a major boost to the winner. Oklahoma was on probation and would not be considered in the UPI vote, Ohio State had already secured a spot to meet USC in the Rose Bowl, and Alabama was looking at an Orange Bowl date with Notre Dame.

Working in USC's favor was the fact that, for the first time in its history, the UPI vote was to be taken *after* the bowl games were played. That would give the Trojans another opportunity to impress pollsters on a national stage against a highly ranked team, prior to the final vote.

The pieces for a USC national championship puzzle were all on the table, though very scattered. Several games would have to play out perfectly for the dream scenario to come to fruition and it all started with a must win against their bitter rivals from South Bend.

The lead-up to the game had the usual hype of the matchup, which was being played for the forty-fifth time, but the intensity of the rivalry had seemed to pick up a notch in recent seasons. The Trojans beat the Irish and won the national championship in 1972, the Irish beat the Trojans and won it all in 1973 and both were very much in the hunt for the title as the game approached in 1974. But only the winner would be alive afterward.

There were several stand-out players on each team, but as much as any of them, both coaches knew the game could very well hinge on the performance of Anthony Davis. Two years previous, he had scorched the Irish with those two kickoff returns. The following year Notre Dame limited Davis' touches on special teams and made him the focus of their defense, holding the Trojans star back to a season-low fifty-five yards on nineteen carries. Davis was back in the spotlight with a tremendous season in 1974, and rolled into the Notre Dame game on the heels of a 195-yard shredding of UCLA. In a *Los Angeles Times* article published the morning of the game, Mal Florence wrote, "It isn't realistic to believe that he can repeat his six touchdown feat of 1972, but the five-foot-nine, 183-pound tailback is always a threat. It remains to be seen whether Parseghian will elect to kick off to Davis as he did two years ago. The Irish were on the verge of upsetting McKay's national champions when Davis broke open the game with his second kickoff return for a touchdown."

Despite the fact that AD had broken OJ Simpson's Pac-8 single-season yardage record the week before, and checked in with a season total of 1,306 yards, there was reason to believe Notre Dame could at least contain him. Statistically, the Irish defense was the best in the country. The unit was particularly tough against the rush, allowing an average of a minuscule 2.2 yards per carry. The USC offense averaged five yards per carry, but hadn't seen defensive talent considered anywhere close to that which they were about to see come Saturday afternoon.

The party in the parking lot of the Coliseum started long before the two p.m. kickoff on a cloudy and cool late November morning. Footballs flew, flames nipped at burgers on grills and six-packs turned into no packs. Students were out in full force, good seats were at a premium and even the fashionably late crowd arrived noticeably early.

Notre Dame won the toss and elected to receive. They churned out one first down before punting, but any confidence the USC defense gained was only temporary. After Haden was intercepted on the Trojans' third play from scrimmage, the Irish offense took the field and unleashed a wicked attack that punished an overwhelmed USC defense for much of the first half. Notre Dame went thirty-nine yards in five plays, capped by fullback Wayne Bullock's burst from the two. The conversion made it 7–0 Irish, just 5:40 into the game.

USC's next drive ended as poorly as its first. On fourth down from their own twenty-nine, with about an inch to go for the first down, McKay decided on a quarterback keeper. Haden tried to slip through the hole over right guard, but as he hit the line, there was no hole. That Notre Dame run defense they had heard so much about closed with the power and resolve of a bank vault door. Haden needed an inch, but didn't even get a millimeter. Suddenly, Parseghian's crew was looking at a short field again, and they didn't waste any time capitalizing.

On first down, quarterback Tom Clements fired to split end Pete Demmerle, who made the grab in the end zone for a quick-strike touchdown, making the score 14–0.

Used to their team being ahead at almost all times throughout the season, the USC faithful in the stands checked the Coliseum clock to see that the midpoint of the first quarter was still nine seconds away, but nobody was sure whether that was a good thing or a bad thing. On one hand, there was still plenty of time to catch up. On the other hand, their team was already down fourteen points and the game was only 7:21 old.

Notre Dame's kicker, Pat McLaughlin, wearing number 99, had gotten his first kickoff through the end zone, showing the Irish were at least willing to challenge Davis on special teams. His second kickoff went to Davis at the two, but AD didn't do much with it, and was dropped after a seventeen-yard return.

USC then put together its best drive of the game to that point, picking up a couple first downs before punting. Then it was here we go again for Notre Dame. The Irish set out on a monster march, racking up six first downs while going seventy-seven yards in sixteen plays down to the three yard line. They were in position to score with a first and goal on the four, but the Trojan defense stiffened and held them to a field goal. Can that be considered a moral victory? Could that inspire any confidence? Sure, they kept them out of the end zone, but only after the game-long trend of Irish dominance continued with a mammoth drive that extended the lead to 17–0. Two Notre Dame series later, another touchdown made it 24–0 with less than a minute remaining in a disastrous first half for USC. You never heard 83,000 people make so much quiet.

With fifty-three seconds to play, Notre Dame's plan was

likely to keep the ball far away from Davis to avoid the big play, but McLaughlin kept it *too* far away. The kickoff went out of bounds, drawing a flag and sending Notre Dame back five yards to rekick from the thirty-five. At that point, they decided to go with a squib kick, which was fielded by sophomore Ricky Bell on his twenty-eight. He returned it to the forty-one, leaving the Trojans fifty-nine yards to go and forty-five seconds to get there.

A first down draw play that picked up three yards made it look as if USC was content to head into halftime having taken a pretty severe beating and thankful that it wasn't any worse. On the next play though, Haden completed just his second pass of the half, a twenty yarder to flanker Shelton Diggs, down to Notre Dame's thirty-six. Two plays later, it was Haden to Diggs again, this time for twenty-nine yards, down to the eight. Two plays after that, with seventeen seconds remaining in the half, Haden hit Davis circling out of the backfield on a swing pass for eight yards and a touchdown. It had taken them twenty-nine minutes and fifty seconds to do it, but the Trojans had finally found the end zone. The extra point was blocked, but there is no way to overstate how important the drive might have been. It was as if a defibrillator were brought in to jolt the barely beating collective Trojans heart back to life.

The teams headed off to their respective locker rooms with drastically different outlooks, but due to the late touchdown, USC was undoubtedly far more upbeat than it would have been. Still, the score was 24–6, and the stats were skewed heavily in favor of the Irish. Notre Dame had built the lead by racking up eighteen first downs to USC's seven, and 257 yards compared to the Trojans' 145, but as McKay addressed his team, he showed very little concern and no cause to be alarmed.

"Everything in our dressing room was calm," remembers assistant coach John Robinson. "McKay told them, 'We are really a very good football team. That wasn't us out there. We have to just go out and be us, and believe in ourselves, do what we do instead of worrying about the score or worrying about them.' "

Anthony Davis didn't hear that part of McKay's speech because he was conferring with team doctors about a gash in his palm, which he suffered late in the first half. He says he missed the meeting with the offensive coaches and walked in to join his teammates as Coach McKay was talking. Davis remembers, "He said, 'Gentlemen, in 1964, Craig Fertig and Mike Garrett [who were both present in the locker room] were down seventeen at halftime to Notre Dame, and if they could come back to win twenty to seventeen, we can come back to win today.' We all looked at each other and said, 'This man has lost his mind.' We're talking about one of the best teams in the nation, the number one defense in the nation and we're gonna come back and beat Notre Dame?

"He took one puff off his cigar, blew the smoke off to the side, looked up and said, 'OK, in the second half, they're gonna kick the ball to AD and he's gonna bring it all the way back.' "

In a thinly veiled shot at the Trojan special teams unit, the coach is said to have added, "And remember, guys, there's no NCAA rule against blocking on kickoffs!"

In the locker room, Richard Wood remembers thinking how much pressure McKay's declaration must have put on Davis. On the way out of the tunnel, Wood caught up with AD, and before the star linebacker could say a word, Wood recalls, "He said to me, 'You watch. I'm gonna do it. I'm gonna take this bad boy right down their throats.' "

Asked in 2006 to confirm Woods' story, Davis did. He said, "Yeah, that happened, but I want to be clear that I didn't say 'bad boy.' I said 'I'm gonna bring this *motherfucker* right down their throats!' "

Davis adds that, as he walked onto the field, he was within earshot of a Notre Dame player who yelled out, "This ball's going right to Davis and we're gonna kick his ass." AD says he then shared that little nugget with his teammates as they left the sideline to line up for the kickoff.

There are exact moments in life and in sports where everything seems to change. Some of those moments, like the birth of a child or a walkoff grand slam in the World Series, are obvious in their magnitude the instant they happen. Others are not so clear. Some instances, like Earl Woods putting a golf club in the hands of his two-year-old son, or the Chicago Bulls selecting a junior out of North Carolina with the third pick of the 1984 NBA draft, are viewed more clearly as the defining moments they are with the benefit of long-term retrospect. And others still, like the kick that sent the ball in motion to begin the second half, seem entirely innocuous at the time but, soon thereafter, are revealed to be moments that set in motion a cosmic shift in a given universe.

For those not in the Coliseum, ABC announcer Keith Jackson welcomed back the television audience from a commercial and wrapped up his comments by saying simply, "I'll tell ya this. The men of Troy have got themselves a problem." As if on cue, with those words hanging in the air to be shot down like a pheasant in hunting season, the second half began. The kick was a good one, high and deep and, as promised, right to Davis, who retreated into his own end zone to field it two yards deep. Five Trojans converged to form a line of blockers at the four, and in unison they began upfield with the synchronization of a Broadway chorus line and the force of a fleet of army tanks. AD steamed forward, full speed ahead along the left hash marks. Several Irish players were buried beneath the charging wall, while three others behind them zeroed in on Davis around the twenty. Two of those men were swarmed under by additional blockers, and the other got caught up in the resulting traffic. The speedy return man caught a glimpse of daylight through the mass of humanity and made a move toward the left sideline. When he hit the thirty-five, all eleven Golden Domers were behind him. He kicked it into overdrive and by the time he hit midfield, all the nonbelievers in the locker room suddenly had blind faith in the words and psychic powers of Reverend McKay.

102 yards after it started, the ride of a lifetime for Anthony Davis came to a joyous end in the Coliseum's west end zone. He extended the ball with his left hand to acknowledge the raging crowd, then turned to celebrate with his teammates, letting the ball fall to the turf. The Trojans were still a couple touchdowns behind, but as second halves go, there was certainly no better way to start. A two-point conversion attempt failed, but the score was suddenly a respectable 24–12, and whatever momentum remained with Notre Dame at halftime quickly joined its more perceptive front-running brethren on the home team's sideline.

Just about everybody involved in the game points to the kickoff return as a turning point, but McKay himself claims the ensuing kickoff was equally meaningful. "The Notre Dame back [Mark McLane] came out of the end zone and started running laterally," McKay remembered, "and one of our young linebackers, Dave Lewis, gave him a shot [drilling him at the Notre Dame eight] that got the crowd on its feet. And you know what? That crowd never did sit down from there."

McKay's son, JK, a highly productive receiver, remembers it well. "I had been going to SC games since 1962, and I was looking around, thinking that I'd never seen the Coliseum like that. Everybody was on their feet. It was really an amazing experience and different from any other game I had seen or played in."

After the big hit on the kickoff return, Notre Dame went three and out, giving USC possession on the Irish thirty-eight. Invigorated from the momentum swing and focused on the job at hand, the Trojan offense jogged on the field with a new sense of purpose and the urging of a suddenly raucous crowd with a major shift in attitude, now expecting the best instead of fearing the worst.

On second down from the thirty-seven, Haden faded back and got great protection. McKay had broken free downfield and was headed toward the left sideline. Haden uncorked a strike, which the lanky receiver took in over his outside shoulder at the ten before being dragged down at the six. The next play, Davis took a pitch around right end, busted through a few tacklers and dived for the end zone, extending the ball over the goal line as he was going down. The already boisterous crowd let out yet another deafening roar as their Trojans were unquestionably back in the game. The touchdown was USC's third in a 2:35 span over the second and third quarters, bringing them to within five at 24–19.

Three plays after the kickoff, the Notre Dame team, which had seemed so solid and unshakeable in the first half, continued to fall apart, fumbling on its own thirty-one. Five plays later, the Trojans made the unlikely comeback complete as AD punched in his third touchdown of the day on a four-yard run over the left side. USC again went for two, and this time, naturally, with the way things were going, they were successful. Amazingly the Trojans had the lead at 27–24. Scribes in the press box weren't sure what to make of it, Notre Dame coaches didn't know what do next, and USC players could barely believe it themselves. Just 6:23 of game time after Davis looked him in the eye and confirmed that he was indeed going to return the second half kickoff for a touchdown, Richard Wood saw his team actually take the lead from a dominant team they had once trailed 24–0. "I said to the guys on the sideline, 'Are we in the same place? Or am I dreaming?' This cannot be the same football game I started out in a couple of hours ago. This cannot be that game!'"

It was. And it was far from over.

Notre Dame stumbled through another three and out, and when Marvin Cobb, who described the second half as "thirty minutes of goose bumps," returned the ensuing punt fifty-six yards to the Irish nineteen, the Trojans were in business yet again. And again they capitalized quickly. From the eighteen, Haden hooked up with McKay, throwing his third touchdown pass of the game. It was the USC's fourth touchdown of the quarter, increasing the lead to 34–24.

On their next possession, there was actually some fight to the Fighting Irish. They managed to string together a couple first downs and move the ball down to the USC thirty-five. It was all for naught though, because on the eleventh play of the drive, Trojan defensive back Charles Phillips, who would later return an interception for a touchdown, stopped the drive cold by picking off Clements and taking the ball back to midfield. The Trojans offense, which had finally gotten a chance to catch its collective breath, headed out to strike what would certainly be a death blow to the suddenly retreating Irish defense. After allowing a first down inside their own territory, Notre Dame's top-ranked defensive unit mustered everything it had left, forcing USC into a third and fifteen from the Irish forty-four with just a few seconds remaining in the quarter.

The Trojans were throwing and everybody knew it. The moment was significant and everybody knew that too. A stop by Notre Dame would be their first of the half and would get them the ball. A first down by USC would be a continuation of the demolition and would surely squeeze whatever life was left in the Irish right out of them.

Notre Dame went with a four-man rush as they dropped seven into coverage. The pass rush, though, was entirely ineffective because the line of scrimmage was completely controlled by USC's offensive line. The Irish were so conscious of protecting the first down line at their own twenty-nine, they barely noticed JK McKay streaking down the middle past their free safety. Haden reared back and fired a laser that traveled fifty yards in the air and was taken in by McKay on the three.

"One of those magical moments in sports," remembers Haden. "Things seemed to slow down. We were in kind of a time warp. I had plenty of protection, and John was wide open. Everything was absolutely perfect. You couldn't have asked for anything better."

By the time McKay caught the ball and got his head back around to look forward, he had crossed the goal line with the Trojans' *fifth* touchdown of a quarter for the ages.

The Coliseum crowd went nuts yet again, and the USC sideline was alive in celebration. The Trojans had scored on both the first and last plays of the third quarter, and three times in between. Incredibly, they added two more scores in the first two minutes of the fourth quarter, turning Notre Dame from simply beaten to completely and utterly demoralized. Paradoxically, the numbers are now familiar yet still shocking: eight touchdowns, fifty-five points in seventeen minutes against the number one defense in the nation.

Anthony Davis, who had a stellar career at USC, scoring forty-four touchdowns in thirty-five games, obviously saved his best for the Irish. Although he met Notre Dame just three times, one quarter of his collegiate touchdown total came against USC's most bitter rival. "A person does not score eleven touchdowns in those games against just those three Notre Dame teams," Davis insists. "You score them against the *legacy* of Notre Dame."

Even to this day, thirty-two years after what he calls "undoubtedly the greatest game in college football history, and don't be talkin' to me about no Doug Flutie," Davis swears that somebody mentions the 1974 game to him on a daily basis.

The game was ranked number three in the 1995 book *Unforgettable: The 100 Greatest Moments in Los Angeles Sports History*. The rankings were compiled through a poll of more than five thousand area media and sports enthusiasts, and covered the period from 1880 through 1995. Kirk Gibson's home-run in the 1988 World Series and the Los Angeles Olympics of 1984 were the only two moments listed above the magical game against Notre Dame.

After the game, as reporters crowded around Ara Parseghian in the Notre Dame locker room, the coach snapped, "Well, c'mon! Let's get this over with." As Parseghian was questioned about the Irish collapse, he actually used the game conditions, which were perfect, as an excuse. Yep, old Ara played the weather card. In the next day's *Los Angeles Times*, the Notre Dame coach was quoted as saying, "We've never played a good second half out here and there's more significance to that than meets the eye. You saw what happened to the Vikings out here against the Rams last weekend. They had a good first half but a poor second half.

"We did not have a good week of preparation. Our problem," Parseghian explained with a straight face, "is that it was twenty to thirty degrees all week in South Bend and the cold weather seems to thicken the blood or something."

In that week's issue of *Sports Illustrated*, the article on the game jokingly pointed out that, late in the game, Parseghian "contemplated hara-kiri with a yard line marker."

The afternoon of November 30, 1974, holds an unwavering, immovable place in the hearts and minds of everybody associated with USC, whether they were in attendance or watching on television, got game updates by smoke signal or have simply heard stories of the game told and retold. Pat Haden has said that it is the only game of his college career about which he has ever told his sons. Richard Wood, who went on to coach a Florida high school team to a state championship and World League teams into World Bowls, said in 2006, "To this day, sometimes I relay to my players that I don't care how far you're behind in a game—or in life. There are times when God makes miracles. Miracles happen. The way that it opened up like that against Notre Dame, I mean, I couldn't believe it myself."

The following day, a *New York Times* article by Leonard Koppett started this way:

> In a truly fantastic turnabout that will rank among the most retold legends of an already legendary rivalry, the University of California [sic] spotted Notre Dame a 24–0 lead, then demolished the Irish in a 55–24 victory. . . .
>
> A crowd of 83,552 in the Coliseum screamed itself silly during this remarkable rally, then started yelling up at the television booth, "We want Woody!" Up there was Woody Hayes, the coach of Ohio State, which will play USC in the Rose Bowl for the third straight year on January 1.

	1	2	3	4	F
Notre Dame	14	10	0	0	24
USC	0	6	35	14	55

SCORING:

First Quarter

Notre Dame: Bullock, 2-yard run (Reeve kick)

Notre Dame: Demmerle, 29-yard pass from Clements (Reeve kick)

Second Quarter

Notre Dame: Reeve, 20-yard field goal

Notre Dame: McLane, 9-yard run (Reeve kick)

USC: Davis, eight-yard pass from Haden

Third Quarter

USC: Davis, 102-yard kickoff return (Limahelu kick)

USC: Davis, 6-yard run (Limahelu kick)

USC: Davis, 4-yard run (Davis run)

USC: McKay, 18-yard pass from Haden (Limahelu kick)

USC: McKay, 44-yard pass from Haden (Limahelu kick)

Fourth Quarter

USC: Diggs, 16-yard pass from Haden (Limahelu kick)

USC: Phillips, 58-yard interception return (Limahelu kick)

Passing:

Notre Dame: Clements, 14–22–180, 3 interceptions, 1 touchdown

USC: Haden, 11–17–225, 1 interception, 4 touchdowns; Evans, 2–2–29

Rushing:

Notre Dame: Bullock, 10–40; Parise, 17–47; Samuel, 5–26

USC: Davis, 18–61; Haden, 10–26; Bell, 3–24

Receiving:

Notre Dame: MacAfee, 5–62; McLane, 3–32; Demmerle, 2–40

USC: McKay, 4–110; Diggs, 4–78; Davis, 3–37; Lee, 2–29

POSTSCRIPT

Ah, yes, Ohio State. The Buckeyes were led by Archie Griffin, who, by the time the teams played, had picked up the first of his two consecutive Heisman Trophies, beating out Anthony Davis for the award. The team had blown through its schedule at 10–1, winning by an average margin of more than thirty-one points per game. They were clearly the class of their conference and had ripped apart teams on their schedule by marching through a three-year stretch with an overall record of 29–3–1, including a 42–21 thumping of USC in the Rose Bowl the previous year.

The Buckeyes had racked up a gargantuan total of 437 points over the course of the 1974 season, but it was their defense that gave the Trojans the most trouble on the first day of 1975. USC had managed just ten points through fifty-five minutes and trailed by seven with the ball late in the fourth quarter. They had gone forty-one yards in seven plays and faced a fourth and one from the Ohio State forty-two. Allen Carter, who had replaced Davis when AD left the game in the second quarter with a rib injury, got the call and powered forward for four yards and a first down at the thirty-eight.

With less than three minutes to play, Haden went to the sideline to discuss play options with the Trojan brain trust. Years later he said, "I remember talking with coach McKay and we agreed the 96X corner to John [JK] was the play to call." JK, obviously not quite the coach his father was, added, "I tried to talk them out of it. I said, 'I don't think I can beat my guy on the corner. He's looking for that.' They said, 'Shut up, get in the huddle and run the corner.'"

Several factors suggested to the Buckeyes that the Trojans would be running. They had a fresh set of downs, and they had already torn up the Ohio State defensive front, rolling for 280 yards on the ground compared to just 143 in the air. Also, with more than two minutes left, if they scored too quickly, the Buckeyes would have time to retaliate. The Buckeyes had to be thinking run, but chances are, if a team was thinking run and John McKay was on the opposing sideline calling the plays, that team was going to see a pass, and that was exactly what was in store for the Buckeyes.

Haden faded back and got the protection he needed from his big offensive line. The Rose Bowl crowd was in a frenzy as the future Rhodes Scholar, NFL star and TV commentator looked left for an instant, then let the ball fly deep downfield to the right.

The ball in flight looked as if it would sail beyond the end line and perhaps beyond the sideline, but as it began its descent, McKay streaked toward the corner. With his man a half step behind him, and the receiver quickly approaching the back right corner of the end zone, he reached out with both arms, stretched in full stride and snagged the pass for the touchdown about six inches before he hit the sideline.

"The most accurate pass I ever saw," beamed the elder McKay.

Unable to stop his momentum, JK unknowingly invented a phenomenon that would become all the rage a couple thousand miles away, in another bastion of football twenty-five years later. As he sped toward the stands a few yards beyond the playing field, McKay jumped into the air and came down on the railing, which separated the field from the seats. The fans welcomed McKay with open arms. Some held him up while others whacked him with congratulatory slaps on the back and helmet. What has become known as the "Lambeau Leap" may live in Green Bay, but it was indeed a West Coast baby born in Pasadena.

The Trojans trailed 17–16 with 2:03 left. Coach McKay, known for despising tie games, was of course going to go for two. He would joke years later that it wasn't that he had a philosophical aversion to tying a game in the final minutes with a PAT, as much as it was that his kicking game often failed him when he needed it most.

The call was a rollout option, which allowed Haden to get on the move and either find a receiver or run the ball in for the lead. Taking the snap from the three, the Trojans line held as Haden moved in an arc backward and to his right. He got as far back as the eleven yard line before he started moving forward. It looked for an instant as if he was going to run—and maybe he was, but any perceived hole closed and two defenders charged hard. At the seven yard line, Haden stopped on a dime, pulling up so quickly that he actually got a couple inches of air underneath his spikes as he fired a wobbly mess of a sinking line drive toward Shelton Diggs. Diggs, about three yards in front of the end line, and smack-dab between the "S" and the "C" of the huge "USC" painted in the end zone of the Rose Bowl, fell to his knees, turned his palms upward, watched the ball drop into his arms a few inches above the turf and cradled that sucker as if it were a newborn. As the referee next to him extended his arms skyward, the Trojan contingent in the stands erupted. Diggs rose to his feet and was swallowed up by a swarm of ecstatic teammates as the Trojans took the lead 18–17.

Two minutes still remained, and for an offense the caliber of Ohio State's, that was enough to score twice, let alone once. The problem for the Buckeyes was that the ultrareliable Archie Griffin, who came into the game with an amazing streak of twenty-two straight hundred-yard games, had been contained by the Trojans the entire day and was limited to seventy-six yards on the ground. Ohio State managed to get the ball out near midfield, but were forced to settle for a sixty-two-yard field goal attempt on the final play of the game. Tom Dempsey being ineligible, the Buckeyes had to instead turn to their own kicker, Tom Skladany, who predictably came up short. USC had pulled out a one-point victory against a top-ranked opponent in a well-played, hard-fought and memorable Rose Bowl.

While USC was winning in Pasadena, the Trojans' dream scenario played out in Miami as Notre Dame took care of Bear Bryant and previously undefeated Alabama in the Orange Bowl, pulling out a 13–11 victory. All those pieces to the USC national championship puzzle were, as unlikely as it had seemed a month earlier, snapped into place. In the two-game stretch between the final Saturday of the regular season and the bowl games, all four teams ranked above the Trojans were either beaten or negated. USC did most of the dirty work, taking care of Notre Dame and Ohio State, while Notre Dame in turn took care of Alabama. Oklahoma, with its NCAA violations and resulting ineligibility in the UPI poll, had taken care of itself, despite an impressive and undefeated season. The Sooners did end up with the Associated Press national title, a spot ahead of once-beaten USC. UPI, though, went with the Trojans who earned twenty-seven of the thirty-four first-place votes, making them a clear-cut number one over Alabama, which ironically was knocked from the top spot by Notre Dame, a team that certainly wasn't looking to do USC any favors.

The title was especially sweet for a pair of Trojans, who had, for years, seemed destined for stardom at USC. Pat Haden actually lived in the McKay household during his senior season in high school, and JK McKay was the coach's son. The pair knew each other like they knew themselves. On the field, they were intimately familiar with each other's tendencies, trends and timing. Through thousands of passes thrown and caught in games and practices from high school to college, they had built an unmistakable, unshakable, unspoken communication. They were Stockton and Malone in helmets, Gretzky and Messier in cleats, Tinker and Evers with pads. Their final coauthored story was perhaps the most meaningful of all: a clutch and precise thirty-eight-yard touchdown connection leading to a victory on their sport's grandest stage and ultimately a national championship.

Haden once said of his 1973 team, "When I'd get to the line of scrimmage, I'd look to my left and there was Lynn Swann, tall, fast, great hands, an all-American. On the other side was this scrawny little kid, JK McKay. So who do I throw to? The little guy, of course. He was the coach's son!"

In beating Ohio State, the coach's son caught five passes for 104 yards. Haden threw for 181 yards and two touchdowns. "The Rose Bowl was the game, as a kid, I always wanted to play in," the quarterback says. "Here, winning the game, winning the national championship and being co-MVP with your best friend—I mean, you couldn't have scripted it any better."

The Ohio State game was the last important win of John McKay's USC coaching career. His Trojans were a perfect 7–0 the next season when he announced he would be leaving the school to coach the NFL's expansion Tampa Bay Buccaneers. Either as a direct result of the announcement, or by sheer coincidence, the 1975 Trojans went on to lose their remaining games, finishing the season 7–4.

McKay might have left his heart at Troy, but his physical body and that great coaching mind went to the NFL to lead one of two expansion teams entering the league. He walked away from USC having won 127 games and four national championships in sixteen seasons. After his departure, a popular bumper sticker began appearing on cars all around Los Angeles: GOD ISN'T DEAD. HE JUST MOVED TO TAMPA.

Initially, it appeared it actually would take divine intervention for the coach to succeed in the NFL. McKay's Buccaneers lost their first twenty-six games and were the joke of the league. Just two seasons later, though, he had turned the team around completely, leading the Bucs to the NFC championship game, where they lost to the Rams, falling one game short of reaching the Super Bowl. He retired from coaching following the 1984 season.

John McKay died of kidney failure on June 10, 2001, and was remembered in a touching memorial service on campus later that year.

"He was one of the greatest football coaches of all time," said athletic director Mike Garrett. "He made us all play beyond ourselves. He was a man we could look up to."

Son JK paid tribute, saying his father had "lived the American dream" by working his way out of a coal-mining town and finding fulfillment and success through football.

Haden read a posthumous letter he wrote McKay, saying, "I went to the Coliseum a few days ago, and it wasn't quite the same. To me, that memorable site and you are inexorably connected. It was your stage for sixteen years. What La Scala was for Caruso, the L.A. Memorial Coliseum was for John Harvey McKay."

Indeed, McKay will always be a part of the very turf at the Coliseum. Shortly after his death, his wife, Corky, was involved in carrying out the coach's wish that his ashes be scattered over the stadium at which his legacy of greatness was forged.

USC's first great
coach, Howard Jones.

Johnny Baker's
kick crushed the
Irish in 1931.

Wide receiver Rod Sherman catches Craig Fertig's game-winning touchdown
pass in the Trojan victory over Notre Dame in 1964.

OJ Simpson breaks into his legendary sixty-four-yard
touchdown run against UCLA.

Legendary Trojan Mike Garrett is greeted by adoring fans.

The great coach John McKay led three undefeated teams and won five Rose Bowls over his sixteen seasons at USC.

Linebacker Richard Wood, the only Trojan to be named first-team all-American three times.

Sam "Bam" Cunningham goes over the top.

USC legend Anthony Davis, whose speed helped the Trojans defeat the Irish in 1974.

Quarterback Paul McDonald hands off to Charles White.

Coach John Robinson speaks with his 1981 Heisman Trophy winner, Marcus Allen.

Carson Palmer,
USC's fifth Heisman
Trophy winner.

USC quarterback Matt Leinart celebrates another bowl victory.

The Trojans' sixth Heisman winner, Reggie Bush.

CHAPTER EIGHT

USC

VS.

ALABAMA,
1978

THE SETUP

If losing Howard Jones was like losing its soul, then for USC, watching John McKay walk away was like losing its very heart. The wins, the great comebacks, the Rose Bowl invitations and the national titles could all be quantified. What McKay meant to the school and its football program could not be. Finding a quality coach—the right coach—is never an easy task. Replacing John McKay was nearly impossible.

To fill the spot, USC turned to former McKay assistant John Robinson, a young coach who had grown up in Daly City, California, starring in football and baseball at Serra High School in San Mateo. He played his college ball at Oregon, where his first action as a player came in the Coliseum against the Trojans in the mid-fifties while McKay was an assistant coach on Oregon's staff.

Robinson, who played in the 1957 Rose Bowl, was an assistant coach for the Ducks for a dozen years before joining McKay's staff as USC's offensive coordinator in 1972. He parlayed the success the Trojans enjoyed in that glorious three-year run into an NFL offensive assistant job with the Raiders in 1975. Shortly after McKay announced that he was taking the job in Tampa, Robinson says he received a phone call from USC president John Hubbard, who was calling from a pay phone at the airport in Washington, D.C.

According to Robinson, the brief conversation went something like this:

Hubbard: Hi, John, John Hubbard.
Robinson: Hey, John. How ya doin'?
Hubbard: I'm fine. You want a job?
Robinson: Yeah.
Hubbard: Well, you got it.

In Robinson's book, *Conquest*, written with Joe Jares in 1981, he remembered the days surrounding his hiring.

There were concerns in some quarters about me following a legend, but USC still had the belief system, the attitude. I think a good definition of tradition is an organization that is more important than the individuals in it. The organization outlasts individuals. John McKay left me fine players and a winning tradition when he went off to the National Football League.

Part of the tradition was his love of big games. Coach McKay was always at his best for them and the feeling filtered down to the assistants and players. There was not a lot of talk. There was almost quiet on our practice field and a gleam in everybody's eye. I never saw us worried. I've never been worried going into a big game with a USC football team.

Maybe Robinson should have been worried heading into the season opener in 1976, but on the surface, there really wasn't anything to worry about. USC had scheduled a night game at the Coliseum to begin the season and the Robinson era. The opponent was an unranked Missouri team that had limped to a 6–5 record by losing three of its final four games the previous season, and had no reason to expect much better in the new year. The Trojans, on the other hand, started the season with the number eight ranking and had high hopes and expectations as team captains Ricky Bell, Vince Evans and Eric Williams strode toward midfield for the opening night coin toss.

The game, played in large part in a bothersome rain and on a sloppy field, turned out to be a disaster. Missouri racked up forty-five points while smashing USC to its most lopsided regular season loss in six years and worst opening game loss ever. Senior running back Curtis Brown ran for 101 yards in a 45–26 thumping that stunned Trojan players and fans. According to a *Las Vegas Sun* article written in 2003, "The only boos louder than the ones for Robinson that night were for Vince Evans, a black quarterback in an era that was almost void of any other black college quarterbacks."

"I'm telling you, the fans were booing like you would not believe," Evans said. "But Coach Robinson, as manly and as with as much courage that he had, stood up and said, 'Hey, it's my fault. We weren't prepared. But I guarantee you that we'll play extremely well the rest of the season.'"

As hollow as that guarantee might have seemed to the nation of Troy at the time, it proved to be as good as gold, as was the remainder of the year.

USC bounced back in a huge way, rolling through the next three games by a combined score of 139–13. Through the season, the defense held opponents under double digits five times, including three shutouts.

UCLA went down 24–14, and then Notre Dame was beaten 17–13. A season that started so miserably ended beautifully with a 14–6 win over Michigan in the Rose Bowl, a sparkling 11–1 record, and a consensus number two national ranking.

Much like McKay did in the third year of his tenure, Robinson solidified his spot at USC in the first year of his. The next year wasn't as strong, as the Trojans ended up with a blue bonnet instead of red roses when an 8–4 season was capped with a 47–28 win over Texas A&M in the Bluebonnet Bowl. Robinson's second USC team wound up ranked thirteenth in the final poll.

Howard Jones won his last national championship in 1939, and McKay won his first in 1962. The twenty-three-year drought between titles was far too lengthy of a span. With their latest new coach, it wouldn't be nearly that long.

John Robinson's third season at the helm began on September 9, but out there in the distance, looming like an impending root canal, was a week three matchup, which had USC flying cross-country to hook up with the nation's top-ranked team.

THE GAME (SEPTEMBER 23, 1978)

The Trojans touched down in Birmingham having won the season's first two games, but USC's football history against the Tide was rather forgettable, with the Trojans winning just one of the five previous meetings.

The year before, USC had started with four straight victories to increase its overall streak to fifteen in a row, and capture the nation's top ranking. The fifth game was at home against Alabama, and it was tight throughout. They went to the final minute with the Trojans trailing 21–14 when USC scored a touchdown to bring them to within a point. Like McKay, Robinson was all about victories, and especially as the number one team in the country, settling for a tie would not do. USC's two-point conversion attempt with thirty-five seconds remaining failed, setting in motion a stretch in which the Trojans lost four of six games prior to a season-ending victory against UCLA.

When you look at the 1978 schedule, Alabama may as well have been printed in big-face, bold type red—or rather, crimson—ink, because that was undoubtedly the glamour game on the docket and a significant challenge for what appeared to be an overmatched USC team. The Tide finished the previous season as a consensus number two in the polls and steamed into the stadium as the number one team in the rankings. They were strong on both sides of the ball and led on offense by a tough, versatile speedster named Tony Nathan.

Nathan, who would later be drafted by John McKay's Tampa Bay Bucs, was one of twenty black players on the Alabama squad. A *Washington Post* article the day before the game praised the university for its progress in racial equities on both the athletic fields and around campus in general. The story made no mention of Sam Cunningham.

In preparation for the game, Robinson left little to chance. The oppressive heat and humidity of the early-fall Alabama afternoons had taken their toll on visiting teams for years.

A few days before heading to Birmingham, Robinson was quoted as saying, "I noticed in Alabama's televised game with Nebraska a few weeks ago that 'Bama had air-conditioning units while the Nebraska players on the other sideline were fanning each other with towels." With temperatures expected to be in the nineties, Robinson arranged for USC to bring along their own air-conditioning units to place behind their bench.

When Robinson took the job at USC, he insisted he would make the quarterback position more significant than it traditionally had been. That claim was significant in itself at a school that had long ago earned the nickname Tailback U. In that vein, another concern for the Trojans was the new wrinkles in the offense implemented that spring by Robinson and passing coach Paul Hackett. A seemingly endless variety of complex blocking schemes—shifts and motion that were so sophisticated it was being used by only a handful of *professional* teams—was the backbone of the USC attack. Quarterback Paul McDonald, who just like Pat Haden had come out of Bishop Amat High School, was the on-field brains behind the operation.

As the game drew near, Robinson spoke of McDonald, saying, "You won't believe this kid. I've never seen a young man so into a game. He's fascinated by it. I worry sometimes that we're giving him too much to do, that we'll blow up with our own weapons. But I don't worry about him handling himself— even against this club—and nobody plays a more sophisticated defense than Alabama. It's going to be something to see."

Sports Illustrated reported that on the eve of the game, the entire USC team went to a movie theater in Birmingham to see *Hooper,* a film starring Burt Reynolds. The movie included a spectacular bar fight featuring Steelers quarterback Terry Bradshaw, who played a rugged loner. McDonald was quoted about the inspiration he got from Bradshaw's character's toughness, saying, "In that fight scene, he got whacked in the mouth with a chair and hardly blinked. He just spat out a few teeth and kept coming. When Burt Reynolds saw that, he said, 'Uh-oh, I think we're in trouble.' It was great. I thought to myself, 'That's what you have to do against Alabama. Spit 'em out and keep coming.'"

The day of the game, a Mal Florence article in the *Los Angeles Times* noted that the Crimson Tide, a 10.5-point favorite, would enjoy the usual boost from the hometown crowd and likely benefit from other factors as well.

> Alabama should be at emotional peak because a victory today before an anticipated record stadium crowd of 80,000 would be a giant step in Bryant's quest for a fifth national championship.

As usual, Bryant has been pouring syrup on the Trojans all week, saying Robinson's team is awesome—the best collection of athletes in the country. "Why, they are as big as skinned mules," Bryant said Friday. The Trojans may well be skinned mules after meeting Alabama.

On game day, under a scorching Southeastern sun, McDonald walked back through the tunnel after pregame warm-ups. Entering his ninth season as the Trojans' award-winning radio analyst in 2006, McDonald remembered the scene. He couldn't believe his eyes as he opened the door to the locker room.

"Everybody was exhausted. The floor was concrete and most of the team was just sprawled out with ice packs on their necks and cold, wet towels on their heads. I'm looking at these guys lying there, thinking, 'Oh, my God! We haven't even played the game yet—these guys are dead tired. What's gonna happen when we get into the fourth quarter?'"

The air-conditioning units on the Trojans sideline were blowing full-blast about a half hour later—kicked *on* even before kick*off*.

Alabama won the toss, and Tony Nathan rode the energy of the Legion Field emotion to a forty-five-yard kickoff return. The Crimson Tide, though, was unable to score and punted to USC, which took over on its own twenty-five and immediately began an impressive march, mixing the pass and run beautifully. Ten plays and seventy-three yards later, on first and goal from the two, McDonald turned to hand off to Charles White, who had already racked up thirty-eight yards on five carries. This time, White went nowhere as he fumbled the handoff and watched helplessly as Alabama recovered. It was a solid drive and a good start, but giving away goal line opportunities while visiting the top-ranked team in the country is usually a formula for disaster.

'Bama's following possession consisted of two runs, which

gained a total of four yards, an incomplete pass and a thirty-four-yard punt. White, who had been on the bench replaying the fumble in his mind, had a bounce in his step as he took the field for a run at redemption, and then he heard his number called in the huddle. He focused forward, anticipating the snap count and, with the enthusiasm and determination of a man who had just been pardoned from a serious crime, shot out of his three-point stance. White bolted forward and to his right where he took a handoff from McDonald, burst through the line, broke a couple of tackles and cut back against the grain into the secondary. He wasn't touched again until his own teammates caught up to him to celebrate in the end zone. The run covered forty yards and ended in front of a small USC cheering section making more than its share of noise in the stands of the packed stadium.

Early in the second quarter, still trailing 7–0, the Tide finally got rolling. Alabama went seventy-eight yards in nine plays and was on the brink of tying the game. Coming out of a time-out, on third down from the one yard line, running back Major Ogilvie was stuffed for no gain. Down a touchdown, Bear Bryant didn't hesitate; he was going to go for it. As if in motion itself, the crowd became increasingly louder as Alabama broke its huddle and moved toward the line of scrimmage. USC's defensive line dug in and, at the snap, thrust forward. The give was to Nathan over right guard, but the slippery senior couldn't get beyond the line of scrimmage. The Trojan linemen stood as firm as lampposts to stop the run and kill the drive. The Trojans defensive unit hustled off the field, past the human wall of cardinal-and-gold encouragement on the sideline and straight toward the humming, inviting waves of cool comfort emanating from the air-conditioning unit.

The offense took over on its own one yard line and started football's version of a triathlon, using speed, strength, stamina and determination to travel a great distance in three different ways. They ran, passed and advanced on penalties, holding the ball for eight and a half minutes while lining up for twenty-three snaps!

Most of the damage was done on the ground with Charles White, Dwight Ford and Lynn Cain carrying the load, while Mc-Donald found Calvin Sweeney and Raymond Butler through the air. Linemen Anthony Munoz and Pat Howell owned the line of scrimmage, muscling their way through the Alabama defensive front. The drive was officially recognized as eighteen plays, but five others were nullified by penalties, including a USC punt that was wiped out by a flag on Alabama for an illegal block, resulting in a Trojan first down. The drive was so time-consuming and so grueling that at one point, deep in Alabama territory, fullback Lynn Cain had had enough. McDonald remembers, "We're in the huddle, I call the play and Lynn starts walking off the field. Of course, on 'student-body right' and 'student-body left,' the fullback leads the way, and Lynn was out there every play, running sideline to sideline, blocking anyone in his path, and he was just spent. He's walking off and I'm yelling, 'Lynn. Come on! Where are you going? Lynn!' He couldn't even talk he was so tired. He just kind of threw his hand up and waved at me as if to say, 'You go on. I'm out of gas.' We took a time-out, Lynn got some fluids and we went back on the field and kept going."

They ended up moving eighty-five yards before settling for a Frank Jordan field goal. It was as if they were making a dizzying trek through the desert and the end zone was merely a mirage. They only came away with three points, but the drive was like a long, silent, energy-sapping taunt directed at a proud, stubborn defense. The field goal made it a 10–0 game, which was the score at halftime.

In the locker room, players pulled off their sweat-soaked gear, knowing they were halfway home. Some of them put on dry T-shirts under their jerseys; others just figured a change of clothing would be as pointless as toweling off between laps of a swim race.

"When you're up ten to zero at the half and playing the number one team in the country, first of all you feel pretty good about yourselves. We were dominating the game at that point," recalls McDonald. "The adrenaline kicked in and our attitude was 'Hey, we got it going. Let's keep it going.' If we were *down* ten, it would have been an entirely different story, but we were rejuvenated."

It didn't take long for Alabama to get the crowd into the game in the second half. On the opening possession, White, who had shredded the Tide defense for 142 yards in the first half, fumbled on a third-and-ten play, giving Alabama the ball on USC's forty-one. Needing desperately to capitalize, the Crimson Tide offense got a huge lift from Ogilvie, who took a handoff through the right side of the line and rumbled all the way for a touchdown. The drive: one play, forty-one yards in seven seconds. The Trojans' lead was cut to three at 10–7, and Legion Field was alive.

The rest of the third quarter was controlled by the defenses. USC's stud inside linebacker Dennis Johnson racked up several of his eleven tackles on the afternoon, while outside 'backer Eric Scoggins made eight stops and assisted on three others. In all, the Trojans forced six turnovers, including four interceptions of Alabama quarterback Jeff Rutledge.

In its next issue, *Sports Illustrated* noted, "USC's defense gets to the ball quicker than Cinderella's stepsisters and doesn't appear to have a pass defender under 6'6"."

Also helping out the Trojans was Alabama punter Woody Umphrey, who had a miserable day. Alabama fans had seen better legs on a coffee table. His first punt went sixteen yards. He averaged a mere thirty yards per punt, ensuring USC relatively good field position all day.

On the first play of the fourth quarter, old Woody checked

in again. From Alabama's eight yard line, he rocked a real boomer: a thirty-one-yard punt that gave the Trojans the ball on the Tide's thirty-nine. White gained six on the first play, and McDonald then scrambled for eight. "I'm faster than they think," he'd say afterward.

Five plays later, on a first and goal from the six, Robinson sent in a play that continued the daylong trend of confusing the Alabama defense. The Trojans broke the huddle and lined up with flanker Kevin Williams, weighing all of 155 pounds, in the tailback spot. Seconds earlier, as Hackett sent the wisp-thin Williams in from the sideline, the coach's final instructions were "Scrunch over so they don't get a good look at you."

On the snap, McDonald faded back and looked left while Williams sprinted out to the right. He then angled quickly back inside, underneath the defense, where McDonald zeroed in and hit him with a pinpoint-accurate dart for a touchdown. While the receiver celebrated, McDonald ran off the field, where he was met by two huge bear hugs: the first from Robinson, the second from the air-conditioning units. The Trojans had extended the lead back to ten at 17–7.

Alabama once again needed to retaliate, but this time, they got nothing. Tony Nathan and Lou Ikner converged to receive the kickoff and dropped the ball. Ikner recovered, but went nowhere and the Tide was forced to start on its own seven. After an incomplete pass, Rutledge and Nathan, looking like Harpo and Zeppo, collided in the backfield on a draw play, losing four yards back to the three. As boos began to rain down from the stands, Rutledge hit Nathan on a swing pass out of the backfield, but safety Dennis Smith sniffed it out and dropped Nathan after a gain of four, and once again, it was time for Woody Umphrey to do his thing.

Umphrey got off his best punt of the day: a whopping thirty-nine yarder fair caught by Ronnie Lott at the forty-six, again allowing the Trojans to start a possession in Alabama territory. On third and four from the forty, McDonald looked for Williams again. He found him and fired, but the pass was a bit underthrown. Defensive back Don McNeal was thinking interception as he went up for the ball, but managed only to tip it. A moment later, the ball settled into the waiting arms of Williams, who took it the rest of the way for the touchdown. Heads dropped on the Alabama sideline while arms raised across the way. Everything was working. The PAT gave USC a commanding 24–7 lead with 8:34 to play.

Now desperate, the Crimson Tide finally showed some signs of being the number one team in the country. Starting from their own fourteen, they chewed up forty-five yards in five plays, and then on a first down at the USC forty-one, 'Bama departed from the local and got on the express. Rutledge found Barry Krauss on a perfectly executed post pattern to finish the impressive drive, which went eighty-six yards in just six plays, taking all of 1:19.

A game that, a minute earlier, had looked all but over was now suddenly worth watching. More than seven minutes remained and the lead was ten. But the fans in Alabama had seen their share of comebacks, and they were whooping it up in the stands, doing what they could to help start another one.

After an unsuccessful onside-kick attempt, the Crimson Tide defense stepped up in a big way. USC started at its own forty-five, but went backward. A nine-yard sack was made worse by a fifteen-yard clipping penalty. Without picking up so much as a single first down, USC had to punt the ball away, and Alabama took over again on its forty-four with five minutes to play. They moved the ball steadily toward the goal line, the crowd's noise level and faith growing with every yard gained. With 3:30 left, they had worked their way down to the Trojan eighteen, but their momentum and their chances were killed right there when Nathan was drilled by defensive tackle Myron Lapka and fumbled on the twelve, where the Trojans recovered. Nathan also fumbled on a punt return a few minutes later, sealing the deal for USC and starting a Southern California–style party two thousand miles from home.

The Trojans had beaten the nation's number one team, racking up 417 yards in offense on a day they never trailed. Paul McDonald completed nine of his sixteen passes for 113 yards, but in that regard, the stats didn't begin to tell the story.

That was best left to John Underwood of *Sports Illustrated*, who wrote, "What was dumped on Bear and his boys, that put them on their collective carrumpus for the first time in 13 games, was brains." Underwood went on to reason that most Trojan quarterbacks' first order of business is not to throw, or to think, but to simply hand the ball off. Garrett, Simpson, Davis and now Charles White—those are the businessmen carrying the USC briefcase. But he wrote, "McDonald can throw, and when it comes to generating brain waves, Robinson and Hackett consider him a Phi Beta Kappa."

And that "syrup" that Jim Murray wrote about—the kind Bear Bryant had been pouring on the Trojans before the game—apparently had truth as its main ingredient. Bryant insisted afterward that he had not been overstating his view of the Trojans and knew all along that USC was a major threat. After the game, the legendary coach said, "I'm still not sure just how good those USC people are, but I know they're a helluva lot better than us. The final score could have been worse than it was. They were the best-coached, best-prepared, best-run team on that field. They handled everybody we put out there and even made us look a little worse than we really are." Reminded about his pregame comments, Bryant said, "I wasn't tryin' to fool anybody." Apparently there had been no whistlin' in Dixie.

The new-look Trojans were like a steroid-enhanced version of a USC team from the early seventies. The school, so well known for its blazing speed, suddenly had the power of a bulked-up bruiser ready to go *through* any team in its way. "We were just out to physically dominate them," said Munoz, now an NFL hall of famer. "It was nothing fancy, just our basic offense."

As with other power teams, the Trojans did most of their damage on the ground. USC ran eighty-two offensive plays, sixty-five of which were runs resulting in a mammoth 309 yards, for an average of 4.8 yards per carry. Charles White's red-hot start continued as he ran the ball twenty-nine times for 199 yards and a touchdown.

"We played the game on artificial turf," remembered Mc-Donald twenty-eight years later, "and I was used to seeing Charles run on natural grass. He was always fast, but on that turf, man, he seemed a lot faster. When we ran the student-body play to either side, it was like we had the infantry out front and Charles was like a stealth fighter behind 'em. He was one of the most intense competitors you'll ever meet, and he was getting stronger every time he got the ball."

White averaged nearly seven yards per rush and brought his three-game total up to 545 yards, putting him on pace for a 2,000-yard season. Never short on confidence (he had declared himself a Heisman candidate as a freshman!), White said after the game, "I am running more intelligently and aggressively than ever."

Asked about White, Alabama senior linebacker Barry Krauss said, "Wow! Quick, agile, powerful. When we hit him he still had momentum, and believe me, it was hard to get a lick on him. His elusiveness and explosion—it seemed like he could have broken into a long run at any time. He's the best back I've ever played against."

The compliments from future NFL star Marty Lyons went even a step beyond. "White's a super athlete and a super guy. He has a lot of class. In fact, their whole team's like that. When their coach comes in here and shakes our hands, calls us by our first names and says, 'Don't worry. It's not the end of the season. You can regroup and come back'—well, that shows me something."

Meantime, in the USC dressing room, players who had walked in that day ranked seventh in the country shared in a celebration. There were hugs, handshakes and high hopes for a season that was clearly taking shape. Instead of the traditional "We're Number One!" the Trojans began a single-word chant that told the story of whom they had beaten and what they hoped to become.

"One! One! One!" they shouted in unison. Coach Robinson got up on a chair in the middle of the locker room, and as the chant died down, he declared, "Remember what I told you Thursday. We're not number one and I'm not voting us number one. I'm voting us number six. But you're the greatest bunch of human beings I have ever been around, and you're going to be a great team. I sense it. I feel it. You're not number one now, but in January . . ."

	1	2	3	4	F
USC	7	3	0	14	24
Alabama	0	0	7	7	14

SCORING:

First Quarter

USC: White, 40-yard run (Jordan kick)

Second Quarter

USC: Jordan, 40-yard field goal

Third Quarter

Alabama: Ogilvie, 41-yard run (McElroy kick)

Fourth Quarter

USC: Williams, 6-yard McDonald pass (Jordan kick)

USC: Williams, 40-yard McDonald pass (Jordan kick)

Alabama: Krauss, 41-yard Rutledge pass (McElroy kick)

Passing:
USC: McDonald, 9–16–113, 1 interception, 2 touchdowns
Alabama: Rutledge, 8–19–119, 4 interceptions, 1 touchdown

Rushing:
USC: White, 29–199; Cain, 18–97; Ford, 8–20
Alabama: Ogilvie, 11–75; Nathan, 12–64

Receiving:
USC: Williams, 2–46; Sweeney, 3–37
Alabama: Krauss, 2–58; Pugh, 2–34

POSTSCRIPT

Two short weeks after the huge win over Alabama had Robinson thinking of January greatness, USC was handed its first loss of the season, going down 20–7 in a shocker at Arizona State. The loss killed chances for an undefeated season, and despite an overall record of 5–1, the Trojans were just 1–1 in conference, putting even a Rose Bowl berth in jeopardy.

After the loss, the Trojans pulled together, defined their personality as a team and established themselves as the class of the Pac-10. Four games and four victories later, they were back up to number five in the rankings when a win over UCLA clinched the conference championship and improved the season record to 9–1. The new poll had them sitting pretty at number three as they prepared for a visit from their old pals from South Bend.

Notre Dame strutted into the Coliseum on a late November Saturday, ranked eighth. USC had its way most of the day, but a quarterback who would build his reputation on precision and execution under pressure led a comeback that threatened to knock the Trojans out of national championship contention.

White scorched the Irish for 205 yards on thirty-seven carries, and USC held a seemingly comfortable 24–6 (sound familiar?) lead through three quarters. The Irish rallied in the fourth though, when a kid named Joe Montana first threw a fifty-seven-yard touchdown pass and then led a ninety-eight-yard touchdown drive to pull his team within five, at 24–19. Notre Dame took possession again with 1:35 left, and needed just forty-nine seconds to score again on Montana's second scoring pass and Notre Dame's third touchdown of the quarter, giving the Irish a 25–24 lead with forty-six seconds remaining. Joe Cool, indeed.

After the kickoff, USC took over on its own thirty. McDonald appeared to fumble, but the referees ruled an incomplete pass. The Trojans then marched into field goal range, largely on the strength of a thirty-five-yard completion from McDonald to Calvin Sweeney. With two seconds to play, kicker Frank Jordan, who had earlier missed an extra point and a short field goal attempt, drilled a thirty-seven-yard game winner as Rose Bowl–bound USC escaped with a memorable 27–25 victory.

In his column the next day, veteran *New York Times* great Red Smith wrote,

> Notre Dame and Southern California have met at football 50 times, and now they might as well knock it off. No use trying. If they played another 50 years, they could not match the gaudy theatrics of Saturday's fourth quarter.

Later in his article, Smith looked ahead to the previously set Rose Bowl matchup between USC and Michigan, suggesting that Wolverines coach Bo Schembechler better find a way to put pressure on the quarterback.

> Maybe between now and Jan. 1, he can discover a route that his pass rushers can follow to reach Paul McDonald. Secure as a cloistered nun behind the monsters in his offensive line, McDonald took his own sweet time throwing to receivers like Kevin Williams, whom the Notre Dame secondary shunned like pollution.

Michigan, the Big-10 champ, was headed to Pasadena for the third straight time. USC was going for the second time in three years. In 1977, Michigan met with the Trojans, winning 14–6.

As the teams prepared to face each other, practices and possibilities raged at other schools around the country, as well, with several teams thinking national championship. Heading into the bowl games, the AP and UPI polls were stacked identically:

1) Penn State (11–0)
2) Alabama (10–1)
3) USC (11–1)
4) Oklahoma (10–1)
5) Michigan (10–1)

The Bowl game matchups were as follows:

Sugar: Penn State vs. Alabama
Rose: USC vs. Michigan
Orange: Oklahoma vs. Nebraska

Many thought that the Sugar Bowl winner would also take the national championship, which seemed logical given the participating teams' first and second rankings, but with USC's win over Alabama earlier in the season, and a potential Alabama win over Penn State in New Orleans, both the Trojans and the Tide would finish with just a single loss.

In that case, who are *you* voting number one: the team that came into its bowl game with the higher ranking (Alabama) or the team that won a head-to-head matchup between the teams (USC)?

In order for that question to even apply, the Trojans had to get by a strong Michigan team in the Rose Bowl.

Bo Schembechler had put together an impressive record of 96–9–3 in ten seasons in Ann Arbor, but bowl season was a different story, with the Wolverines going 0–5 under his guidance. USC, on the other hand, came into the game with the best winning percentage (.738) of any team in the country that had played in at least ten bowl games, and they were listed as 5.5-point favorites to keep Michigan winless.

A couple of left-handed quarterbacks led the way out of the respective tunnels: Rick Leach for the Wolverines and Paul McDonald, who was nursing a sprained ankle, for USC. The main concern for the Trojans was the Michigan defense which had allowed an average of just eight points per game.

Early in the first quarter, though, it was the USC defense that made a difference. Ronnie Lott, one of the greatest to ever play the game on any level, intercepted a Leach pass on Michigan's first possession. Lott hauled it in at midfield and, after a thirty-three-yard run back, came within one broken tackle of taking it in for a touchdown. A few plays later, McDonald, limping noticeably, rolled to his left and hit tight end Hoby Brenner with a nine-yard touchdown toss to give USC a 7–0 lead.

Midway through the second quarter, with a 7–3 edge, the Trojans struck again, but this time with controversy. Finishing off a seven-play, fifty-yard drive, Charles White banged it over from the three. Replays and still photographs clearly show that the future Heisman Trophy winner fumbled just shy of the goal line on a dive into the end zone. Michigan recovered on the one and White pounded the turf with his fist in frustration. However, line judge Gilbert Marchman raised his arms signaling a touchdown while umpire Don Mason signaled that it was Michigan's ball. The officials huddled for a few seconds and head linesman Lee Joseph ruled that the call was indeed touchdown.

The ruling set off an angry protest from the Michigan side of the field and made it 14–3 in favor of the Trojans, whose defense took over from there, leading USC to a 17–10 victory. The offensive statistics weren't very impressive—pathetic, actually, as the Trojans managed just 157 yards in total offense, and the hobbled McDonald completed a mere four passes for twenty-three yards. The only numbers that matter, though, are the big ones on the scoreboard, and those put the finishing touches on USC's 12–1 season.

Thoroughly bored in the press box, Jim Murray made no secret of his thoughts in his *Los Angeles Times* column the next day.

The game was distinguished because it managed to cram more in-action into 60 minutes of football than the old Pitt-Fordham score-less ties.

Michigan scored in the 3rd quarter, but spent most of the rest of the 2nd half on its own 10 yard line looking like a fly trying to get out of a spider web.

Frankly I wouldn't want to get into the same lifeboat with this Michigan team. In fact, I would not get into an elevator with them. Wouldn't want to back their play at a casino, but I would bet the limit against them even if they had three aces showing. Because these guys would have to get luckier to even be considered snakebit. I'm sur-prised they didn't bring rain. These are the kind of guys who would be just lucky enough to get a last-minute reservation on the *Titanic*.

Whether by hook or by crook, through good calls or bad, with excitement or lack thereof, USC pulled out the win and turned its attention to New Orleans, where Alabama was taking on undefeated Penn State. The Trojans, of course, were pulling for 'Bama, knowing the only way they could possibly get the number one nod was with a Nittany Lions loss, leaving the country without an unbeaten team.

Alabama led it 14–7 midway through the fourth quarter when a fumble recovery gave Penn State a first down, nineteen yards from the tying touchdown. Six plays later they were a yard away. On third down, Matt Suhey banged through the middle to within a foot of the goal line, and on fourth down, the Alabama defense stood like a stack of sumo wrestlers, ston-ing Penn State and leaving Joe Paterno twelve inches short of a national championship. There was no more scoring as Alabama held on for a 14–7 win.

Meantime, in Miami, Oklahoma avenged its only loss of the season with a 31–24 win over Nebraska in the Orange Bowl (the Sooners had fumbled *nine* times, losing six of them, in their regular-season loss to the Cornhuskers), and suddenly, with four one-loss teams laying claim, the national title was up for grabs. Alabama, USC, Penn State and Oklahoma—four of the most storied programs in the history of collegiate athletics— all had arguments, albeit some better than others. After a season's worth of on-field combat, the championship would be decided by a vote as the eyes of the college football nation turned toward the AP and UPI polls.

A Sugar Bowl game story by Bob Oates in the *Los Angeles Times* the next day ended with a case for USC.

> The key fact in the debate, possibly, is that USC's offensive team wrecked a defense that Penn State could hardly budge. In September, Trojan tailback Charles White ran through Alabama for 199 yards as USC breezed 24–14. By contrast, the entire Penn State backfield gained a net of 19 yards rushing against Alabama, proving that Bryant's defense is indeed a majestic weapon—except when contending with the Trojans.

The Alabama players anticipated a close vote and many of them started campaigning in their dressing room in New Orleans, mere minutes after their Sugar Bowl victory. For a guy who had been so unproductive (twelve carries, two fourth quarter fumbles, one botched kickoff return) against USC, Tony Nathan sure was vociferous. In a thinly veiled shot at the Trojans, Nathan said, "We just beat the best team we played all year. Penn State is strong and well-coached and we just took it to them."

Tuesday, January 2, was the first workday of 1979. Lawyers, bankers, janitors and dancers all reported to their respective offices. The focus of the sports world, though, was on the thirty-five men who made up the United Press International board of coaches. The secret votes began trickling in early that morning, and much like most of the relevant bowl games, it was close the whole way. USC would take a one-vote lead; then three straight votes would come in for Alabama to turn the tide for the Tide. Then USC would capture a flurry of votes, Oklahoma would pop up here and there and then the edge again tilted in 'Bama's favor. When the ballots were all counted, it was a dead-heat; both USC and Alabama had fifteen first-place votes, with Oklahoma taking the other five.

The key to the vote was USC's and Alabama's respective rankings on the ballots in which they were *not* voted number one. On those, USC had a slight edge, picking up more second-place votes, and ultimately more total points. The call came into the Trojan athletic offices shortly before the news became public. The voice on the other end started the conversation simply by saying, "Congratulations."

USC had won its eighth national championship with a final tally of 496 points to 491 for the Crimson Tide in one of the closest UPI votes in history.

Robinson, who had led his teams to a sparkling 31–5 record since the opening night debacle three years earlier, was glowing in the satisfaction at the announcement. "I think this team might have accomplished more than any team in USC's history, considering how tough our schedule was. We beat the Sugar Bowl champion [Alabama], the Cotton Bowl champion [Notre Dame], the co-Big-10 champions [Michigan and Michigan State], the Bluebonnet Bowl winner [Stanford] and the team [UCLA] that tied for the Fiesta Bowl championship.

"At the start of the season, people questioned our talent. Then, all of a sudden, we were called awesome," Robinson said.

The reaction, of course, was far different in Tuscaloosa. Bear Bryant, who after his team's loss to the Trojans a few months earlier admitted, "I don't know just how good these USC people are, but I know they're a helluva lot better than us," suddenly had a change of opinion.

"My heart bleeds for our players," Bryant said quietly. "I don't think any other team played the tough schedule we did with as much success. The UPI demonstrated a lack of consistency with this vote. Their number one and number two teams played in what the vast majority of the nation viewed as the national championship game. All I can say is that we've won a hell of a lot more games than we have popularity contests recently."

Bryant was in fact somewhat justified in his feelings toward the polls. The previous season Alabama was ranked second heading into the bowl games, but even after a win over Ohio State in the Sugar Bowl, the Tide was leap-frogged by number three Notre Dame, which beat top-ranked Texas in the Cotton Bowl. The Irish won the national title while 'Bama stayed put at number two.

The day after UPI named USC national champions, it was the AP's turn, and that vote went to Alabama. The Crimson Tide beat out the Trojans, with Oklahoma and Penn State finishing third and fourth. The split national title allowed both schools to claim a championship.

In a way, polls are like poles. They are, on their own, useless. They both exist only to hold up something more relevant. And you know all those guys who were screaming and yelling for a playoff when USC and LSU shared the title after the 2003 season? Well, their fathers were screaming and yelling back in 1979 for a Trojan-Tide rematch. The more things change, the more they remain the same.

In fact, just as the Trojans would have been favored against LSU in the new millennium, the head oddsmaker at Harrah's in Las Vegas went on record saying that, if USC and Alabama were to meet, the Trojans would be the choice. He put the number at six points if the game was played in Los Angeles, three at a neutral site and two in Birmingham.

As far as USC was concerned, though, the season was over and there was no need to play another game. The Trojans looked at it this way: *We were voted number one in one of the polls. And the number one team in the other poll? We beat them, fair and square, on their own field. Any more questions?*

CHAPTER NINE

UCLA

VS.

USC, 2001

THE SETUP

The darkness that had fallen over the Coliseum as the Trojans made their way to their locker room was symbolic to say the least. Freshmen scurried to the showers while seniors lingered, some catching a final field-level glimpse of a college football stadium on game day. Several players milled about, congratulating counterparts from Notre Dame on their 38–21 season-ending victory. Coach Paul Hackett, in his most optimistic thoughts, focused on the positive aspects of the Trojans' loss as something to build on for next season, but in his most realistic consciousness likely saw his march through the Coliseum's southwest tunnel as something akin to a final trudge into the gallows. Dead man walking.

The previous three hours, just like most of the past five seasons, had been torture for the Trojan diehards among the

81,342 in attendance. The on-field beating was bad enough in itself, but the idea that what they were witnessing had become the norm around these parts was downright maddening. Notre Dame ran the ball sixty-two times against the once proud Trojan defense, racking up 246 yards on the ground. In comparison, the Trojans rushed thirty times for a mere seventy-eight yards. Future Heisman Trophy winner Carson Palmer connected on fewer than half of his thirty-five passes and was intercepted twice.

The loss was USC's seventh of the season against just five wins and their 2–6 mark in the Pac-10 left them dead last in conference for the first time in school history. Over the past five seasons, the Trojans managed to stay above .500 with a record of 31–29, but since when was staying above .500 anything to be proud of at USC? Their conference record over that span, 17–23, was downright embarrassing. There was a cool November breeze blowing through the old stadium, but the winds of change weren't far behind.

Forty-eight hours later, on November 27, 2000, exactly three-quarters of a century since Gwynn Wilson and Knute Rockne connected on that eastbound train, Paul Hackett was fired. USC's loss to the school with which Rockne is still heavily identified simply made what was already an easy decision for the administration a bit easier. A coaching search was on, and there was no room for error. The Trojans needed a difference maker. They were looking for a big-name, big-game coach who could recruit, teach and dance in rhythm with autumn Saturday afternoons. They were in search of a man to lead the school in the new century to the same level of glory it had enjoyed for much of the old one.

Since the end of John Robinson's first tenure at USC in 1982, Trojan coaches Ted Tollner, Larry Smith and Paul Hackett had combined to go 89–63–4. At some schools, that would be considered a dynasty. At USC, it is unimpressive, uninspiring and unacceptable. Robinson was brought back for a five-year stint in the mid-nineties and had modest success, taking the Trojans to one Rose Bowl, but never finishing higher than twelfth in the final polls.

Names of coaches started flying around campus like kites on a windy day. It seems every year a few coaches are perceived as hot commodities, because of recent successes, expiring contracts, media-created buzz or a combination of those or other factors. This year, three West Coast–based coaches were in strong demand and each had a contingent of supporters in the nation of Troy.

* Dennis Erickson, winner of two national championships at the University of Miami, and at the tail end of an 11–1 breakout season at Oregon State, which was capped off by a Fiesta Bowl victory. Through 2000, Erickson had compiled a collegiate coaching record of 131–46–1.
* Mike Bellotti, head coach of an Oregon team that made rock-steady progress toward elite status in the Pac-10. Bellotti's Ducks won six games in 1996 and increased its victory total in each successive season through 2001. That year, Oregon won the conference championship after going 11–1 and winning the Fiesta Bowl. In 2000, he piqued USC's interest with a 10–2 season and a cochampionship in the conference.
* Mike Riley, a USC assistant coach from 1993–96, who left the Trojans for the head job at Oregon State. After two years in Corvallis, he took over as head coach of the San Diego Chargers and went 8–8 in his first season. From there, it was all downhill as Riley suffered through a 1–15 year with a miserable Chargers team in 2000, prompting speculation that he would soon be available.

Several good candidates and one great program in need of restoration. It would seem like a foolproof process. If you are USC, you identify the man you want and make him an offer he can't refuse. You pull out all the stops. You walk him through Heritage Hall and let him breathe the history. You take him into the Coliseum and let him feel the tradition. You stop him in front of the Heisman Trophies, the national championship banners and the list of all-time all-Americans and dare him to say no. He gets phone calls from Marcus Allen and Pat Haden and Charles White and Anthony Munoz and Lynn Swann and Anthony Davis. You'll get your man.

Or maybe you won't.

If the process of finding a coach was not a complete disaster for USC, it certainly wasn't textbook, either. Fans had to be wondering whether even the old Trojan *aura* was gone. Granted, the on-field product hadn't been what it once was, but wasn't the head coaching job at USC still considered one of the great gigs in college sports? In *all* of sports? Elite schools hire elite coaches, and an opening at Troy would, once upon a time, setoff the football equivalent of Hollywood's high-voltage casting call. But there didn't seem to be much of a line forming outside the athletic offices on campus.

After flirting with several coaching candidates and actually offering the job to Erickson, the news broke on December 15, 2000. The Trojans' new hire was Pete Carroll, a man who had turned down USC three years earlier and had made his living, for the most part, in the NFL. He had been the head coach of the Jets and Patriots and on staffs with the Bills, Vikings and 49ers. His last college job was with his alma matter, Pacific, in 1983.

Asked about his new gig, Carroll said, "I believe I am tailored for this—it's quite clear. I'm going to a place where there are great expectations. That's where I want to be." And pressed for a time frame to return the Trojans to glory, the coach refused to be nailed down. "We'll be good when we're good," he said. "My goal is to win right now."

As word started to circulate throughout the USC community, Internet message boards were overloaded with responses—almost exclusively negative. At his introductory press conference, Carroll was informed of the adverse reaction to his hiring and calmly said, "I've been an unpopular choice at times. It is a challenge. I'm going to prove [the USC hierarchy] right. I want to make the fans proud. I don't need anybody to give me pep talks or fire me up."

For his part, Athletic Director Mike Garrett admitted that he had heard from a lot of angry alumni and supporters of the program. When asked what he would like to say to those who had called, he smiled and said simply, "Have faith."

Faith had become less of the defining quality it once was and more of an ideological concept in the world of USC football. Instead of faith, which in the nineties had dissipated like early-morning fog, Trojan fans were desperate for *proof* of a turnaround. Until they saw something concrete, they had become inclined to take a wait-and-see approach. And what they were seeing, they didn't like. What Mike Garrett was selling, they weren't buying. And whatever promises came along with Pete Carroll appeared to be worth about as much as the wind on which they were spoken.

The Trojans started the season with a 21–10 win over San Jose State on a steaming hot Los Angeles afternoon in front of 45,568, the smallest opening day Coliseum crowd since 1984. Sultan McCullough, to that point the fastest man ever to wear a Trojan uniform, led the way with 172 yards and three touchdowns on twenty-five carries. It was a solid start for Carroll, but it was, after all, just San Jose State.

From there, it got bad. And then it got worse. The Trojans

lost their next four in a row and, after breaking the losing streak, were beaten at Notre Dame, 27–16. Their record stood at a dismal 2–5 with four games left to play.

Carroll, who had been in the line of fire from the beginning, was unmistakably in the crosshairs. *Los Angeles Times* page two columnist T.J. Simers, never one to allow a good deed to go unpunished, expressed his thoughts on Carroll the day after the loss to the Irish.

> Put a baseball cap on Carroll's head, pull it tight over his eyes, and USC fans would be screaming this guy can't hack it in crunch time. (Get it?)
>
> USC was the better team on the field, but Carroll allowed another close game—20–16 with less than two minutes to play—to get away. Given the chance to be bold, he played it safe at a key point in the third quarter—this after declaring last week he intended to show the Irish what to expect in the next few years from the Carroll-coached Trojans. Well, he did.

As the dissatisfaction with the coach and criticism mounted, out there in the distance was a matchup with UCLA. As had long been the case at USC, if the year was a failure and the Notre Dame game didn't quite work out, there was always a potential season saver against the Bruins. In fact, after the loss in South Bend, as the Trojans were preparing to face Arizona, an article entitled "Westwood, Ho!" written by Bill Plaschke appeared in the *Los Angeles Times*. The point was simple, and at the time valid.

> For most of the last six years, those helmeted kids from a basketball school have improbably bullied opponents, wowed fans and impressed voters nationwide. But now the UCLA football team has done the impossible. It has won the neighborhood. When it comes to college football, Los Angeles clearly belongs to the Bruins. Not USC,

not anymore, not even close, and not only just this year. This is a Bruin football town, and has been a Bruin football town, and will continue to be a Bruin football town as long as the Bruins continue running the consistent, directed program so lacking across town. Certainly there are some USC alumni who will disagree. But surely not even that constant digital recording of "Conquest" blaring from their dashboard can distract them from the facts.

The article went on to point out several positives about UCLA and the corresponding negatives about USC, but ignored the fact that since losing eight straight to the Bruins, the Trojans had won the last two games between the schools. The meeting with UCLA was still twenty-three days away, and the Trojans were having a hard enough time beating the team it was facing each week to worry about the inner-city rivalry still four games ahead on the schedule.

USC hadn't had a successful season since 1995, and on the surface, at 2–5, 2001 seemed like another lost year. A closer look, though, revealed a team with several quality players that had been competitive in every single game. The first four losses came by a *total* of fourteen points. Three of the teams that had beaten USC were ranked in the top twelve. And two of the losses came on the road, late in the fourth quarter (seventh-ranked Oregon won in Eugene on a field goal with :12 remaining, and number eleven Washington pulled out a home victory on a field goal as time expired). Through seven games, it seemed as if every crucial break had gone against USC.

Then everything changed. USC not only started winning, but winning in different ways. A touchdown in the final two minutes got them past Arizona, 41–34. The next week, they went to overtime before pulling out a 16–13 win over Oregon State, and followed that with a 55–14 blowout victory at Cal. Suddenly the record stood at 5–5 with a chance to go over .500 in the regular-season finale.

THE GAME (NOVEMBER 17, 2001)

While the Trojans were getting knocked around early in the season, the Bruins were rolling through opponents like a bowling ball over bobble-head dolls. Four of their first five victims were ranked in the top twenty-five, but UCLA tore through them as if they were all, well, San Jose State. The Bruins dominated just about every team on their schedule, racking up six straight wins, four of them by more than twenty points. On the same day that USC was losing to Notre Dame, UCLA was putting a thirty-nine-point stomping on Cal, to solidify the Bruins' number four national ranking.

There is nothing on record that indicates any unexplained happening in Los Angeles between October 20 and 27 of 2001, but there must have been some kind of cosmic shift or unusual weather pattern that transposed the fortunes of the city's two prominent universities. Whatever had been going right for UCLA and wrong for USC suddenly changed. Fate switched uniforms. It was as if the northwesterly winds of destiny blew through Westwood, taking with them whatever good karma remained, depositing it on the campus at Troy.

While the Trojans' high-speed U-turn was taking them in the right direction, the Bruins applied the brakes, hit the skids and then ran off the road entirely. It started with a loss to Stanford, followed by a loss to Washington State. A few days later, Heisman Trophy candidate DeShaun Foster was declared ineligible after admitting he had been driving a car leased by a Hollywood director suspected to have ties to the UCLA program. The NCAA later ruled that Foster would be suspended for the rest of the season. After another loss, UCLA's third straight, the Bruins began to prepare for the game against USC. On Thursday of game week, the story broke that starting quarterback

Cory Paus had been arrested on a drunken driving charge over the summer. In late August, Paus was sentenced to serve four days in jail after the season, but the quarterback never informed the school or coach Bob Toledo. Many were calling for Paus to be suspended, but with Foster already gone and the season slipping away, Toledo decided not to take action, saying, "This is a twenty-one-year-old guy who thought he could handle it himself. He didn't want to disrupt the team, and he was scared. I'm not going to suspend him for this. He thought he could handle it. He wasn't lying to me. There's a difference."

So, with three straight losses, their best player suspended, their on-field leader involved in a brewing controversy and their national ranking plummeting like a tech stock, UCLA made its way across town to face a surging USC team in the Coliseum.

Three seniors playing their final game at USC—running back Charlie Landrigan, safety Troy Polamalu and cornerback Antuan Simmons—were captains for the game and represented the Trojans at midfield for the coin toss. It went the way of the Bruins, which actually might have been the highlight of the day for UCLA, because from there, it was all downhill. In fact, UCLA began its poor performance right then and there, opting to defer their choice of ball or side until the second half and gave the first decision to the Trojans.

USC, of course, chose to receive and didn't waste much time setting the tone. On the third play from scrimmage, a third and thirteen from their own seventeen, quarterback Carson Palmer hit tight end Kori Dickerson. The six-foot-four, 235 pounder out of Los Angeles maneuvered around the left side, broke a couple tackles and, as the crowd started to roar, headed down the sideline. It looked like clear sailing, but as a guy who simply didn't have occasion to run eighty-plus yards very often, Dickerson ran out of gas and was taken down from behind by Bruins standout cornerback Ricky Manning Jr. Still, the play covered sixty-six yards, going from one seventeen yard line to the other.

The Bruins called a time-out. It had not started well for them to say the least. Just 1:28 into the game, they were already being threatened in their own red zone and had burned a time-out on defense. They regrouped, refocused, then receded. Five plays later, USC was in the end zone as Palmer found Keary Colbert, a future NFL teammate of Manning on a touchdown pass from the four. The drive went eighty yards in eight plays and took the Trojans just 3:14. David Davis added the extra point, to make it a 7–0 lead as the Coliseum crowd rejoiced in a guarded celebration.

The first UCLA drive went eight plays as well, but it was not exactly the same kind of march the Trojans had put together. The Bruins picked up two first downs moving from their own thirty-five into USC territory, and down to the thirty-nine. But then they started going backward. A fifteen-yard face-mask penalty was followed by back-to-back sacks. Shaun Cody, who terrorized the Bruins offense all day, got Paus for seven yards, and Lonnie Ford got him for four more. UCLA had moved twenty-six yards forward and then twenty-seven yards backward and, staring at a fourth and thirty-seven, punted from its own thirty-four. It was your basic eight-play minus-one-yard drive, which took nearly six minutes. Worse yet, a thirty-seven-yard punt was returned forty-two yards, but thankfully for UCLA, the return was nullified by a blocking-in-the-back penalty. The Bruin contingent among the 88,588 in attendance was silent and squirming.

UCLA got the ball back on its own nine yard line late in the quarter and began hammering away with running back Manuel White. He picked up five yards, then eight, then four. As the Bruins headed to the line for a second and six from their twenty-six yard line, the clock was ticking down to the end of the quarter. Paus took the snap, faded back and looked to his left, about ten yards downfield. He had Brian Poli-Dixon open and fired, but the big receiver couldn't make the catch. The ball hit off his hands, and as it was falling to the turf in front of him, Poli-Dixon dejectedly began to turn away. Cornerback Antuan Simmons reached down and to his left, and the ball, about a foot off the ground, just kind of stuck between his left hand and left calf. Simmons reached through his legs with his right hand, gathered the ball and took off around a stunned and stationary Poli-Dixon. Simmons checked his rearview mirror, saw he was in the clear and began high stepping his way to a joyride of an interception return, striking a pose as he crossed the goal line and dancing in the end zone to the beautiful music of a roaring stadium. He was flagged for an excessive-celebration penalty, but you'll have to excuse him if he got caught up in the moment. To him, the thirty-six-yard romp was really more a personal celebration of triumph than an interception return for touchdown.

A 195 pounder out of Sacramento, Antuan Simmons felt the pain of losses to UCLA in each of his first two seasons, 1997 and 1998. Prior to meeting the Bruins his junior season, Simmons had season-ending surgery to repair a herniated disk in his back. During follow-up exams, doctors discovered a benign abdominal tumor, which required two surgeries to remove. Simmons was supposed to be in the hospital for five routine days, but his stay turned into six hellish weeks. Because of complications from the surgery, the muscular junior literally came close to death on three separate occasions. The strain on his body was tremendous, and he lost forty pounds, falling to his junior high school weight of 155. Simmons redshirted the 2000 season while recuperating, had additional surgery in November for a hernia and, through sheer will, courageously battled his way back onto the field the following year for spring practice. Excessive celebration? You be the judge.

The penalty merely made the extra point a thirty-five-yard kick instead of the usual twenty yards. Davis had Antuan's back and banged it through to make it a 14–0 Trojan lead after one quarter. "That play took a little fight out of them," Simmons said in the postgame locker room. "A few of their guys checked out after that."

The Bruins' next possession was a mess. It started at their thirty-four and ended three plays later at their thirty after two incomplete passes and another Shaun Cody sack forced a punt. Nate Fiske got the snap, took two steps forward, released the ball, whipped his leg forward and heard the sound that punters hear in their nightmares: the dreaded double-thud. The first thud was his foot making contact with the ball, the second was the ball being blocked by all-America safety and special teams standout Troy Polamalu. USC's Ryan Kaiser covered the loose ball at the twenty-three, and the Trojans were in business again.

Palmer completed a couple passes to Sunny Byrd, setting up a fourth and first on the Bruins three. The Trojans called a time-out, discussed the situation and decided to kick the field goal, taking a 17–0 lead.

The next two UCLA drives went for negative yardage, and the rest of the half was controlled by the respective defenses. The halftime statistics looked like numbers you might see in an early-season game between a highly ranked team and a Division I–AA patsy on the schedule to take a beating and collect a paycheck. UCLA ran twenty-four offensive plays, good for a total of twenty-three yards. Their longest play of the half went for nine yards, and their leading rusher, Manuel White, was averaging 2.6 yards per carry. Time of possession was actually close with the Trojans holding a two-minute edge, but that was more of a function of USC scoring quickly than anything else.

In the Trojan locker room, there was no celebrating. The seventeen-point lead was indicative of the domination, and a UCLA comeback seemed pretty unlikely, but there was still a businesslike approach. "Whenever you're up like that, you want to put the pressure on," Palmer says. "You want to double your first half output. We wanted to make it thirty-four to zero. It was loud in the locker room. Pete's always in your face and very intense."

"We just thought about it like the score was zero–zero," remembers tight end Alex Holmes, who caught three passes for thirty-seven yards. "You can't win the game in the first or second quarter. We just wanted to continue to execute our game plan."

The third quarter began much the same way the second quarter ended. Both defenses were strong and neither offense could string together more than a couple first downs. Trojan cornerback Kris Richard kept the momentum on the USC side of the field, delivering a crushing tackle on Bruins tight end Matthew Clark in the open field. On the fourth possession of the half, the Trojans took over on their own seventeen and erased any doubt about the direction the game was headed. On third and seven from the twenty, Palmer hit Dickerson for thirteen yards to pick up a first down and keep the drive alive. A face-mask penalty on UCLA the following play took USC out to midfield, and then four plays later, tailback Chris Howard struck like a bolt of lightning. Howard, out of Banning High in Los Angeles, utilized a great surge by the offensive line and sped through the Bruins defense on a thirty-four-yard touchdown burst to cap off an eight-play, eighty-three-yard drive. The arrow on UCLA's emotion meter settled in somewhere between miserable and embarrassed as the extra point sailed through to make it a 24–0 Trojans lead. The Coliseum crowd was convinced. Several years of frustration were, at least for the day, wiped away in the celebration of a systematic butt kicking of their crosstown rival.

Craig Bragg returned the ensuing kickoff to midfield, but the thirty-one-yard return did absolutely nothing to spark the

Bruins offense. On the first play from scrimmage, Paus fired a pass that could have easily been intercepted, but was dropped by safety Jason Leach. Given a reprieve, Paus came out throwing on the next play. This time, he was picked off by Polamalu, the future NFL all-pro and a huge contributor to the 2006 Super Bowl champion Pittsburgh Steelers, who returned the interception thirty-four yards. Bob Toledo immediately took football's version of a trip to the mound, making a call to his bullpen where right-hander Scott McEwan was warming up. Paus was done for the day after completing just seven of his fifteen passes for a mere forty-five yards. He was intercepted twice, sacked five times and knocked down another five, and he had seen enough of the Trojan defensive front to last a lifetime. "It was a pretty tough game for the offense and myself," he said afterward. "USC was throwing a lot of heat at us." Ya think?

The interception led to another USC field goal, but it was really academic at that point. McEwan was intercepted by Kevin Arbett in his first series, but overall, with the game clearly out of reach, he was a bit more effective than Paus had been. As the fourth quarter wound down, strangely, there was still a bit of drama left to play out. UCLA took possession on its own twenty-eight, and three plays later, facing a fourth and eight with 1:03 remaining, they called a time-out. Instead of running the ball into the line and turning it over on downs, or punting, the Bruins were going to fight until the bitter end. The objective had become avoiding the shutout.

They did convert the fourth-down play, picking up eleven on a pass that got them out to their forty-one. Three plays later, though, after another time-out, UCLA was looking at a fourth and fifteen. Typical of the suffering, McEwan was forced out of the pocket and, after scrambling for eight yards, tried to lateral and was called for an illegal forward pass. The Trojans took over and killed the clock to wrap up a 27–0 annihilation, their first shutout against the Bruins in fifty-three years.

"I like that stuff, finishing the game right," said an elated Pete Carroll, speaking of the shutout in the postgame press conference. "It was our first one and we'll remember it for a long time."

After Carroll left the interview room, UCLA's coach entered. A month earlier, Bob Toledo was coaching the fourth-ranked team in the country, but in the past few hours had witnessed the final phase of a demolition. A cardinal-and-gold wrecking ball had taken down what remained of a promising UCLA season. "I'm kind of speechless right now," he said. "We got out-played today. We were totally inept out there. There were too many turnovers and we just couldn't make any plays. You've got to give credit to USC. We got beat by a better team."

Throughout the Trojan locker room, the players circulated, laughing, joking and congratulating one another. As media members asked them questions, they addressed the game that was just played, but notably, many also spoke of the bigger picture.

"Coach Carroll is building this program," said Carson Palmer. "I wish I were a freshman. It's too bad I only have one more year."

"Coach told us the game was going to be like this," Antuan Simmons relayed. "He said we were laying the foundation for something special at USC."

Carroll himself was glowing in the euphoric aftermath of a thoroughly dominant victory on a night he could have desperately used one. Three seasons and two national championships later, he reflected, "That was an extraordinary night. It was my first chance to taste the rivalry and feel the magnitude of it. To have such a tremendous game really did jump-start this program in the direction we're going. It was so exciting to be at the

Coliseum for the first time with the kind of crowd and excitement that we have seen so many times since then."

The 2001 team's potential might not have been clear to the casual observer, but it was certainly evident to anybody paying close attention. Late in the season, the defense was among the best in the country, showing early signs of the greatness to come. In the final four games, the Trojans intercepted eleven passes, sacked the quarterback twenty-three times and scored five defensive touchdowns. Most of the defensive players were coming back the next season, and an ultratalented defensive line was stacked with collegiate infants. Shaun Cody, Kenechi Udeze, Omar Nazel and Mike Patterson were all underclassmen with multiple seasons to terrorize opposing college quarterbacks still ahead.

Offensively, there were some stars departing, but most of the skill position players like Palmer, Colbert, Kareem Kelly and Alex Holmes would be returning. Pete Carroll shook off the early-season criticism and a rough start, blazing to a strong finish and bringing the precious commodity of realistic promise back to USC football.

	1	2	3	4	F
UCLA	0	0	0	0	0
USC	14	3	7	3	27

Scoring:

First Quarter

USC: Colbert, 4-yard pass from Palmer (Davis kick)

USC: Simmons, 36-yard interception return (Davis kick)

Second Quarter

USC: Davis, 20-yard field goal

Third Quarter

USC: Howard, 34-yard run (Davis kick)

Fourth Quarter

USC: Davis, 20-yard field goal

Passing:

USC: Palmer, 14–23–180, 1 interception, 1 touchdown

UCLA: Paus, 7–15–45, 2 interceptions; McEwan, 3–8–29, 1 interception

Rushing:

USC: Howard, 8–49; Byrd, 20–40; Kelly, 2–6

UCLA: White, 9–23; Harris 6–14; Clark 2–4

Receiving:

USC: Dickerson, 3–92; Holmes, 3–37; Colbert, 3–26

UCLA: Bragg, 6–29; Lepisto, 2–11; Smith, 1–23

POSTSCRIPT

The game against UCLA can be looked at in the long run as either a meaningless win or as a history changer. It is kind of like playing Mozart for a baby. Some think it's just background noise, while others claim that classical music helps long-term brain development in more ways than we can know. If the baby turns out to be a genius, who is to say whether the music was a factor? If the Trojans go on to dominate college football over the next five years, who's to say the 27–0 spanking of the Bruins had anything to do with it?

The truth regarding the victory is that while there is really no quantitative way to measure the game's impact, some at USC insist that those sixty minutes at the Coliseum were a springboard to Trojans greatness in the new millennium.

There is an entire city stocked with young football talent watching the USC/UCLA game every year, and those who saw the 2001 game likely got a pretty good feel for which of the teams was the up-and-comer. Yes, there could be hundreds of variables that go into the final decision of a heavily recruited player, but some speak louder than others. Any kid who witnessed the Trojans control just about every minute of the action that day must have, at least to some degree, wanted to be part of that winning program.

"You don't really understand the rivalry until you experience a USC/UCLA game," says a kid who was a redshirt freshman watching from the sidelines that November day in 2001. "Winning can definitely change someone's perspective on what school they want to go to, especially if they're from Los Angeles and want to stay here. When you watch that game and you see USC roll like that, it's just as simple as that. They say, 'OK, I want to go to SC now.' A win like that really helps, and putting together seasons like we have will definitely help in recruiting.

The young kids think, 'Oh, SC is my dream school.' It will definitely help." The redshirt freshman who spoke those words is now an NFL quarterback named Matt Leinart.

Matt watched the game against UCLA, perhaps wondering whether he would one day lead the Trojans just as Carson Palmer was doing. Palmer is a firm believer in that game's long-term impact, saying, "There was domination all over the place that day: offense, defense and special teams. Being a recruit, you don't want to go to the school that is getting dominated. You want to be with the dominator."

Pete Carroll says of the victory, "It has been extremely meaningful. You look at kids when they're twelve and thirteen—what teams are they really excited about? Before we got going here, I think it was Miami and Florida State, schools like that. I think at least in our state, we've changed that. Kids don't have to go out of state to get into a big-time college program and position themselves to be playing in big games and big-time high-lighted matchups."

Whether or not it laid the groundwork for the phenomenal stretch that lay ahead, 2001 was undeniably a positive step for USC. After their 1–4 start, the Trojans finished with a flurry, reeling off five wins in their final six games, bringing their victory total to six to become bowl eligible.

The Las Vegas Bowl, of course, will never be confused with the Rose Bowl, but given where the Trojans had been two months earlier, an invitation to any bowl, including a bowl of soup, would have been thought of as a major accomplishment.

After a couple practices in Las Vegas, some of the Trojans players showed up at Sunrise Children's Hospital to spread a little holiday cheer. The hospital was an all too familiar place to Antuan Simmons, but the scrappy cornerback, who sports a thick scar through the length of his abdomen as a result of his stomach problems in 1999, approached the outing with a unique perspective. "I like visiting," he said, "because I know how it was for me when I was in the hospital. When people visit, it helps you get through some of those hard days. You really wouldn't understand until you lay in that bed. It means a lot."

On Christmas Day, the Trojans lost the bowl game to Utah, 10–6, suffering their sixth loss of the season and, incredibly, their fifth by fewer than six points. Of note, Troy Polamalu capped off his all-American season and said good-bye to college football, making *twenty* tackles on his way out.

The next season, 2002, was a continuation of the progress USC made in 2001. After a 3–2 start, the Trojans ran off eight straight wins and again finished the season in a manner so electric that it illuminated the future. They ended with a pair of impressive blowout wins: 52–21 over twenty-fifth-ranked UCLA (the fourth in a row over the Bruins) and 44–13 over number seven Notre Dame.

Still, the best was yet to come. The Bowl Championship Series rankings sent them to Miami for the Orange Bowl where the number five Trojans chewed up and spit out the third-ranked Iowa Hawkeyes 38–17. It was the crowning performance of that "one more year" that Carson Palmer spoke about having at USC. The fifth-year senior out of Laguna Niguel went out in style, smashing any doubt about his ability as a quarterback and team leader. Palmer was named the game's most valuable player, finishing off an outstanding season in which he led the Trojans to an 11–2 record and the number four national ranking. Palmer threw for 3,942 yards with thirty-three touchdowns and was named the fifth Heisman Trophy winner in USC history.

Like John McKay four decades before him, and John Robinson a quarter century before, Pete Carroll put together an amazing season to solidify his standing inside the Trojan nation. Boosters and alumni who took a stance against the hiring of the former NFL coach just two years earlier would hardly admit their objections, let alone express them again, after the 2002 season. When he took the job, Carroll inherited a fantastic re- cruiting class from Hackett, but he didn't let the trail of great players end there. With the strength of both 2001's and 2002's late-season marches behind him, Carroll pulled in some of the best players from around the city, the state and the country. With potential recruits in attendance on game day, Pete had set them up, and the players' performance on the field knocked them down. And whatever hesitancy remained, the head coach erased. He was, like Dennis Eckersly in his prime, an all-star closer. "Once guys met Coach Carroll," says Alex Holmes, "and saw his enthusiasm and saw how he acted toward our players, that sold 'em. It was over."

USC football was certainly in good hands as it moved into year number three under its new leader.

USC

VS.

OKLAHOMA, 2005

THE SETUP

With 2002, a step in the right direction, behind them, the Trojans were ready to take a giant leap in 2003. Palmer had graduated and changed his cardinal-and-gold stripes to Bengal Orange as Cincinnati made him the number one pick in the NFL draft. In his absence, spring practice became as much about the battle for the starting quarterback position as it was about anything else. Four young guns—Matt Cassel, Brandon Hance, Billy Hart and Matt Leinart—all had designs on the spot. The winner would get the wonderful prize of stepping into the role vacated by one of the most prolific passers in USC history, who, three months earlier, had been acknowledged as the best college player in the country.

Pressure? What pressure?

Even before naming a quarterback, the Trojans were the

odds-on favorite to win the Pac-10 and were listed in the top ten of every national preseason poll. Cassel had been Palmer's backup, and although he didn't play much, he did see some game action in 2002. Having started nine games for Purdue as a freshman in 2001 before transferring, Hance was the only player in the quarterback quartet with significant experience. Hart was getting most of the early reps in practice because he was a two-sport athlete planning on playing baseball. He was to meet with Carroll after two weeks of practice to get a read on his chances of starting, which would determine whether he would focus full-time on baseball for the remainder of the spring. Leinart was the most celebrated of the quarterbacks coming out of high school, but he hadn't thrown a single pass the previous season. He was so unaccomplished as a college player, his bio in the Trojans media guide listed among his duties "backup holder on place kicks."

Looking back to the days when he was buried behind Palmer, Leinart said in 2005, "There was a low point where I was just over football. There were parts of my redshirt freshman year where I was thinking I didn't even want to play anymore. I was third string. I didn't care. I was one of those guys who just kind of hung in the back.

"I had talent. They knew I had talent. Coach Norm Chow always knew, but when was I going to get the chance to show it? You want to play, and when you know you can play, it's a humbling experience when you are not the guy right away."

During his sophomore year, when he was involved in the competition for the starting job, Leinart was asked about the requirements of the spring. He answered, "What we discussed is just being efficient, which means not making turnovers. Putting our team in a position to score and to win games is really what it comes down to. They're not asking us to go out there and make plays or be the next Heisman."

The next Heisman? Who in their right mind could expect

a guy taking over for a Heisman Trophy winner to win it himself?

As the spring wore on, each candidate did whatever he could to impress whoever he could. On April 5, with Billy Hart unavailable because of an illness, the Trojans finished spring practice with an eighty-nine-play scrimmage in which the coaches got a good look at the other three quarterbacks. Leinart got the most reps, going eight for twenty-one with 102 yards passing and Carroll said if the season opener was the next day, Matt would get the nod.

An Internet article on FOXSports.com acknowledged Leinart's edge over the others, but went on to say, "However, the race is still wide open and a starter for the first game is unclear. Stay tuned."

In preseason practice, nothing changed. Leinart was the most impressive of the quarterback choices, so Pete Carroll made the decision to start the inexperienced lanky left-hander out of Santa Ana's Mater Dei High School.

"Even when I was named the starter, I was still kind of looking over my shoulder," Leinart remembers. "Once fall came, Mike Williams said publicly that 'This is our guy. I'm following him.' He was really the one player on the team who had my back. Mike's a smart guy. He probably just wanted to give me confidence because he knew I was going to be his quarterback."

Often, major colleges schedule what is known as a "cupcake" or a "patsy" to get their season started. Nebraska, for example, might set a date with Akron. Florida State might open against Louisiana Tech. It is a way to ease into the schedule and get players some seasoning, game experience and a victory before facing a legitimate opponent.

That was not the case for USC in 2003. The Trojans started the season against Auburn, the sixth-ranked team in the country, and they did so not only on the road in front of 86,000 wild fans, but also at night and on national television. That is a tough situation for any team, but especially for one starting an unproven, untested quarterback.

As Leinart said in the spring, his job was merely to take care of the football. The USC coaches figured their defense was strong enough to keep them in any game, and a couple of touchdowns should be enough to win.

That night, August 30, the defense was spectacular. Forget the fact that Auburn's highly touted offense didn't score a single point; it didn't even come close. The USC defense allowed just 164 total yards and the best penetration the Tigers got all night was to the Trojans' thirty-three yard line!

Freshman safety Darnell Bing, wearing Mike Garrett's previously retired number 20, intercepted Jason Campbell on Auburn's opening possession, and Leinart, on his first collegiate pass, made it count by hitting Mike Williams for a five-yard touchdown. Leinart completed seventeen of thirty passes for 192 yards with no interceptions and helped convert three Auburn turnovers into seventeen points in a 23–0 victory—the Trojans' first road shutout of a top ten team in school history. The twenty-three points USC scored against Auburn were their lowest total of the season. The next two weeks, they combined for ninety-six in wins over BYU and Hawaii.

Game four had the third-ranked Trojans visiting Cal in an emotional roller coaster of a game, ultimately won by the Bears in triple overtime, 34–31. USC's ranking fell from third to tenth, and talk of a national title at Troy, although not completely silenced, was certainly reduced to a whisper.

The next day, a wire-service story ran in newspapers across the country, and the picture it painted of USC and its fans was not pretty.

Southern California picked the wrong town and the wrong time for an early celebration. Several Cal players got all the motivation they needed after hearing reports of a raucous informal parade by Southern California's boosters and band on the streets of Berkeley on Friday night. "They were marching down our streets, partying in our town," Cal running back Adimchinobe Echemandu said. "That's just the way USC is. They're so arrogant. They think they're better than everybody else on the West Coast before they even play a game."

"They came out and punched us in the mouth," USC defensive tackle Shaun Cody said. "We didn't have an answer for anything."

To an extremely talented team, an unexpected loss is kind of like an antibiotic. It cures a lot of things. The defeat snapped an eleven-game Trojan winning streak dating back to the previous season, and from that point on, the humbled USC squad talked a lot softer and practiced a lot harder.

The following week, they were on the road at Arizona State and were tied 10–10 at halftime. At that very moment, Division I games were going on all over the country, but right there in Tempe, Arizona, on a 100-degree afternoon in the desert, one half of one football game was about to take a twist that would have implications throughout the nation. The next thirty minutes would shape the season. Lose, and all hopes for a national title and a Pac-10 title were gone for USC. Win, and who knows?

Concern number one in the locker room was Leinart, who had left the game early in the second quarter after injuring his right knee and ankle while getting sacked, forcing him to miss almost the entire second quarter. Cassel stepped in at quarterback, but completed just four of his ten passes and had trouble moving the ball. At the break, Leinart, who had been questionable even before the game with a groin injury *and* sprained ligaments in his left knee, had his ankle taped heavily and jogged lightly in the locker room, feeling the pain in his newly injured right knee with every step. "They said it was up to me. If I could go, I could go," Leinart said after the game. "I was running on it a little bit and limping, but sometimes you just have to block out the pain and go. I knew my team needed me, so I just went out there and got the job done."

ASU took a 17–10 lead on the first possession of the second half, but their fun ended right there. The Trojans took the field with their starting quarterback wounded, but back under center, and came together. It was a half of football that defined a team.

Facing the prospect of a second straight loss, and an 0–2 start in the Pac-10, each unit—offense, defense and special teams—played to its potential and perhaps a bit beyond. With Leinart hobbling but in command, the offense suddenly looked like a powerhouse, going eighty yards in six plays for the tying touchdown. The defense flexed its muscle, holding the Sun Devils without another point the rest of the way, and special teams kept the battle of field position tilted in the Trojans' favor. Leinart completed thirteen of twenty-three passes for 289 yards and two touchdowns, and USC reeled off twenty-seven straight points to bury Arizona State 37–17 and set the tone for a dominating run through the rest of the schedule. The quarterback's courageous performance was inspirational to every man on the roster. His insistence on playing might have been standard operating procedure to him, but to his USC teammates, it was a first true look into the toughness and resolve of a player who had just *earned* the role of team leader, which is simply *given* to so many quarterbacks.

"They were playing us really tough. Then we had Matt go out with an injury in the second quarter and weren't sure whether he would be able to play in the second half. It was gut-check time," said all-American offensive tackle Jacob Rogers.

"That's when we found out what we were made of," added star defensive tackle Shaun Cody. "Going into that second half, a lot of guys were questioning where this team was at."

Pete Carroll, who had been in coaching his entire adult life, saw the game for what it was and realized the long-term value of a team being tested on so many levels. "This was one of my favorite games since I've been here," the coach said, "under the circumstances of losing last week and having a young team, not knowing how they're going to respond. The second half was the kind of football that we are capable of playing. I was really proud of Matt. I thought that it was a fantastic effort to come back when he easily could have not finished that game. The coaches challenged him a little bit, and he said that he was playing. He never wavered on the fact that he was going to play. He just didn't *look* like he was going to play."

In 2005, figurative light-years from that comeback in Tempe, Leinart remembers the significance of not only that game, but also the one that followed.

"Everyone goes back to the Arizona State game. That's definitely a point when they saw me as a leader because I was playing hurt and they could tell. We came back to win that one, but as for me being comfortable, it was the next week against Stanford [18–27, 260 yards, three touchdowns]. I was throwing the ball well, didn't throw an interception. I was comfortable in the system and wasn't afraid to make a mistake or throw the ball away. The span of those two games, ASU and Stanford, was the turning point in my career.

"I was reading some of the quotes in the paper the day after the Arizona State game, and guys were saying, 'He showed a lot of guts and a lot of fight and we're gonna follow him.' Stuff like that made me think, 'Wow, this is my team now,' and I think that confidence carried over into the rest of the year. As a team, that's when we really took off, that Stanford game. That was the first real complete game that we had."

It was also a breakout game for tailback LenDale White, who broke loose for 140 yards and two touchdowns in a 44–21 victory. "People have been saying we don't have a running game," said Leinart at the time. "I don't think that's true. We started to click, and maybe this game sets the tone for the rest of the season."

The tone was set all right. From there the Trojans put together one of the most incredible runs in school history. In the seven regular season games that remained, they were as explosive as they were consistent, scoring 44, 45, 43, 43, 45, 47 and 52 points. They beat Notre Dame by thirty-one, and UCLA by twenty-five, finishing the regular season with eleven wins and only the triple-overtime loss to Cal. They went into the Rose Bowl as the number one–ranked team in the country by the AP, and after a 28–14 win over Michigan, showered, sat back and waited for the controversy to roll in.

In a standing agreement with the Bowl Championship Series, the coaches' poll is contractually bound to award the final number one ranking to the winner of the BCS championship game, which in 2003 was LSU, 21–14 over Oklahoma in the Sugar Bowl.

The AP poll, however, went to the Trojans, giving USC its tenth national title, and first in twenty-five years. If not completely satisfying because of the split element, the season was a launching pad for one of the most dominant teams in recent memory.

The main difference between 2003 and 2004 for USC was expectations. Coming off the co–national championship, and returning, well, just about everybody, the Trojans entered 2004 as the preseason number one. And they played like it. Reggie Bush, a future Heisman winner himself, emerged as a superstar in the making in the opening game win over Virginia Tech. LenDale White grabbed the headlines in the week two romp over Colorado State, and Leinart displayed his trademark efficiency the following Saturday at BYU.

The two weeks that followed were a bit dicey, but certainly got the attention of Trojan nation. USC first had to roar back from an eleven-point deficit to beat Stanford and then hold off a last-minute rally by Cal to avenge the previous season's only loss, in a game statistically dominated by the Bears.

They won their next six rather easily, five of them by thirty points or more including 41–10 over Notre Dame in the rain to make Anthony Davis Day a true celebration at the Coliseum.

The final regular season hurdle, as it often is, was the crosstown rivalry. UCLA was 6–4 and having a mediocre season, but of course had been targeting the USC game as a way to change the fortunes of the present and future of both schools. Leinart came out smoking, completing his first ten passes, and Reggie Bush left the Bruins defense in his dust with sizzling touchdown runs of sixty-five and eighty-one yards. Reggie looked like he was freewheeling on the Autobahn while UCLA was stuck in rush-hour traffic on the 405. The Trojans went on to beat the Bruins for the sixth straight time in a somewhat unspectacular game, 29–24, to put the cap on a perfect 12–0 regular season as Pete Carroll became the first Trojans coach to beat Notre Dame and UCLA in three straight years.

From the first day of spring practice to the last day of the regular season, the Trojans were widely considered the best team in the country. They were number one in the first AP poll, the last AP poll and every one in between. Same with the BCS rankings.

On Friday, December 10, six days after the season finale against UCLA, Matt Leinart and Reggie Bush were three thousand miles from home. Sent to New York to report on the event for Fox Sports Net's *Southern California Sports Report*, I met up with the pair in a third-floor media room of the New York Hilton, where the next night the proud pair of Trojans would be onstage with three other players for the presentation of the Heisman Trophy. I asked Leinart whether he was nervous. He answered, "No, not really because I'm not going to be disappointed if I don't

win. It means a lot, but at the same time, it's just an honor to be
here with the five guys and a teammate in Reggie." Having seen
numerous Heisman winners trembling onstage as they expressed their feelings upon winning the award, I made a mental note to ask him the same question the following night if his
name was called.

Also nominated were Utah quarterback Alex Smith, and two
Oklahoma players: Jason White, who had won the award the
previous year, and freshman running back Adrian Peterson.
The five elite players all seemed supportive of one another,
and there was no discernible undertone of competitiveness between the Trojans and the Sooners, who would meet again three
weeks later in Miami for the national title in the Orange Bowl.

As the moment of truth arrived, the packed ballroom was
silent. And then the announcement was made. "The winner of
the 2004 Heisman Trophy is . . . Matt Line-hard from the University of Southern California." There are times when a slight
mispronunciation of a person's name might bother him. This
was not one of those times for the six-foot-five Trojan star, who
describes himself as a child as "a cross-eyed fat kid with
glasses." Upon hearing his name (or a reasonable facsimile
thereof), Leinart first bowed his head for an instant, then was
embraced by Bush, who was sitting to his right. The friends and
teammates shared a few quiet words, and then Matt stood and
hugged his fellow nominees. Leinart then surprised most of the
audience by stepping down from the stage and making his way
toward his parents to embrace them and then his brother Ryan
before walking back up to the stage to make his speech.

Once at the podium, he thought back to an evening two
years earlier. Before he had ever thrown a collegiate pass,
Leinart was sitting on his couch in Southern California, watching a teammate accept the same trophy. At that moment, the
idea that Matt would be standing in that exact spot on this night
must have seemed like a million-to-one shot. "I remember

when Carson was sitting up here. He said his heart was beating out of his chest. I think mine's about to do the same thing."

He continued by saying, "First I would love to thank my teammates and coaches back home and Reggie also. We get to represent USC. Charles White and Mike Garrett are here as well and it's just a great honor to play for that program."

About a half hour after he won the award, I caught up with Matt to do an interview that would be sent back to Los Angeles to air on that night. It started like this:

Barry LeBrock: All right, thanks. I'm with Mr. Big Shot himself. Matt, you told me yesterday you weren't going to be nervous. As the moment approached, what were your thoughts and emotions?

Matt Leinart: I definitely lied to you about that. [Laughs] I don't even know what to say. It's just an honor to be here, and when my name was called, I was just in shock and disbelief. You don't go into it thinking you're going to win. I was at a loss for words up there and I just did the best I could.

And the final exchange:

Barry LeBrock: It's back-to-work time now. As significant as this award is, there is still the issue of a rather important game coming up in about 3.5 weeks at the Orange Bowl.

Matt Leinart: Yeah, when I get back to LA, it's all business. I'll be back Tuesday and I'll be out there Wednesday at practice. School is out and I plan on working hard this month. I'll be ready. I realize people win the Heisman and then they don't finish strong, but I plan on playing how I have all season and I'm excited about the matchup.

Yes, the matchup. Twenty-four days away: USC against Oklahoma in the Orange Bowl for the undisputed national championship.

A few days after the UCLA game, the Trojans got some great national run in *Sports Illustrated*. The magazine featured Reggie Bush on the cover, photographed in midsomersault crossing the goal line against UCLA. The caption read *Trojans Roll*.

Pointing out that the Trojans had won twenty-one straight games, and thirty-two of thirty-three, writer Austin Murphy wondered, "Is Southern California on the verge of doing what was supposed to have been impossible after the NCAA whittled scholarships to 85 a decade ago: building a dynasty?"

The article contained quotes from several coaches who had faced the Trojans and expressed the difficulty Oklahoma would have slowing down a USC offense that had gotten stronger throughout the season. Arizona head coach Mike Stoops, who would see the task of beating USC fall on his brother's shoulders, said of Leinart, "You put eight in the box, he throws. Put seven in the box, he gets them in a running play. You roll over to cover Jarrett, he finds the tight end. He's back there, saying, 'You take away this guy, I'll throw to that guy.'"

Cal's defensive coordinator Bob Gregory, who actually had some degree of success against the Trojans, said, "Sometimes you bring four, sometimes five. Sometimes bring three and drop eight. You can't blitz every time because if you do, Leinart's gonna kill you. You can't sit back and play cover three either, 'cause he'll kill ya that way too. What you want is a mixture of playing zone, playing man, combination man zone, blitz and blitz zone." Oh, OK.

Another big problem that Pac-10 coaches spoke of regarding all the USC talent was mismatches. In one of the most colorful quotes of the year, Washington State coach Bill Doba succinctly summed up one of the Trojan threats, "If you end up with a linebacker covering Bush, you might as well start singing the USC fight song."

THE GAME (JANUARY 4, 2005)

As if a game like this needed any more hype, it got it two weeks prior to kickoff. After an Oklahoma practice, Sooners defensive end Larry Birdine was asked about the game, specifically the Trojans offense. His answer, as shocking as it was off base, was more in line with the rhetoric you'd hear from a professional wrestler than from a player from one of the more well-respected football programs in the country. "I feel like they're, I'd say, a 1.5-man team," Birdine said. "I want to respect them just because I have to play them, but when I watch them on tape, I realize that they're an average team. Besides Reggie Bush, he's a great athlete. He's a fast back. He makes plays or whatever, but nobody else stands out to me. Matt Leinart, he's the Heisman Trophy winner, but he hasn't been driving them—or he hasn't been winning games. We feel like if we take Reggie out of the game, we're gonna win."

Birdine also insisted Leinart should not have won the Heisman Trophy, and perhaps forgetting that his own team's quarterback Jason White was also nominated, Birdine went on to say, "Alex Smith [of Utah] was better than Leinart. I don't think Matt should have won. He's definitely overrated. Like I said, he's a good quarterback, but he's not a Heisman-winning quarterback."

Asked for a response, USC players declined. They refused to be dragged into any trash talking. You couldn't even get a good, old-fashioned "Who is Larry Birdine?" out of them. When

Bush was pressed for his feelings on the subject, he simply said, "We weren't coached to go out there and give our personal opinions to the media. We were coached in more of a team aspect, to remain humble. We'll just leave it at that."

Both teams arrived in Miami with perfect 12–0 records and bad memories of bowl season a year earlier. The Trojans, of course, felt they should have been unanimous champions after the Rose Bowl victory, while Oklahoma was knocked out of the number one spot by virtue of their upset loss to LSU in the Sugar Bowl. There were the usual photo ops, parties and beach events in the days leading up to the game, but USC kept its focus and seemed loose and productive at their daily practices.

The Trojans were listed as a three-point favorite from just about the time the matchup was made official, but as the bowl season wore on, the spread started to fall and then, amazingly, swung the other way with the Sooners becoming a 1.5-point favorite. USC might have been losing support at the windows in Las Vegas partly because of a high ankle sprain to leading rusher LenDale White, who managed to climb out of the "doubtful" category and into "questionable" a few days before the game. The public also saw some teams that played close games with the Trojans (Cal, UCLA) lose rather unimpressively in their bowl games, suggesting perhaps USC would have its hands full with a powerhouse like Oklahoma.

On the first day of the new year, the Trojan practice at the Miami Dolphins facility became a star-studded event. Former Trojan great and longtime broadcaster Frank Gifford, USC baseball coaching legend Rod Dedeaux, lifetime Dodger Tommy Lasorda and pop singer Nick Lachey all attended USC's workout. Lasorda told a story to the gathering media about the day four years earlier that he called a radio sports talk show to defend the hiring of Pete Carroll, directing his comments toward several callers who had been critical of the move. "So I say what I have to say, the host thanks me and I hang up. I go back to listening to my radio and the next caller calls in and says, 'What does Lasorda know about football? He's the guy who traded away Pedro Martinez. He doesn't even know anything about *baseball*!' "

January 4 was a beautiful day and a gorgeous, calm 70-degree night in Miami. Despite several bouts of rain and high winds in the days leading up to the game, conditions were perfect at Pro Player Stadium as the Trojans took the field wearing their cardinal jerseys with gold pants. If Pete Carroll had any anxiety during pregame warm-ups, it certainly didn't show. He was like a hyperactive kid, bouncing around from player to player, flashing a smile and offering hand slaps. In the on-camera interview just prior to kickoff, he said, "This is a great opportunity. This is all we ever wanted right here. We've worked like crazy. This is the night."

The spirited stadium, filled with nearly 78,000 fans, seemed close to evenly divided in allegiance with Oklahoma perhaps owning a 60–40 split. Shaun Cody, Matt Grootegoed and Matt Leinart went to midfield where Shaquille O'Neal flipped the coin. Oklahoma called heads, and Shaq, who had been getting back at all things Southern California since being traded from the Lakers six months earlier, tossed a heads. The Sooners elected to defer their choice until the second half, and the Trojans decided to take the ball first.

Reggie Bush was deep to receive the opening kickoff, but didn't get a chance to make a play. Sooner kicker Garrett Hartley, trying to keep the ball away from Bush (Anthony Davis, anyone?), kicked it out of bounds, giving USC possession on the thirty-five.

The Sooners might not have wanted the ball in Reggie's hands, but the Trojans sure did. On the first play from scrimmage, Bush lined up wide to the left and Leinart hit him on a quick pop, which he turned into a twenty-seven-yard opening-play gain. From there, though, it was three and out, with Tom Malone dropping a punt on the Oklahoma eight.

The Sooner offense, which was led by the pair of guys Leinart and Bush had been with a few weeks earlier in New York, took the field. Jason White had a miserable time of it in the national championship game the previous season, hitting just thirteen of his thirty-seven passes in the Sugar Bowl, and was determined to perform well in this, his final collegiate game. Running back Adrian Peterson, a freshman who finished second in the Heisman balloting, brought a potentially deadly mix of deceptive speed and raw power. The USC defense ex-pected a grueling battle with him all night long.

Oklahoma began a long and steady march converting on two separate third-and-eight situations when White twice scrambled to elude pressure and then found a receiver down-field for a first down. On the list of weapons that opponents of the second-ranked Sooners had to worry about, Jason White's mobility was near the bottom, but his second scramble and throw was good for thirty-four yards down to the USC six. Two plays later, White hit Travis Wilson to cap off OU's impressive twelve-play, ninety-two-yard opening-drive march, making it 7–0 Sooners.

For Oklahoma fans, it was the perfect start. For USC fans, it was a march that went too far, too fast, too easily. As early as it might have been, they were antsy for a response as the Tro-jans took over on their own twenty-five midway through the first quarter.

USC picked up one first down, but a few plays later faced a third and eleven from their own thirty-six. At the snap, Leinart rolled to his left as a blitzing linebacker made a beeline toward him. Bush stepped up from his spot in the backfield and threw a textbook block, stopping the 'backer in his tracks. Steve Smith, who had lined up in the slot to the right, cut across the middle beyond the first-down marker, and Leinart, whose arm strength had actually been a question mark in spring camp, drilled a perfect strike with a Peyton Manning–quality bullet. Smith got his arms around the ball at the same instant the defensive back drilled him from behind, but held on for fourteen yards and a first down at midfield.

On the next play, Leinart hit tight end Dominique Byrd, who went up high to make an impressive fingertip catch on the right sideline for seventeen yards to the thirty-three. Then, throwing on first down again, Leinart rolled out of trouble and fired deep down the middle. The pass was intended for Byrd, who was running full stride with a step on his man. Byrd was looking back over his right shoulder, but the ball was thrown a bit to his left. Instead of breaking eye contact with the ball by turning to his left so he could keep running, Byrd did a complete 180 to his right, backpedaling for a couple steps in the transition, never losing sight of the football. As the ball came down, Byrd left his feet and, while still spinning, extended his big right arm and made the sweetest one-hand grab you'll ever see by a six-foot-three, 270-pound tight end. Dominique's momentum carried him into the end zone, where he fell, popped back up, raised both arms and was mobbed by his teammates. The band played, the stands rocked and the cheerleaders danced.

The final three of the six plays on the drive were passes, covering sixty-four yards. Leinart made the throws; Steve Smith and Dominique Byrd made the catches. Larry Birdine walked off the field after the touchdown, probably wondering, "Who are *those* guys?" It was the first touchdown the tough Oklahoma defense had allowed in its last thirty-nine possessions on the field, and it tied the score at seven.

Late in the first quarter, the Trojans crossed midfield again, but were forced to punt from Oklahoma's forty-eight. Malone didn't kick it well, but after landing at the twenty-two, the ball took a great Trojan bounce, spinning forward inside the fifteen, inside the ten, inside the five. At the three yard line, the Sooners Mark Bradley threw a block on Greig Carlson who was closing in to down the ball, and then Bradley hurriedly picked it up at the two.

Big mistake.

As Bradley touched it, Trojan reserve linebacker Collin Ashton hit him, jarring the ball loose. No less than six Trojans converged, and covered the ball as if it was a treasure chest full of gold. "Just a bonehead play on my part," Bradley would say after the game. It was, indeed, a colossal blunder by Oklahoma, and it would cost them. LenDale White made sure of that.

The high ankle sprain is an injury that is notoriously slow to heal. White suffered that injury in the season's final game against UCLA and, until a week before the Orange Bowl, was counted out by just about everybody. A few days before the game, Pete Carroll's wife, Glena, half jokingly placed what Pete called her "healing hands" on White's ankle.

"Mrs. Carroll did her thing. It's crazy," White told the media. "Everyone was standing around. She came up and asked how my ankle was. She performed a short prayer with her hands in the vicinity of my injury. The next morning I woke up and it felt great."

The coach's wife—the new twelfth man.

Taking over on the six after the fumble, White lined up seven yards behind the line of scrimmage and moved forward on the snap, taking a handoff at the eleven. The offensive line held pretty well, and White powered through a couple defenders around the five, kept his legs pumping and squeezed his big body between a pair of converging linebackers at the two. As he went down, he stretched the ball as far as his right arm would reach, and barely broke the plane of the goal line for a touchdown. One play, six yards, six points, and an opportunity cashed in by USC, making it a 14–7 game after one quarter.

The Sooners were moving the ball well to start the second quarter, but on a second and six from the Trojan thirty-six, Jason White faded back and felt the pressure. The sixth-year senior made a play you wouldn't expect from even a semi-disciplined freshman, throwing the ball up for grabs deep down the middle. The odds were clearly stacked in USC's favor. As the ball came down, four Trojans and one Sooner were in the vicinity. Jason Leach, USC's steady senior safety, went up high and pulled it in for the interception. It was a horrible decision by White, but served the same purpose as a well-placed punt for Oklahoma, giving the Trojans possession on their eleven yard line. Thing is, not many championship-caliber teams punt on second down.

Leading 14–7, the USC offense took the field. They knew they were looking at a great opportunity and went right to work. On second down, White broke through the middle for fifteen yards to pick up a first. Three plays later, on third and eight, Bush went in motion out of the backfield to the right. And like Mike Garrett in 1964 versus Notre Dame, Bush attracted his share of attention, and then some. Not only did the linebacker who was spying the versatile back go with him, but Oklahoma's safety, mirroring Bush, left the middle of the field, as well. The defensive shift left six-foot-five freshman receiver Dwayne Jarrett and five-foot-eleven freshman cornerback Marcus Walker all alone on the left side of the field. Leinart, who instantly picks up even subtle changes in the defense, was smacked in the face with the obvious movement in the coverage, and knew he'd have his receiver one on one, covered by a defender six inches shorter. For a guy with Leinart's accuracy, it was like throwing to Andre the Giant running a route in man coverage against Danny DeVito. At the snap, Jarrett faked an inside move, then bolted to the outside around Walker. Leinart lobbed a pass about fifteen yards downfield along the sideline. Jarrett raced ahead, leaped and pulled in the ball, which came down over the outstretched arms of the undersized cornerback. The play yielded eighteen yards and a Trojan first down at their forty-six.

As Jarrett jogged back to the huddle, Walker got up favoring his right arm. He was slumped slightly to his right side with the arm dangling gingerly from his shoulder. It is unclear exactly what the problem was, but replays appear to show him jamming his wrist against Jarrett as he tackled him. The Trojans approached the line again, and the same pair of freshman faced each other as they lined up about five yards from the sideline. As Leinart got the ball, Jarrett headed downfield, but instead of following the receiver, Walker made a move toward the offensive backfield. He didn't seem to be rushing with the speed or urgency of a blitzing cornerback and, a half second later, was caught in no-man's-land. When Leinart faked a handoff to Bush and it was clear the Trojans were running play action, Walker stopped in his tracks, turned around and began a futile chase of Jarrett, who had blown by him and was already twenty yards downfield. Leinart, of course, saw the whole thing develop and zipped a perfect spiral, hitting Jarrett in stride at the fourteen. Free safety Brodney Poole was assigned to pick up Jarrett when Walker made his move, and was stride for stride with the speedy receiver until the defender turned to the inside to look for the ball, which was thrown to the outside. He was a good three yards behind when Jarrett made the catch and didn't even attempt to make a tackle as Dwayne went untouched into the end zone to finish off the fifty-four-yard hookup for another USC touchdown.

Leinart stood comfortably in what had been the pocket, eyes fixed downfield watching his man motor in for six. He was like the architect of a magnificent building, standing outside admiring his work as the last brushstroke of paint was being applied. Matt lifted his arms skyward as the Trojans extended the lead. It was 21–7, but USC was just getting warmed up.

Oklahoma found itself in a third and fourteen from its own sixteen on the next possession, and once again, White made an ill-advised throw. Under immense pressure from USC's talent-rich defensive line, led by Shaun Cody, Mike Patterson and Frostee Rucker, he fired into double coverage.

As White was cocking his arm, his receiver, Mark Bradley, planted to cut, but slipped. Cornerback Eric Wright, who was facing the quarterback, saw the pass coming the whole way and made his move. He cut in front of Bradley, who had managed to regain his balance. The timing on the play was entirely off, though, because of the slip. Wright darted forward and caught the ball about eye level at the thirty-two, then snaked between Oklahoma players toward the goal line before being taken down at the ten. The Trojan defense, which led the nation in takeaways, had yet another one and set up the offense with a gimme.

On third down from the six, USC put six men on the line of scrimmage, with Bush in the backfield behind Leinart and three receivers staggered, but packed in relatively tight to the left. Bush began moving laterally to his right, and on the snap, Bush, the three receivers and tight end Alex Holmes, who was stacked on the right side of the line, ran in unison toward the end zone. The middle linebacker was coming on a blitz, so naturally Leinart threw to the receiver who had dashed to the middle of the field. It was Steve Smith, who was so open he was lonely. Leinart had to hurry the throw, which sailed low and to Smith's right. Turning to face the quarterback, the sophomore out of Orange Park didn't so much dive as he really just *fell* to his right, snagging the pass with his big paws and keeping it elevated off the ground as he lay flat in the end zone. Touchdown Trojans, 28–7. This was fun.

ABC analyst Bob Griese, who was working the game with announcer Keith Jackson, commented that the Trojan play design made it almost impossible to cover all the receivers. "The pencil got Oklahoma on that one," he said. "The guy that drew up that play beat 'em there, and that's Norm Chow."

After an Oklahoma field goal made it 28–10, USC took over and cranked the engine right back up to a sweet purr. Reggie Bush was heard from for the first time since the opening play, taking a pitch and blowing by most of the defense. He picked up forty-four yards, taking the ball into Oklahoma territory. Two plays later, Leinart dusted off the deadly left arm, zinging one deep down the middle for Steve Smith. Smith was covered well and, as he quickly approached the back of the end zone, was pulled down by Poole, but as the pair went to the turf, Smith never lost sight of the ball. With the safety holding on to Smith's left arm, the receiver reached out with his right, trapping the ball for an instant between his biceps and forearm. A split second later, as his body hit the ground, the ball was jarred loose, but by then, he had worked his left arm free and secured the rock as his body skidded within inches of the end line. It.was a great throw and a phenomenal catch. The referee, who was about a foot away, nodded his head and threw his arms up signaling the Trojans' fifth touchdown of the half. A game that was supposed to be an epic battle was quickly turning into an epic blowout.

USC led 35–10, with 1:56 still to play in the first half. Oklahoma was going to get the ball back, but anybody watching had to seriously question whether they really wanted it. At this point, the safe harbor of their locker room was probably looking like a pretty good alternative. Four plays later, "probably" became "definitely" when the most basic play in football turned into another Sooners nightmare.

On third and one, White turned to hand off to Kejuan Jones for a run up the middle. Jones, though, stumbled forward out of his stance and never controlled the ball, which hit him in the hip and shot forward. Matt Grootegoed covered it, and incredibly the Trojans had yet another chance, taking over on the Oklahoma thirty-six with fifty-three seconds remaining. After getting as far as the sixteen, they settled for a forty-four-yard Ryan Kileen field goal to make the score 38–10.

38–10. At halftime. Number one against number two 38–10 at halftime. Unbelievable.

The Sooners trotted off the field, beaten, battered and undoubtedly embarrassed, having already allowed more points in a bowl game than any team in school history. A nightmare of a first half had mercifully ended and Oklahoma's team of trash-talking tough guys couldn't get away from the national television cameras fast enough. The Trojans gathered in the end zone as they waited for the Sooners to clear the field, and grooved to Outkast's "Hey Ya!" blaring over the stadium's speakers.

The carnage was considerable. USC's linemen were dominating the game on both sides of the ball. The demolition was largely unquantifiable, but the statistics did tell some of the story with the Trojans rolling up 314 yards to 197 for Oklahoma. Time of possession was slanted greatly toward the Sooners, who had held the ball for more than eighteen of the thirty minutes, but that was largely a function of USC's propensity to score quickly. Six of their eight first-half possessions ended with points—five touchdowns and a field goal—and four of them took less than a minute off of the clock.

USC's first-half scoring drives:

PLAYS	YARDS	TIME	RESULT	SCORE
6	75	3:11	TD	7–7
1	6	0:07	TD	14–7
6	89	1:33	TD	21–7
3	10	0:45	TD	28–7
4	79	0:59	TD	35–10
7	8	0:39	FG	38–10

In his ABC interview on the way off the field, Pete Carroll was asked whether he was surprised at what had transpired in the first thirty minutes. He answered, "Yes. I'm surprised that we're out ahead like this right now because we have so much respect for Oklahoma and they're a great football team. We scored thirty-eight in the first half, and they might be able to score a bunch too."

As the coach walked away, ABC put a graphic on the screen indicating the Trojans were 33–2 under Carroll when leading at halftime. There was no statistic given, though, regarding their record when leading by twenty-eight points.

It was a rather upbeat USC locker room at halftime, to say the least. While pop singer Ashlee Simpson shrieked her way through a miserable and heartily booed performance on a makeshift stage at midfield, the Trojans sang and chanted in an impromptu miniconcert of their own. It is one thing to be cautiously optimistic, and another thing for a team to know when it has its opponent entirely overmatched and outclassed.

Taking the field for the second half, USC got its kickoff team ready. Remember, Oklahoma won the coin toss and deferred its choice until the second half. Well, here they were, about to get the ball and, at this point, down four touchdowns—it didn't really seem to mean much. The Sooners ran four offensive plays and then punted, giving USC possession on its own fifteen.

On first down, they got a first down. Leinart hit running back David Kirtman for fifteen yards to the thirty. Then, again on first down, they got another first down as White broke through the middle for fourteen more. Six plays later, the Trojans were in familiar territory: the end zone. Smith, who had caught a forty-eight-yard pass a few plays earlier, grabbed a four yarder on the same exact play he had scored on in the second quarter for another touchdown. The hookup capped off

USC's longest drive of the game: an eight-play, eighty-five-yard "don't even think about a comeback" kind of march.

A couple months later, Leinart recalled an incident that played out on the next Trojan possession. "The guy that was doing all the talking before the game, umm, one of their d-line-men."

"Larry Birdine?" I asked.

"Yeah, Birdine." Leinart had truly, and symbolically forgotten his name. "It was the third quarter and we were up 45–10. I rolled out and he was chasing me. I just threw the ball away and he started talkin' again. I couldn't understand a word he was saying—he was just mumbling something—but it seemed like he was talking crap to me and I just kind of laughed at him."

Although Birdine might have been unintelligible at that point, some of the other Oklahoma players were speaking very clearly, and the USC players could not believe what they were hearing.

"They gave up," Leinart recalled. "Third quarter a lot of their players were saying, 'C'mon, just run the ball so we can run the clock out. Don't throw the ball anymore.' They were saying it to the offensive line and even saying it to me. They were like 'Man, just get the game over with,' and we were thinking, 'Wow! This is unbelievable. This has turned into a joke!'

"I have never heard anybody on any level of football say anything like that, and this is the national championship game! But they gave up. They were embarrassed. It was really incredible and I remember thinking, 'They've given up.' They gave up in the second quarter! When we went up 28–10 on that catch by Steve, I remember coming off the field and Coach Carroll was hugging me, saying, 'Good throw,' and I said, 'Coach, they do not *want* this game,' and he said, 'Yeah, I don't think so either.' I just kept walking. That was a cool feeling. I remember that as clear as day."

It is a memory that will likely live with Leinart for the rest of his life, regardless of what else he accomplishes on or off the football field. The same goes for all of the Trojans who participated in the 2005 Orange Bowl. It was that kind of a night.

The Trojans went on to finish off Oklahoma 55–19 and gathered on the field afterward to take possession of the Waterford crystal BCS championship trophy. Leinart climbed on a nearby stage to get the Orange Bowl trophy, and perhaps instinctively, his left arm kept firing. He grabbed the oranges out of the trophy's bowl and threw to any teammate who was looking, unofficially completing eight of nine oranges for 123 yards and three more touchdowns.

"We knew we had them beat from the time we watched them on film," said Alex Holmes. "We spent all month listening to them talk, but we didn't respond. We're gentlemen. We knew we'd come out and punch them in the mouths."

Across the way, Bob Stoops had to agree. "Nothing you could say other than we just got whipped."

"We thought we could get the ball downfield against them," understated offensive coordinator Norm Chow said. "Matt was as sharp as a tack."

When a team puts up fifty-five points, the defensive effort tends to be overlooked. In the season's biggest game, the Trojans' defense was spectacular, controlling the line of scrimmage, keeping the powerful Oklahoma offense out of the end zone for a stretch of nearly fifty minutes of game time and holding game-breaking back Adrian Peterson to an average of 3.3 yards per carry. Junior linebacker Lofa Tatupu, playing in what would turn out to be his final collegiate game, made seven solo tackles and twelve total. "It's just unreal," he said. "We worked hard and believed in the system and Coach Carroll. We felt if we took away the run early and made them pass, pressure them, it would work out."

It worked out, all right. Following a season in which they won just a share of a national championship and extended their win streak to twenty-two straight, the Trojans now had a title all to themselves. Sure, there was some chirping out of Auburn, where the Tigers finished a 13–0 season with a three-point Sugar Bowl win over Virginia Tech, but anybody who witnessed the power of the USC machine that destroyed the number two team in the nation on January 4 could not objectively say that there was any question as to the best team in the country. The Trojans racked up 525 total yards while working mostly on short fields as the result of five takeaways. Leinart completed eighteen of his thirty-five passes for 332 yards, with no interceptions and five touchdowns. White shook off the ankle injury and ran for 118 yards on fifteen carries, while Bush chipped in with 149 all-purpose yards.

It was a crowning achievement, a dazzling victory at a dizzying pace, marking a magnificent end to a perfect season. Thirteen wins, no losses and a unanimous national championship.

Four months later, as Pete Carroll left the practice field on a cool Los Angeles evening following a spring practice session in 2005, he reflected on the magical night in Miami that ended the 2004 season.

"This is a cool story," he said with a smile. "There's a lot to this. The story of this game is the epitome of what I dreamed would happen in this program. We were in the biggest setting of all time, and we played great. We had this dream opportunity. I don't know if it was the greatest game we ever played, but relative to Oklahoma, it sure looked like it.

"The number one objective in running this program is trying to develop an attitude with our team that we *know* we're going to win. All that it takes to get that done is what makes us really strong and really hard to beat. We had been through a great season of challenges that we just took one right after another and played really good, solid football. We were always playing great by the end of the game, not always throughout the whole game, but by the end of the game, we played terrific and were able to win all those games really in the same manner and the same style with the same formula. We didn't have to luck out. It was just good solid play the whole time. That put us in the position for this great matchup with this great Oklahoma team that was loaded and experienced and fast and athletic.

"The hype and the buildup, the last game of the year—everything was riding on it," the coach continued, seemingly transported to that magical Miami evening. "What we set out and did was practice really well. I mean, every day was a productive day—the focus, the effort, the intensity, it was all there. We were healthy. Everything was clicking. It was just obvious. We couldn't get any more ready. We couldn't be any more prepared. We had no reason to think anything other than we were going to win. We just didn't know by how much.

"The night before the game, we talked about it, just like that. We had done all the things we needed to do and we weren't going to expect anything but to play really well and have fun doing it and not worry one bit about what they had to say. We really wanted to make them look ordinary like we had to so many other good teams along the way, and that happened. What was cool during the game is that we knew *really early*. You could tell really early in the game that we had 'em. Guys were coming off the field to the sideline and were so excited because they knew there was no way Oklahoma was gonna hang with us. We knew it was gonna be a great night of playing football from very early on. It was an extraordinary opportunity for us to show what our philosophy was: just go out and do what we do, and disregard whatever the other guys could do or whatever factor they could play in it and play football the way we were capable of playing and have the time of our lives doing it.

"They scored first, and I chuckled because two years before in the Orange Bowl, Iowa scored on the opening kickoff [C. J. Jones went a hundred yards for a touchdown], and I thought, 'Hey, it took 'em seven or eight plays to score this time. We're doing much better this year!' It didn't faze us at all. We went back to work, they made a couple of mistakes, we capitalized on 'em and from there we got better and stronger.

"I remember Lofa came off the field one time and said something like 'Coach, it feels like we're on a racehorse just riding away from these guys.' They didn't have a chance.

"It was a night of great fun. You can't have any more fun in a game, in a setting, in an environment, under all the scrutiny and the buildup to have that much time when you know you're going to win, and you just enjoy the heck out of it."

	1	2	3	4	F
Oklahoma	7	3	0	9	19
USC	14	24	10	7	55

Scoring:

First Quarter

Oklahoma: Wilson, 5-yard pass from White (Hartley kick)

USC: Byrd, 33-yard pass from Leinart (Killeen kick)

USC: White, 6-yard run (Killeen kick)

Second Quarter

USC: Jarrett, 54-yard pass from Leinart (Killeen kick)

USC: Smith, 5-yard pass from Leinart (Killeen kick)

Oklahoma: Hartley, 29-yard field goal

USC: Smith, 33-yard pass from Leinart (Killeen kick)

USC: Killeen, 44-yard field goal

Third Quarter

USC: Smith, 4-yard pass from Leinart (Killeen kick)

USC: Killeen, 42-yard field goal

Fourth Quarter

USC: White, 8-yard run (Killeen kick)

Oklahoma: safety (Leinart tackled in end zone)

Oklahoma: Wilson, 9-yard pass from White (Hartley kick)

Passing:
USC: Leinart, 18–35–332, 5 touchdowns

Oklahoma: White, 24–36–244, 3 interceptions, 2 touch-downs

Rushing:

USC: White, 15–118; Bush, 6–75

Oklahoma: Peterson, 25–82; Wolfe, 7–40

Receiving:

USC: Smith, 7–113; Jarrett, 5–115; Byrd, 3–58; Bush, 2–31

Oklahoma: Wilson, 7–59; Clayton, 4–21; Bradley, 2–66; Jones, 2–30

POSTSCRIPT

Longtime NFL coach Bill Parcells once made a point regarding the fleeting enjoyment derived from a hard-fought football victory. He said that after one late-season win he celebrated with his players on the sidelines, but by the time he made his way to the tunnel, the fun was over. He had already started mentally game planning for the following week's game.

For the Trojans, there was no game the following week, but out there in the distance were question marks already presenting themselves regarding the next season. For Matt Leinart, it didn't take long for the questions to come pouring in about 2005. He was four months away from turning twenty-two, had just won his second straight national championship and had a Heisman Trophy waiting for him at home. Would he, *could* he, find a reason to come back to school for his senior season?

The Trojans' celebration was not yet an hour old when Leinart was confronted with that very issue in the postgame news conference. "I still plan on coming back," he said. "It's going to take a lot for me to leave. It's something special that we're a part of, to have a chance to win a third national championship in a row at the Rose Bowl in our backyard. The young guys that we have . . . I can't answer right now. It's gonna take a lot for me to leave."

Sure it would, but a lot of what? Money? That wouldn't be a problem.

Many had Leinart pegged as the top overall pick in the upcoming NFL draft. Virtually everybody had him projected to go somewhere in the top five. The financial aspect of his situation was only one of the variables that would, over the next couple months, tumble continuously through Leinart's head like clothes in a dryer. The football season had ended, but with the

Orange Bowl's final whistle, the clock began ticking on the star quarterback's decision about his football future. As the party died and with the Miami sun about an hour away from rising, the MVP of the Orange Bowl finally fell asleep. The NFL's deadline for underclassmen to declare eligibility was just ten days away.

Speculation ran rampant. Talk radio was abuzz. The Great Leinart Watch of 2005 was on. People who would never, under any circumstances, find themselves in Matt's position were insisting on what *they* would do. Of course, society being what it is, and money meaning what it does, the great majority of the public had Leinart written in indelible ink on the NFL draft board. Some close to him, though, spoke of his love of the college life and desire to try to win a third straight championship. Several newspaper and Internet columnists opined that it would be pointless for him to stay. CBSSportsline.com ran an article the day after the Orange Bowl pointing out that Leinart probably threw what they were calling "a five-touchdown farewell," adding the rhetorical question that many were asking, "What else does he have to accomplish in college?"

Carroll, perhaps just preparing himself for the probability of his quarterback's departure, seemed resigned to the fact that Leinart was stepping out and stepping up. After the game, he said, "If you get to a point where you're relying on one guy to get it done, then you're not a strong program. We're Trojans forever but the program is bigger than any one guy. That's the way we established it and we can't wait to see who's going to do something special next."

As the pages on the calendar turned, the quarterback wrestled with his options. He sought the opinion of, well, just about anybody he came across. "I got advice from different people: NFL quarterbacks, coaches, people who played in the NFL. I even asked my friends, who couldn't possibly have known all the factors. I'd say, like, 'What do you think I should do?' [Laughs] I just wanted to get insight. I was even asking them, 'What do you think I'm *gonna* do?' "

USC set up a press conference for Matt and two of his teammates, linebacker Lofa Tatupu and punter Tom Malone, for Thursday, January 13. Each of the three had just finished his junior season, and they were all entertaining thoughts of jumping to the NFL. Tatupu, a third-team all-American and son of former Trojan Mosi Tatupu, had a monster game in the Orange Bowl and was expected to go pro. Malone's forty-nine-yards-per-punt average had led the nation in 2003, but he failed to qualify for the official punting title because, due to USC's efficiency on offense, he didn't have the required number of punts. After another solid season in 2004, Malone was on record saying he'd leave USC if Leinart stayed. With Matt back, he joked, his punting opportunities in 2005 would be almost nonexistent.

The Tuesday before the announcement, the quarterback said his decision sometimes changed hourly. Wednesday, Leinart was the topic of choice at watercoolers all around Los Angeles. There was even word of office pools popping up with odds established and friendly wagers made on whether the quarterback was staying or leaving. Late Thursday morning, an announcement came from USC, but it wasn't the one people had been anticipating.

Leinart needed more time to decide. Forty-eight hours before the NFL's deadline, the press conference was being moved to the following day. "There's just so much stuff," Leinart said. "It's almost like I learn something new every day, so it makes the decision a lot harder. If I declare for the draft, then I have to think of every possible thing. You've got to think of what other quarterbacks are going, where do you want to train, things like that."

Friday was D-day. "The day before I announced, I was ready to go," Matt recalled in March 2005. "I didn't have my mind completely made up, but I said to myself, 'Y'know what? Just go. I'm ready. I can do this.' That night, I actually slept well. I was fine. The day of my press conference I woke up about ten thirty and just laid in my bed for a couple hours. The whole time it was like 'What am I gonna do?'"

So as Trojan nation wondered which decision Leinart had made, he, in fact, hadn't made one at all. If there wasn't a deadline staring him in the face, perhaps he still wouldn't have made it!

On the afternoon of January 14, 2005, the Trojan quarterback strode into Heritage Hall with his heart racing and his mind spinning. He joined Tatupu, Malone and Carroll at a table facing a slew of cameras. As the Heisman Trophy winner walked toward the podium, microphones awaited, cameras flashed and scribes scribbled. Outside, the scene was a bit surreal. A gathering crowd of about five hundred USC students had crashed the party, pushing forward for a glimpse of the star quarterback while those in front actually pressed their ears to the glass.

Like a seasoned rock star, or the lead actor in a long-running Broadway play, Leinart spoke deliberately, knowing he had the audience in the palm of his hand. He made the press conference equivalent of a bit of small talk and then matter-of-factly spit out the words for which Trojan nation had waited.

"I would like to announce that I'm coming back for my senior season."

The crowd went wild.

"It was the toughest decision of my life," Leinart continued. "I realized the opportunity to support my family by going to the NFL early, but to me, I think college football and this whole atmosphere of being here with my friends and teammates that I have been with for four years is ultimately more satisfying and will make me happier than any amount of money could make someone happy."

The sentiment was refreshing if not shocking. He had built himself a path to the riches of the NFL and standing at a fork between that path and his college life, he took the road less traveled. For poet Robert Frost, that same choice made all the difference.

Respected scouting expert Gil Brandt projected Leinart as the top pick overall, a spot that would likely have netted the kid out of Mater Dei High School around $15 million. When asked about the money, Leinart referred to his NCAA stipend saying, "Hey, I get nine hundred fifty dollars a month." Speaking a couple months after making his decision, Leinart said, "A lot of people think Coach Carroll influenced me. There are underclassmen who can make it, like Kenechi Udeze [who left following his junior season in 2003], who obviously has the tools physically, but they wanted him to stay in school. No disrespect to Coach Carroll. It's only natural. He wants his guys—that's all it is. A lot of people think he swayed my decision. He gave me a lot of information on staying and on going. He said, 'If you leave, I don't know where you'd go. You could be top five, you could be number one, you could be top ten, top fifteen, anything.' I said, 'You're right.' But then he said, 'If you stay, you could increase your value even more. You could have another good year, get bigger, get stronger.'"

Leinart pondered the issue of returning and added, "A lot of people say, 'Well, what if he has a bad season?' I'm not cocky, but I don't think I'm gonna have a bad season. Why would I? The only negative to me coming back is the risk of getting hurt, and to me that's not really even a big deal. It sounds stupid, but I could get hurt any day. We've had guys get hurt lifting weights. They tear a muscle and they're out for the year. I don't play scared. I'm not gonna play scared next season. It's all part of the game. If ya get hurt, ya get hurt."

Of the decision, Carroll said, "All of a sudden you can become a multimillionaire—that's hard to just turn away from and not many guys would do that, but this is a very unique person and a great character kid, and he's willing to postpone that to do something that's really in his heart, that he loves doing."

All-time Trojan great Frank Gifford was going about his business on January 15 when his cell phone rang. Gifford answered to the sound of his teenage son Cody yelling, "He's gonna stay, Dad. He's gonna stay!"

"I said, 'Who the hell is going to stay?'" laughs Gifford. "I didn't know who he was talking about. He said, 'Leinart's gonna stay.' I said, 'Ohhh.' I was really happy. I was wondering what he would do, and I think it's a great decision. No matter what he does, and of course, there's a risk that he might get hurt, but I don't think you can compare that to the legendary role he might play in college football. All he has to do is have his ordinary year. He's been just incredible."

Some in the media actually criticized Leinart's decision, saying he made the wrong move by passing up the money. Mike Garrett, who played in the pros for eight seasons, said of those taking shots at the quarterback, "What amazes me is that people make decisions for money and we all become cynical and we all accept that that's the way to go. Then someone shows a bit of class, a bit of integrity, a bit of character and enjoyment, and others belittle that decision. Those people don't know anything about football, and apparently they don't know much about life either. That was a *life issue* with that young man. It took courage for him to do it, and it took courage for his parents to support him. Everybody who criticized him missed the mark, and that's kinda how it works most of the time. The quality people, they always stand out, and other quality people recognize it.

"I have a friend who is in the stock market, and when the computer boom hit, he was invested. Stocks were shooting up and he got out. I asked why he got out and he said, 'When the masses start following, I get real nervous.' The real leaders are sometimes out there all by themselves."

Having had time to relax a little bit and accept numerous compliments on his decision, Leinart points out, "Other than a few teammates, everybody's been real respectful. And the only reason those teammates are bummed is because they thought I was going to buy them cars."

If there were any cars to be bought for the boys at USC, Lofa Tatupu was to do the buying. On the day that Leinart announced he was coming back, Tatupu made public his decision to jump to the NFL. Punter Tom Malone, on the other hand, decided to play the role of Maytag repairman, announcing that, as lonely and inactive as he might be on fall Saturdays in 2005, he would be staying for his senior season.

CHAPTER ELEVEN

THE FUTURE

Change in collegiate sports is inevitable. It is part of what defines the industry. The changes at USC after the 2005 Orange Bowl, though, were not confined to the roster. The copycat world of corporate America has made its way to the country's athletic fields. If a business or a movie or a restaurant is successful, you can expect a whole slew of followers to duplicate the formula. Look at reality television. Check out clothing trends. Remember Buddy Ryan's championship defense? Two years later, it was everywhere. And why the hell does everybody in the United States under the age of forty suddenly have a tattoo?

If imitation is indeed the most sincere form of flattery, teams all over the country, on every level, are going beyond flattering the current Trojans; they are downright stealing from them. Four coaches were wooed away to higher-paying jobs within a month of the 2005 Orange Bowl. Offensive coordinator Norm

Chow, quarterback coach Carl Smith, offensive-line coach Tim Davis and defensive-line coach Ed Orgeron all skipped town. You don't have to be a forensic scientist to see their fingerprints all over the Trojans' recent national championships. Now they are all on to their next challenge with higher expectations and bigger bank accounts.

Many thought Chow's departure would have a strong negative impact on Leinart, but the quarterback worked with coaches Steve Sarkisian and Lane Kiffin to create an offense that racked up more than forty-nine points per game in 2005. He did have some ups and downs, and a couple rough stretches, but mostly the quarterback delivered his trademark trifecta of efficiency, effectiveness and victories.

The returning Heisman Trophy winner completed nearly 66 percent of his passes for more than 3,800 yards and twenty-eight touchdowns in 2005 while leading USC to another undefeated regular season. The highlight was a thrilling 34–31 win at Notre Dame, in which Leinart threaded the needle on a fourth-and-nine pass to Dwayne Jarrett with the Trojans down three and ninety seconds remaining. The play was good for sixty-one yards and led to a game-winning quarterback sneak in the waning seconds as Reggie Bush, in the middle of a monster season, and a couple months away from picking up a Heisman Trophy of his own, actually pushed Leinart into the end zone.

The season seemed to turn into a yearlong quest for a third consecutive national championship, with the title game to be played in the Rose Bowl. As the Trojans finished off every team on their schedule, the University of Texas was doing the same.

On the night of January 4, 2006, in front of nearly 94,000 fans in Pasadena, USC locked horns with the Longhorns in a classic. The Trojans led by twelve with five minutes left to play, but were unable to stop Texas quarterback Vince Young, who, many felt, turned in the most dominant performance in the history of college football.

Young completed thirty of his forty passes for 267 yards, and racked up a mind-blowing two hundred yards rushing. His eight-yard scramble with nineteen-seconds left is all that ultimately stood between USC and a third straight national title. Texas won the game 41–38, marking the end of an era—several eras, in fact, in Trojan football.

Matt Leinart's eligibility was gone. Reggie Bush and LenDale White were gone too, later announcing they would forgo their respective senior seasons to enter the NFL draft. Linemen Fred Matua and Winston Justice declared their eligibility, as did Darnell Bing. Also gone was a win streak for the ages: thirty-four wins in a row.

Thirty-four.

Change being inevitable, a strong football program needs a rock-solid constant. Under Mike Garrett's watch, the constant in USC's phenomenal rebirth has been Pete Carroll. He came in, not so much as an unknown quantity, but perceived as a moderately successful "nice guy" who had never displayed signs of the greatness to come. He, in fact, had never even been a head coach on the collegiate level. He came to USC after being fired by the New England Patriots following a three-year stint with consecutive seasons of declining results.

For a guy who arrived amid so much negativity around him, Carroll sure did turn it around in a hurry. He doesn't actually wear a crown around the USC campus these days, but there is no question that he is already considered Trojan royalty. The system he has created has laid the foundation for a potentially unparalleled stretch of success and supremacy. Still, under that foundation are two concrete building blocks that are the essence of the program's staying power in its return to greatness.

The first one is recruiting. Coaches coach and players play, and without the latter, the former doesn't make much of a difference. Pete Carroll, through sheer determination, relentless pursuit, proper approach, unique personality or a combination of the above, has been consistently able to lure the best of the best to USC.

"I'll never forget being a sophomore and reading through those prep magazines," Carson Palmer says, looking back. "I'd follow the recruiting and nobody would ever have us listed near the top. They would always say UCLA, Michigan, Notre Dame, Texas, Tennessee, all these schools, and USC was never in there. Then, all of a sudden, my senior year, USC was on every list. Every kid wanted to go to USC. We were finally getting the best talent. The reason for the turnaround was Pete. He's a guy that you want to be around. You want to play for him. You want to learn from him. He's been in the NFL, and that's so attractive to young players. He's been a coach in the league and knows what it takes to get there, but I think mainly it's his personality."

The second building block is competition. Heading into each year's spring practice, the Trojans' depth chart is essentially a blank slate. Going into training camp, any names that made it onto the chart in the spring are written in only in pencil. Some coaches abhor the idea of freshmen in a starting lineup. Carroll finds his first-year players eminently usable.

Every spot is vacant; every player is equal. Anybody wearing a number has a shot at starting. It's all about performance. Here's the ball. Go play.

Garry Paskwietz, publisher of *We Are SC* magazine, and among the most knowledgeable of the hundreds of thousands of Trojans fans around the country, says, "It's amazing what they've done here. Recruiting is an inexact science. Even in the NFL draft, there's bust after bust in the first round."

Seeing a player for what he is today is one thing. Seeing a player for what he could be in a couple years is something else entirely. "What they've done here," Paskwietz continues, "is pick the right players and create an environment that is all about competition. I think when you have the elite players, they're built on competition, they want to be the best. When you say to them, 'Hey guys, every job is open. We're all about competition,' that appeals to elite-level guys. They want to be in that situation. They want to be here. The reason behind it is Pete Carroll. There's no other reason. It's Pete selling this thing right now, and as long as he's here, I don't see it ending."

"This thing"—it is a phrase that comes up over and over again around the USC program. As everybody from fans to alumni to players to coaches speak about the Trojan program, they do so by calling it "this thing." It is as if the success, or more specifically the ongoing success and the momentum behind it, is so unique and indefinable that there is no other all-encompassing way to refer to it. It is like a raging monster nobody has ever seen before. This thing is big, it is powerful and it has a distinct personality all of its own.

Regarding USC's incredible run of success, Carroll himself is the most widely credited and certainly the least-impressed person out there. "There's no reason for our program to take a step backward for a season or a couple seasons," he says. "We've created an extremely competitive football team and it doesn't even matter who plays in a lot of cases. We've shown how resilient we've been to losses of players, and that's become our nature. When somebody falls out, that just opens up the opportunity for other guys to do what they can do. We've lived with that mentality and we just won't waver. We're not gonna falter at all in our mind-set. I had a big opportunity to preach to the guys when the Mike Williams situation came up. I said, 'Hey, last year we lost Carson Palmer the Heisman Trophy winner, Troy Polamalu, five running backs, six other starters, and what did we do? We won the national championship.' So hey, never again is any loss going to affect us."

Under Carroll, and his system of competition, the youngest of the young do get a chance, but the life span of a player's importance to the big picture of the program works to the high side as well. The great players of the past—all players of the past—are welcome these days around Heritage Hall. Even a program-changing superstar like Anthony Davis has, at times, felt as if he was forgotten by some of the recent coaching staffs.

"All the credit goes to Pete Carroll," Davis says. "He got there, grabbed the program by the horns and said, 'This is the greatest tradition in college football.' He embraced the program, embraced the older guys and brought us back. He's the only current-day guy who has done that. He says, 'Hey, man, you gotta come back around so these kids can see what this legacy is about.' That's why I do all the fantasy camps and everything. If he calls me, I'm there. I don't care what it is. If Pete Carroll calls me, I'll do whatever he needs me to do. Listen, about the older players, you have no tradition if you don't have us."

As do many Trojans of the past, Sam Cunningham has a similar feeling. "Whatever is going on, he invites everybody," the old fullback says. "There's a line that connects all of us, and Coach Carroll has been gracious enough to want us to come back and want the older players to be seen and have history walking through those halls and hanging out."

Carroll responds to the comments made by Davis and Cunningham, saying, "There's a factor that you can develop and nurture that can help the energy of your program to be positive and uplifting and supportive. I have made a point to bring those guys together to help us all. They all want to win. The more they're around us and the more they talk positive and the more they support us, it just makes everything better. When ya talk about family, Trojan family, you don't ever shut the door on your family. You don't leave them out. You open your doors, and whatever they need, you give it to them. I'm just living the life of being a part of a family that I know exists and I believe in. We owe everything to those guys. Every chance I get, I'll do everything I can for 'em."

Carroll was rewarded for the success he achieved in his first five years at USC with a contract to coach another five. He signed a contract extension in early 2006 that runs through the 2010 season, ending what had become annual speculation that he would jump back to the NFL.

Carroll leaves little doubt about his comfort level at Southern California. "I've lived my life in coaching thinking that the nature of my job is to be a mercenary and to go fight somebody else's wars," he explains. "In the NFL, you get hired by an owner to fight his battles for him, and then after a while, they discard you and you go on. There are a lot of guys who have been mercenaries in their lifetime in other ways, but that's what the NFL felt like. I've already done that and I don't want to deal with that anymore. There is no formula that works for me in the NFL because there are owners and GMs. They couldn't get out of my way so that I could do it the way I am capable of doing it. That's why, when I left, I didn't feel that bad about it. There was no way I could do the best I could do. I didn't have enough freedom.

"I realize in the college setting, the athletic director and the president, they have their own jobs, all this other stuff to do. They can't spend their time looking over my shoulder. I get to do everything. Being at USC feels different. It does. This is a very deep, almost religious experience for me in my football career, and I have this opportunity with this marvelous product of the university and this beautiful setting where we have all this population to support us and this great style about the school, and the great heritage, and the great music, and the color of the uniforms, and the Coliseum—all those things. But it's not too good to be true. That's what I do know. This is the real deal. This is what's happening. This is the life we're living.

This is what we get to do, so let's just squeeze every drop out of this opportunity every step of the way."

Carroll has compiled a record of 54–10 to begin his career at Troy. The average margin of defeat in his ten losses is fewer than five points, and only one of those losses was by more than a touchdown. Just one.

"There are very few schools where this kind of thing can be created," Paskwietz says, "where a coach can come in and really get to that level. SC, Notre Dame, Alabama, schools like that. It comes from tradition. You gotta have it. You just have to be a football school. There are only a handful of schools that are elite. There are others that are a bit below that that think they are, like the Auburns. Yeah, you're a great football school, but are you the elite? No, you're not. I don't really know how it's defined but it's like great art—you know it when you see it."

All those Pete bashers who surfaced when the coach was hired have since seen it very clearly. The University of Southern California *is* the elite. The bashers have been replaced one hundred fold by Pete supporters. The opinion that "this thing" will last as long as Carroll does is pretty prevalent.

It certainly has been fun for the past few seasons, and in order for it to stay that way, Garrett insists that there can be no letting down. "I'm always thinking about how we continue to stay right on the edge," he says. "That's the issue more than anything else. If I felt we were getting complacent, that would really worry me. We talk about it at staff meetings. We have to keep the edge, and that's what we're trying to do."

Are you succeeding, Mike?

"We're kicking ass. But you can't dwell on things. Everything in sports is fundamentals. If you do things fundamentally right, you have a pretty good chance. We have to stay fundamentally sound, so we're always checking ourselves to make sure we are. Staying sound is a state of being. The winning is the result. We're not focusing on the winning. We're focusing on staying on that cutting edge. You start looking at winning, you'll start losing. You can't be too pleased with yourself. I don't celebrate. I acknowledge, but I don't celebrate."

Life experience tells us that all good things must end. The record books confirm that goes for the world of college football as well. Just as Howard Jones and John McKay led teams to periods of greatness, so too has Pete Carroll. But his streak will end, as theirs did, and somewhere down the line there will be the next great coach to lead the next great revival at this elite and unique football school. There is no shame in defeat and there is no avoiding the cyclical nature of sporting success. Any surfer will tell you, it's not what you do between the waves that matters—it's knowing how to identify the big ones, getting on and using every bit of your experience, knowledge and energy to stay on top for as long as you can, riding them for all they're worth.

As a tornado of hype and hyperbole swirls around him, Pete Carroll is, at the same time, basking in and shying away from all attention his program has received.

On a warm spring night in 2005, outside Heritage Hall, the fifty-three-year-old coach acknowledged the extraordinary situation that has been created at USC. "I want to see if we can win for a real long time," he said matter-of-factly. "That's a tremendous challenge in coaching. To win a championship doesn't mean that much. It's fun and all that, but I want to see if we can do it over a long period of time and keep it going. I just want to be on top for as long as we can, and see how long we can stretch this thing out and then just fall apart, waste away and then blow away in the wind, y'know?

"I think I'm smart enough to realize this is awesome. I'm living it. I'm gonna make the very most of it and I'm gonna make it as fun as I can, for as many people as I can, for as long as I can."